W9-CIM-679

SUICIDE:

A Selective Bibliography
of Over 2,200 Items

by

ANN E. PRENTICE

The Scarecrow Press, Inc.
Metuchen, N.J.   1974

Library of Congress Cataloging in Publication Data

Prentice, Ann E
    Suicide: a selective bibliography of more than 2, 200
items.

    1.   Suicide--Bibliography.   I.   Title.
Z7615. P73   016. 3641'522   74-19231
ISBN 0-8108-0773-4

CONTENTS

iii

PREFACE

Our unusual concern about the many aspects of suicide
is reflected in the tremendous output in the publication on the
subject. Articles have appeared in many languages on suicide
and their authors have dealt with the causes, implementation,
and prevention of self-destruction in its various guises.

With the needs of the general researcher in mind, the
following selection of more than two thousand was made from
several thousand possible articles. Sources not available in
English were omitted, as were references to articles of a
very highly technical nature. A further limitation was of those
articles describing variations on a subject as it related to a
specific city or region. Those articles which refer to a particular geographic area were included only if they had approaches or insights which transcended the purely geographic
orientation. A final limitation was made to emphasize materials which were published from 1960-1973, so that the
more current developments in the field could be emphasized.
If, however, certain items which appeared prior to 1960 were
judged to be outstanding, they were included. No such time
limitations were placed upon literary works, as creative expression has no chronological limits.

The literature was searched extensively to locate and
identify relevant sources. Because of the difficulty in la-
belling a particular article as being medically, sociologically,
or psychologically oriented, the largest part of the bibliography is Chapter 8, which includes articles reflecting one or
more of these orientations. The range of topics covered here
is reflected in the subject index which leads the user through
the body of the work to a specific interest.

During the year and a half in which the bibliography
was developed, numerous libraries and other information
sources were used. The librarians were most helpful in
providing me with whatever materials I needed. A special

debt is owed my graduate assistant, Ms. Cheryl Bissinger, who looked up, tracked down, and verified the information relating to thousands of items. Without her able assistance, such an undertaking would have been much more difficult to complete.

Dr. Ann E. Prentice
School of Library & Information Science
State University of New York at Albany

I. BOOKS

1) Adams, John. An essay concerning self-murther. Wherein is endeavour'd to prove, that it is unlawful according to natural principles ... by the author of a treatise, untitled, Beanthanatos, and others. By J. Adams.... London, Printed for T. Bennet, 1700.

2) Adams, J.R. and Rosenblatt, S. Traffic Accidents and Other Symptoms of Social Pathology. Annual Report, Safety Research and Educational Projects. New York: Teachers College, Columbia University, 1966.

3) Alvarez, Alfred. The Savage God. New York: Random House, 1972.

4) American Association of Suicidology. On the Nature of Suicide. First Annual Conference. San Francisco: Jossey-Bass, Inc., 1969.

5) Anderson, Dorothy and McLean, Lenora, eds. Conference on Identifying Suicide Potential. New York: Behavioral Publications, 1971.

6) Andics, Margarethe von. Suicide and the Meaning of Life. London: W. Hodge, 1947.

7) Asinof, Eliot. Craig and Joan: Two Lives for Peace. New York: Viking Press, 1971.

8) Blachly, Paul H. Seduction: A Conceptual Model in the Drug Dependencies and Other Contagious Ills. Springfield, Ill.: Charles C. Thomas, 1970.

9) Bohannan, Paul, ed. African Homicide and Suicide. Princeton: Princeton University Press, 1960.

10) Bosselman, Beulah Chamberlin. Self-Destruction: A

1

Study of the Suicidal Impulse. Springfield, Ill.:
Charles C. Thomas, 1958.

11) Britt, F. E. Felode Se: A Treatise on the Recognition
and Prevention of Suicidal Behavior. New York:
Vantage Press, 1969.

12) Brophy, Brigid. Black Ship To Hell. New York: Harcourt, Brace, Jovanovich, 1962.

13) Bruller, Jean. 21 Delightful Ways of Committing Suicide. For the use of persons who are discouraged or
disgusted with life for reasons which do not really
concern us. New York: 1930.

14) Buckner, H. Taylor. Deviance, Reality, and Change.
New York: Random House, 1970.

15) Burston, Geoffrey R. Self-Poisoning. Baltimore:
Williams & Wilkins, 1970.

16) Cavan, Ruth S. Suicide. Chicago: University of Chicago Press, 1928. (Reprint 1965 - Russell & Russell.)

17) Chesser, Eustace. Living with Suicide. London:
Hutchinson, 1967.

18) Chesser, Eustace. Why Suicide? London: Arrow
Books, 1968.

19) Choron, Jacques. Suicide. New York: Scribner, 1972.

20) Church of England National Assembly. Board for Social
Responsibility. Ought Suicide to be a Crime? A Dis-
cussion of Suicide, Attempted Suicide, and the Law.
London: Church Information Office, 1959.

21) Cohen, John. Behaviour in Uncertainty and Its Social
Implications. New York: Basic Books, 1964.

22) Crancer, Alfred and Guering, Dennis L. Driving Records
of Persons Hospitalized for Suicide Gestures. Olympia:
State of Washington, Dept. of Motor Vehicles, Div. of Research, 1968.

23) Crasilneck, Harold B. An Analysis of Differences between
Suicidal and Pseudo-suicidal Patients through the Use of
Projective Techniques. Houston: Univ. of Houston, 1954.

24) Devereux, George. Mohave Ethnopsychiatry and Sui-
     cide: The Psychiatric Knowledge and the Psychic Dis-
     turbances. (Bulletin No. 175.) Washington: Superin-
     tendent of Documents, U. S. Government Printing Of-
     fice, 1961.

25) Donne, John. Bianthanatos Reproduced from the First
     Edition. New York: The Facsimile Test Society, 1930.

26) Douglas, Jack D. The Social Meanings of Suicide.
     Princeton: Princeton University Press, 1967.

27) Dublin, L. I. Suicide: A Sociological and Statistical
     Study. New York: Ronald Press, 1963.

28) Durkheim, Emile. Suicide, A Study in Sociology.
     Glencoe, Ill. : Free Press, 1951. (Originally pub-
     lished in 1897.)

29) Elbert, Edmund J. I Understand: A Handbook for
     Counseling in the Seventies. New York: Sheed &
     Ward, 1971.

30) Ellis, E. R. and Allen, G. N. Traitor Within: Our
     Suicide Problem. New York: Doubleday, 1961.

31) Elwin, Verrier. Maria, Murder and Suicide. 2d ed.
     Oxford: Oxford University Press, 1950.

32) Farber, M. Theory of Suicide. New York: Funk &
     Wagnalls, 1968.

33) Farberow, Norman L. Bibliography on Suicide and
     Prevention, 1897-1957; 1958-1967. Washington, D. C. :
     Public Health Service, 1969.

34) Farberow, Norman L. , ed. Proceedings: Fourth In-
     ternational Conference for Suicide Prevention. Los
     Angeles: Suicide Prevention Center, 1968.

35) Farberow, Norman L. and Shneidman, Edwin S. , eds.
     The Cry for Help. New York: McGraw-Hill, 1961.

36) Farberow, N. L. , Shneidman, E. S. , and Leonard,
     Calista V. Suicide Among General Medical and Surgical
     Hospital Patients with Malignant Neoplasms. Medical
     Bulletin-9, Veterans Administration, Washington, D. C. ,
     1963.

37)   Farberow, N. L. , Heilig, S. M. , and Litman, R. E.
      Techniques in Crisis Intervention: A Training Manual.
      Los Angeles: Suicide Prevention Center, Inc. , 1968.

38)   Farnsworth, Dana L. and Braceland, Francis J. , eds.
      Psychiatry, the Clergy and Pastoral Counseling: The
      St. John's Story.   Collegeville, Minn. :   St. John's
      University Press, 1969.

39)   Fedden, Henry Romilly.   Suicide, A Social and His-
      torical Study.   London: P. Davies Ltd. , 1938.

40)   Finch, Stuart M.   Adolescent Suicide.   Springfield,
      Ill. :   Charles C. Thomas, 1971.

41)   Finch, Stuart and Poznanski, Elva.   Adolescent Suicide.
      (American Living Chemistry Series.)   Springfield, Ill. :
      Charles C. Thomas, 1974.

42)   Flescher, Joachim.   Suicide--Man's Fate?   Genetic
      Prevention.   New York: D. T. R. B. Editions, 1971.

43)   Forrer, Gordon.   Weaning and Human Development.
      Roslyn Heights, N. Y. :   Libra Publishers, 1969.

44)   Fox, Richard, ed.   Proceedings of the Fifth Interna-
      tional Conference for Suicide Prevention, London, Sept.
      24-27, 1969.   Vienna: International Association for
      Suicide Prevention, 1970.

45)   Frederiksson, G.   The Suicide: Contribution to its
      Psychology.   Stockholm: Stockholm Institute of Sociology
      of Religion, 1970.

46)   Friedman, P. , ed.   On Suicide: With Particular
      Reference to Suicide Among Young Students.   New
      York: International Universities Press, 1967.

47)   Gibbs, Jack P. and Martin, Walter T.   Status Inte-
      gration and Suicide: A Sociological Study.   Eugene:
      University of Oregon, 1964.

48)   Gibbs, Jack P. , ed.   Suicide.   New York: Harper &
      Row, 1969.

49)   Gibbs, Jack P. , ed.   Suicide.   New York: Macmillan,
      1967.

50) Giddens, Anthony, ed. Sociology of Suicide: A reader. London: F. Cass, 1971.

51) Goffman, I. Suicide Motives and Categorization of the Living and the Dead in the United States. Syracuse, N. Y.: M. H. R. U., 1966.

52) Grollman, Earl A. Suicide Prevention, Intervention, Postvention. Boston: Beacon Press, 1971.

53) Hafen, Brent Q. and Faux, E. J., eds. Self-Destructive Behavior. Minneapolis: Burgess Publishing Co., 1972.

54) Hendin, Herbert. Black Suicide. New York: Basic Books, 1969.

55) Hendin, Herbert. Suicide and Scandinavia: A Psychoanalytic Study of Culture and Character. New York: Anchor Doubleday, 1965.

56) Hendin, Herbert. Suicide and Scandinavia. New York: Grune & Stratton, 1964.

57) Henry, Andrew F. and Short, James F. Suicide and Homicide: Some Economic, Sociological and Psychological Aspects of Aggression. Glencoe, Ill.: Free Press, 1964.

58) Hillman, James. Suicide and the Soul. New York: Harper & Row, 1964.

59) Howells, John G., ed. Modern Perspectives in Child Psychiatry. New York: Brunner-Mazel, 1971.

60) Idänpään-Heikkilä, Pirkko. "Student Suicides. Finnish Psychiatry," Yearbook of the Psychiatric Clinic of the Helsinki University Central Hospital, 1970.

61) Israel Central Bureau of Statistics. Suicides and Attempted Suicides in Israel, 1949-1959. Jerusalem: Special Series No. 115, 1962.

62) Israel Central Bureau of Statistics. Suicides and Attempted Suicides in Israel (1960-1966). Jerusalem: The Bureau, 1969.

63) Jacobs, Jerry. Adolescent Suicide. New York: Wiley, 1971.

64) Jan-Lausch, James. Suicide of Children 1960-63;
     New Jersey Public School Students. Trenton: Office
     of Special Education Services, Dept. of Education,
     1964.

65) Kohler, Arthur L. and Stotland, Ezra. The End of
     Hope: A Social-Clinical Study of Suicide. Glencoe, Ill.:
     Free Press, 1964.

66) Landsberg, Paul Ludwig. The Experience of Death.
     The Moral Problem of Suicide. Trans. by Cynthia Row-
     land. New York: Philosophical Library, 1953.

67) Leonard, Calista V. Understanding and Preventing
     Suicide. Springfield, Ill.: Charles C. Thomas, 1967.

68) Lepp, Ignace. Death and Its Mysteries. New York:
     Macmillan, 1968.

69) Lester, David. Why People Kill Themselves. Spring-
     field, Ill.: Charles C. Thomas, 1972.

70) Lester, G. and D. Suicide: The Gamble with Death.
     Englewood Cliffs, N.J.: Prentice-Hall, 1971.

71) McCormick, Donald. The Unseen Killer. London:
     Fred Muller, 1964.

71a) McCulloch, J. Wallace and Alistair, E. Philip. Sui-
     cidal Behavior. New York: Pergamon Press, 1972.

72) Mailer, Norman. Marilyn. New York: Grosset &
     Dunlap, 1973.

73) Mannes, Marya. Waiting for the End. New York:
     Morrow, 1973.

74) Maris, Ronald W. Social Forces in Urban Suicide.
     Homewood, Ill.: Dorsey Press, 1969.

75) Masarynk, Thomas G. Suicide and the Meaning of
     Civilization. Chicago: University of Chicago Press,
     1970.

76) Meaker, M. J. Sudden Endings. New York: Double-
     day, 1965.

77) Meerloo, Joost A. Suicide and Mass Suicide. New
    York: Dutton, 1968.

78) Mental Health Research Fund. Depression and Suicide.
    London: Mental Health Research Fund, 1968.

79) Mintz, R. S. Detection and Management of the Suicidal
    Patient. (Disease-a-Month Series) Chicago: Year Book
    Medical Publishers, Inc., July 1961.

80) Moriyama, I. M. The Change in Mortality Trends in
    the United States. Washington, D. C.: Public Health
    Service, 1964.

81) National Institute of Mental Health, Indian Health Ser-
    vice. Suicide Among the American Indians. Washing-
    ton, D. C.: The Institute, 1969.

82) New Hampshire, Division of Mental Health. Suicide
    and Depression; Second Technical Assistance Project
    Conference. Concord: The Division, 1967.

83) Peck, Michael. "Optimism and Despair in Adolescent
    Suicide." College Student Personnel Abstracts, 1967.

83a) Plath, Sylvia. The Bell Jar. New York: Harper &
    Row, 1971.

84) Porterfield, Austin Larimore. Cultures of Violence:
    A Study of the Tragic Man in Society, Giving Attention
    to Philosophical, Psychological, and Cultural Stresses
    in Acts Against Life. Fort Worth: Texas Christian
    University, 1965.

85) Powell, Elwin H. The Design of Discord: Studies of
    Anomie: Suicide, Urban Society, War. New York:
    Oxford University Press, 1970.

86) Pretzel, Paul W. Understanding and Counseling the
    Suicidal Person. Nashville, Tenn.: Abingdon, 1972.

87) Resnick, Harvey L. Suicidal Behavior, Diagnosis, and
    Management. Boston: Little, Brown, 1968.

88) Retterstøl, Nils. Long-Term Prognosis after Attempted
    Suicide. Oslo: Universitetsforlaget; Springfield: Charles
    C. Thomas, 1970.

89)   Roberts, C. A. Primary Prevention of Psychiatric
      Disorders: The Clarence M. Hincks Memorial Lec-
      tures, 1967. Toronto: University of Toronto Press,
      1968.

90)   Rochlin, C. Griefs and Discontents. Boston: Little,
      Brown, 1965.

91)   Rosten, Norman. Marilyn: An Untold Story. New
      York: New American Library, 1973.

92)   Rush, Warren W. God's Answer to Suicide. New
      York: Vantage, 1970.

93)   St. John-Stevas, Norman A. F. The Right to Life.
      New York: Holt, Rinehart and Winston, 1964.

94)   Samaan, Makram. Suicidal Behaviour in Cairo (a
      psycho-social study). Cairo: Dar Al Maaref, 1963.

95)   Seiden, Richard H. Suicide Among Youth. A Review
      of the Literature, 1900-1967. Washington, D. C.:
      Public Health Service, 1969.

96)   Seward, Jack. Hara-Kiri; Japanese Ritual Suicide.
      Rutland, Vt.: Charles Little Co., 1968.

97)   Shean, Glenn D. Studies in Abnormal Behavior.
      Chicago: Rand McNally, 1971.

98)   Shneidman, Edwin S., ed. Death and the College
      Student. New York: Behavioral Publications, 1972.

99)   Shneidman, E. S., ed. Essays in Self-Destruction.
      New York: Science House, 1967.

100) Shneidman, Edwin S., ed. On the Nature of Suicide.
      San Francisco: Jossey-Bass, Inc., 1969.

101) Shneidman, Edwin S. and Farberow, Norman L., eds.
      Clues to Suicide. New York: McGraw-Hill, 1957.

102) Shneidman, E. S. Suicide: Some Classificatory Con-
      siderations. Special Treatment Situations. Des
      Plaines, Ill.: Forest Hospital Publications, 1962.

103) Shneidman, E. S. and Farberow, N. L. Suicide: The

Problem and Its Magnitude. Medical Bulletin-7.
Washington, D. C.: Veterans Administration, 1961.

104) Shneidman, E. S., Farberow, N. L., and Leonard,
Calista V. Some Facts About Suicides. Washington,
D. C.: U. S. Health, Education, and Welfare Department, Public Health Service Publication No. 852,
1961.

105) Shneidman, E. S., Farberow, N. L., and Leonard,
Calista V. Suicide: Evaluation and Treatment of
Suicidal Risk Among Schizophrenic Patients in Psy-
chiatric Hospitals. Medical Bulletin-8. Washington,
D. C.: Veterans Administration, 1962.

106) Shneidman, E. S., Farberow, N. L., and Litman, R. E.
The Psychology of Suicide. New York: Science House,
1970.

107) Shneidman, E. S. and Mandelkorn, P. How to Prevent
Suicide. Public Affairs Pamphlets No. 406. New
York: Public Affairs Committee, 1967.

108) Silverman, Charlotte. The Epidemiology of Depression. Baltimore: Johns Hopkins University Press,
1968.

109) Sprott, Samuel Ernest. The English Debate on Suicide; from Donne to Hume. La Salle, Ill.: Open
Court, 1961.

110) Steiner, Nancy H. A Closer Look at Ariel: A
Memory of Sylvia Plath. New York: Harper's
Magazine Press, 1973.

111) Stengel, Erwin. Suicide and Attempted Suicide.
Baltimore: Penguin Books, 1964.

112) Stern, Daniel. The Suicide Academy. New York:
McGraw-Hill, 1968.

113) Suicide in the United States, 1950-1964; a Study of
Suicide Statistics Showing Trends for 1950-1964 and
Differences by Age, Sex, Color, Marital Status and
Geographic Area for Selected Periods. Washington,
D. C.: Public Health Service, 1969.

114) Swinn, Richard Michael. Fundamentals of Behavior
     Pathology. New York: Wiley, 1970.

115) Thakur, Upendra. The History of Suicide in India:
     An Introduction. Delhi: Munshi Ram Manohar Lal,
     1963.

116) Thielicke, Helmut. Nihilism. New York: Harper
     & Row, 1961.

117) Tombs, Poole (pseud.). Suicidal Behavior. New
     York: Carlton, 1970.

118) Tucker, G. J. and Reinhardt, R. F. Suicide Attempts.
     NAMI-975. Pensacola, Fla.: U. S. Naval Aerospace
     Medical Institute, 1966.

119) U. S. Health, Education, and Welfare Department.
     Suicide Among the American Indians. Washington,
     D. C.: Public Health Service Publication No. 1903,
     June 1969.

120) Usher-Wilson, R. N. Suicide or Adoration. New
     York: Vantage Press, 1972.

121) Varah, Chad., ed. Samaritans: To Help Those
     Tempted to Suicide or Despair. New York: Macmil-
     lan, 1966.

122) Weiner, Irving B. Psychological Disturbance in
     Adolescence. New York: Wiley-Interscience, 1970.

123) West, Donald J. Murder Followed by Suicide. Lon-
     don & Edinburgh: Morrison & Gibbs, Ltd., 1965.
     (Also - Cambridge: Harvard University Press, 1966.)

124) Whittemore, K. Ten Centers. Atlanta: Lullwater
     Press, 1970.

125) Williams, Glanville. Sanctity of Life and the Crim-
     inal Law. New York: Knopf, 1957.

126) Wolff, Kurt, ed. Patterns of Self-Destruction: De-
     pression and Suicide. Springfield, Ill.: Charles C.
     Thomas, 1970.

127) Wood, Arthur L. Crime and Aggression in Changing

Ceylon: A Sociological Analysis of Homicide, Suicide and Economic Crime. Transactions of the American Philosophical Society, December 1961, 51, 132 p.

128) World Health Organization. Prevention of Suicide. (Public health papers 35.) 1968.

129) Yap, Pow-meng. Suicide in Hong Kong, with Special Reference to Attempted Suicide. Hong Kong: Hong Kong University Press, 1958.

130) Yochelson, L. , ed. Symposium on Suicide. Washington, D. C. : George Washington University School of Medicine, 1965.

131) Yolles, Stanley F. The Tragedy of Suicide in the U. S. Washington, D. C.: U. S. Government Printing Office, Public Health Service Publication No. 1558, 1966.

132) Zusman, Jack and Davidson, David L. Organizing the Community to Prevent Suicide. Springfield, Ill. : Charles C. Thomas, 1971.

II. THESES AND DISSERTATIONS

133) Allen, Adele I. A Study of Suicide and Attempted Suicide to Establish Patterns and Their Implications for Public Health Nursing. University of Colorado, 1960.

134) Amberg, William Frederic. A Cross-Indexed Study of Suicide Intervention Programs and Analysis of Current Models. Brigham Young University, 1970.

135) Bloom, Marshall H. An Analysis of Responses to the "Cry for Help." University of Califronia, Los Angeles, 1971.

136) Callender, Willard Douglas, Jr. A Social-Psychological Study of Suicide-Related Behavior in a Student Population. University of Connecticut, 1968.

137) Campion, Donald Richard. Patterns of Suicide in Philadelphia, 1948-1952. University of Pennsylvania, 1960.

138) Darbonne, Allen R. An Investigation Into the Communication Style of Suicidal Individuals. University of Southern California, 1967.

139) Devries, Alcon G. Methodological Problems in the Identification of Suicidal Behavior by Means of Two Personality Inventories. University of South Carolina, 1964.

139a) Doroff, David R. Attempted and Gestured Suicide in Adolescent Girls. Rutgers University, 1969.

140) Douglas, Jack Daniel. The Sociological Study of Suicidal Actions as Socially Meaningful Actions. Princeton University, 1967.

12

141) Erickson, Gustave A. Effects of Patient Selected Con-
      tingent Verbal Stimuli on Verbal Output of Hospitalized
      Suicidal Males. Arizona State University, 1965.

142) Esler, Harold Dean. An Investigation of the Causes
      of Suicide in Patients Diagnosed as Schizophrenic.
      Michigan State University, 1965.

143) Fisher, Sheila Abugov. Suicide Prevention and/or
      Crisis Services: A National Survey. Case Western
      Reserve University, 1972.

144) Fleischer, Murray S. Differential Rorschach Config-
      urations of Suicidal Psychiatric Patients: A Psycholog-
      ical Study of Threatened Attempted and Successful
      Suicides. Yeshiva University, 1957.

145) Furlong, Paul Thomas. Psychological Assessment of
      Potentially Suicidal Patients at the Community Mental
      Health Center, Salt Lake City, Utah. University of
      Utah, 1970.

146) Ganzler, Sidney. Some Interpersonal and Social Di-
      mensions of Suicidal Behavior. University of Cali-
      fornia, Los Angeles, 1967.

147) Geisel, Robert Lee. Suicide in Missouri: An Empir-
      ical Test of Durkheim's Social Integration Theory.
      University of Iowa, 1972.

148) Hattem, Jack Victor. The Precipitating Role of Dis-
      cordant Interpersonal Relationships in Suicidal Behavior.
      University of Houston, 1964.

149) Henderson, James Taylor. Competence, Threat, Hope
      and Self-Destructive Behavior. University of Mary-
      land, 1972.

150) Hoey, Henry Patrick. The Interpersonal Behavior of
      Suicidal Individuals. Ohio University, 1970.

151) Jacobs, Jerry. Adolescent Suicide Attempts: The
      Culmination of a Progressive Social Isolation. Uni-
      versity of California, Los Angeles, 1967.

152) Jones, Ronald Bennett. Suicidal Out-Patients: The
      MMPI and Case File Data. University of Oregon, 1969.

153)   Kinsinger, John Ray.   The Relationship Between
       Lethality of Suicidal Intentions and Assertive, Aggres-
       sive and Hostile Traits.   University of Texas, South-
       western Medical School, Dallas, 1971.

154)   Kochansky, Gerald Edwin.   Risk-Taking and Hedonic
       Mood Stimulation in Suicide Attempters.   Boston Uni-
       versity, 1970.

155)   Korrella, Karl.   Teen-Age Suicidal Gestures: A Study
       of Suicidal Behavior Among High School Students.   Uni-
       versity of Oregon, 1971.

156)   Krauss, Herbert H.   A Cross-Cultural Study of Suicide.
       Northwestern University, 1967.

157)   Lee, Mercile Johnson.   A Search for Meaning: A Study
       of Threatened, Attempted, and Completed Suicides
       Among Selected College Students.   The Hartford Semi-
       nary Foundation, 1969.

158)   Lettieri, Dan J.   Affect, Attitude and Cognition in
       Suicidal Persons.   University of Kansas, 1970.

159)   Linehan, Marsha M.   Sex Differences in Suicide and
       Attempted Suicide: A Study of Differential Social Ac-
       ceptability and Expectations.   Loyola University, 1971.

160)   McEvoy, Theodore Lee.   A Comparison of Suicidal
       and Nonsuicidal Patients by Means of the Thematic
       Apperception Test.   University of California, Los
       Angeles, 1963.

161)   Maris, Ronald William.   Suicide in Chicago: An Ex-
       amination of Emile Durkheim's Theory of Suicide.
       University of Illinois at Urbana-Champagne, 1966.

162)   Martin, Harry.   A Rorschach Study of Suicide.   Uni-
       versity of Kentucky, 1959.

163)   Miller, Dorothy Hillyer.   Suicidal Careers: Toward a
       Symbolic Interaction Theory of Suicide.   University of
       California, Berkeley, 1968.

164)   Monck, Maureen Finnerty.   The Relationship between
       Bioelectrical Potential Differences and Suicidal Be-
       havior.   New York University, 1968.

165)   Neuringer, C. An Exploratory Study of Suicidal Think-
       ing. University of Kansas, 1960.

166)   Parkin, James M. Assignment of Responsibility for
       Deaths Perceived as Unintentioned, Subintentioned, or In-
       tentioned. Purdue University, 1972.

167)   Pearson, Nils Steven. Identification of Psychological
       Variables Distinguishing Suicide Attempters within a
       Sample of Depressive Individuals. Rutgers University,
       1972.

168)   Porterfield, Austin Laremore. Cultures of Violence,
       a Study of the Tragic Man in Society, Giving Attention
       to Philosophical, Psychological, and Cultural Stresses
       in Acts Against Life. Texas Christian University, 1965.

169)   Praul, Edward John. The Role of the College Coun-
       selor with Regard to the Problem of Suicide Among
       Students; An Exploratory Study. University of Toledo,
       1971.

170)   Reese, Frederick D., Jr. School-Age Suicide: The
       Educational Parameters. University of Ohio, 1967.

171)   Rudestam, Kjell Erik. Stockholm and Los Angeles: A
       Cross-Cultural Study of the Communication of Suicidal
       Intent. University of Oregon, 1969.

172)   Rutstein, Eleanor H. The Effects of Aggressive Stim-
       ulation on Suicidal Patients: An Experimental Study of
       the Psychoanalytic Theory of Suicide. New York Uni-
       versity, 1970.

173)   Sacks, Harvey. The Search for Help: No One to Turn
       To. University of California, Berkeley, 1967.

174)   Sakheim, George T. Suicidal Responses on the Ror-
       schach Test: A Validation Study, Protocols of Suicidal
       Mental Patients Compared with Those of Non-Suicidal
       Patients. Florida State University, 1954.

175)   Scholz, James Andrew. Defense Styles in Suicide
       Attempters. Fordham University, 1972.

176)   Schwartz, Michael B. Suicide Prevention and Suicidal
       Behavior. Tulane University School of Social Work, 1971.

177)   Shagoury, Joan Bonnar. A Study of Marital Commun-
        ication and Attitudes Toward Suicide in Suicidal and
        Non-Suicidal Individuals. University of Florida, 1971.

178)   Snavely, Harry Robinson. Factors Underlying Clinician
        Bias in Decisions About Suicide Potential. University
        of California, Los Angeles, 1970.

179)   Temoche, A. Suicide and Known Mental Disease.
        Harvard University, 1961.

180)   Vogel, Roberta Burrage. A Projective Study of Dy-
        namic Factors in Attempted Suicide. Michigan State
        University, 1968.

181)   Wendling, Aubrey. Suicide in the San Francisco Bay
        Region, 1938-1942 and 1948-1952. University of Wash-
        ington, 1954.

182)   White, Hugh Pelham. The Lethal Aggression Rate and
        the Suicide-Murder Ratio; A Synthetic Theory of Suicide
        and Homicide. University of North Carolina, 1969.

183)   Windsor, James Clayton. An Analysis of the Child
        Rearing Attitudes of the Parents of a Group of Ado-
        lescents Who Attempted Suicide. University of Virginia,
        1972.

III. ARTICLES IN BOOKS

184) Adam, Kenneth S., Lohrenz, John G., and Harper, Dorothy. "Broken homes, suicidal ideation and depression," a preliminary report on university students, in Fox, Richard (ed.), Proceedings of the Fifth International Conference for Suicide Prevention, London, September 24-27, 1969 (Vienna: International Association for Suicide Prevention, 1970), pp. 198-202.

185) Adams, A. C. "Student counselling in a teacher training college," in Fox, Richard (ed.), Proceedings of the Fifth International Conference for Suicide Prevention, London, Sept. 24-27, 1969 (Vienna: International Association for Suicide Prevention, 1970), pp. 186-187.

186) Ansbacher, Heinz L. "Suicide: The Adlerian point of view," in Farberow, N. L. and Shneidman, E. S. (eds.), The Cry for Help (New York: McGraw-Hill, 1961). Chapter 15, pp. 204-219.

187) Ayd, Frank. "Use and misuse of drugs in suicide prevention," in Farberow, Norman L. (ed.), Proceedings: Fourth International Conference for Suicide Prevention (Los Angeles: Suicide Prevention Center, 1968), pp. 54-60.

188) Bagley, Christopher. "Causes and prevention of repeated attempted suicide," in Fox, Richard (ed.), Proceedings of the Fifth International Conference for Suicide Prevention (Vienna: International Association for Suicide Prevention, 1970), pp. 96-101.

189) Bakan, David. "Suicide and the method of introspection," in Bakan, D. (ed.), On Method; Toward a Reconstruction of Psychological Investigation (San Francisco: Jossey-Bass, 1967).

190) Barraclough, B. M., Nelson, B., Bunch, J., and

17

Sainsbury, P. "The diagnostic classification and psychiatric treatment of 100 suicides, " in Fox, Richard (ed.), Proceedings of the Fifth International Conference for Suicide Prevention, London, Sept. 24-27, 1969 (Vienna: International Association for Suicide Prevention, 1970), pp. 129-132.

191)   Barraclough, B. M., Nelson, B., and Sainsbury, P. "The diagnostic classification and psychiatric treatment of 25 suicides, " in Farberow, Norman L. (ed.), Proceedings: Fourth International Conference for Suicide Prevention (Los Angeles: Suicide Prevention Center, 1968), pp. 61-66.

192)   Barraclough, B. M. and Sainsbury, Peter. "The effect that coroners have on the suicide rate and the open verdict rate, " in Hare, E. H. and Wing, J. K. (eds.), Psychiatric Epidemiology (London: Oxford University Press, 1970).

193)   Bender, Lauretta. "Children preoccupied with suicide. " in Bender, Lauretta, Aggression, Hostility and Anxiety in Children (Springfield, Ill.: Charles C. Thomas, 1953), pp. 66-90.

194)   Bernspang, Erik. "Faith problems and suicide prevention, " in Farberow, Norman L. (ed.), Proceedings: Fourth International Conference for Suicide Prevention (Los Angeles: Suicide Prevention Center, 1968), pp. 121-122.

195)   Bill, Aydin Z. "Prevention of hospitalization and suicide in Delaware--a controlled study, " in Fox, Richard (ed.), Proceedings of the Fifth International Conference for Suicide Prevention, London, Sept. 24-27, 1969 (Vienna: International Association for Suicide Prevention, 1970), pp. 239-242.

196)   Bloomberg, Sam G. "Suicide Anonymous, " in Farberow, Norman L. (ed.), Proceedings: Fourth International Conference for Suicide Prevention (Los Angeles: Suicide Prevention Center, 1968), pp. 111-116.

197)   Bogard, Howard M. "Rationale and implementation of a suicide prevention program in a general hospital, " in Farberow, Norman L. (ed.), Proceedings: Fourth International Conference for Suicide Prevention (Los

Angeles: Suicide Prevention Center, 1968), pp. 104-110.

198)   Breed, Warren. "The social psychology of suicide, "
       in Farberow, Norman L. (ed.), Proceedings: Fourth
       International Conference for Suicide Prevention (Los
       Angeles: Suicide Prevention Center, 1968), pp. 286-
       291.

199)   Bucklew, Reba M. "Suicide, " in Proceedings of the
       Southwestern Sociological Association, 14:70-73, 1964.

200)   Bunney, William E. , Jr. and Fawcett, Jan. A. "Bi-
       ochemical research in depression and suicide, " in
       Resnick, H. L. P. (ed.), Suicidal Behaviors: Diagnosis
       and Management (Boston: Little, Brown & Co. , 1968),
       pp. 144-159.

201)   Cain, Albert and Fast, Irene. "Parent suicide and
       suicide prevention, " in Fox, Richard (ed.), Proceed-
       ings of the Fifth International Conference for Suicide
       Prevention, London, Sept. 24-27, 1969 (Vienna: Inter-
       national Association for Suicide Prevention, 1970),
       pp. 187-190.

202)   Cantor, Joel. "Alcoholism as a suicidal equivalent, "
       in Farberow, Norman L. (ed.), Proceedings: Fourth
       International Conference for Suicide Prevention (Los
       Angeles: Suicide Prevention Center, 1968), pp. 328-
       339.

203)   Cantor, Joel M. "The search for the suicidal per-
       sonality, " in Wolff, Kurt (ed.), Patterns of Self-De-
       struction (Springfield, Ill. : Charles C. Thomas, 1970),
       pp. 56-66.

204)   Chen, Ronald. "Community cooperative emergency
       service: the objectives and problems in the organiza-
       tional process, " in Fox, Richard (ed.), Proceedings
       of the Fifth International Conference for Suicide Pre-
       vention, London, Sept. 24-27, 1969 (Vienna: Interna-
       tional Association for Suicide Prevention, 1970), pp.
       64-67.

205)   Chron, Jacques. "Suicide and the notions of death, "
       in Farberow, Norman L. (ed.), Proceedings: Fourth
       International Conference for Suicide Prevention (Los
       Angeles: Suicide Prevention Center, 1968), pp. 268-276.

206)   Cohen, E. "Suicide," A study of definition, in Fox,
        Richard (ed.), Proceedings of the Fifth International
        Conference for Suicide Prevention, 1970), pp. 225-227.

207)   Cohen, Sidney. "The psychedelic way of death," in
        Farberow, Norman L. (ed.), Proceedings: Fourth In-
        ternational Conference for Suicide Prevention (Los
        Angeles: Suicide Prevention Center, 1968), pp. 75-76,
        p. 106.

208)   Connell, P. H. "Suicidal attempts in childhood and
        adolescence," in Howells, J. G. (ed.), Modern Per-
        spectives in Child Psychiatry (Edinburgh/London:
        Oliver & Boyd, 1965.

209)   Crammer, J. L. "Completed suicide as a guide to
        its prevention," in Fox, Richard (ed.), Proceedings
        of the Fifth International Conference for Suicide Pre-
        vention, London, Sept. 24-27, 1969 (Vienna: Interna-
        tional Association for Suicide Prevention, 1970), pp.
        213-216.

210)   Curphey, Theodore J. "Drug deaths: A problem in
        certification," in Farberow, Norman L. (ed.), Pro-
        ceedings: Fourth International Conference for Suicide
        Prevention (Los Angeles: Suicide Prevention Center,
        1968), pp. 22-28.

211)   Curphey, Theodore J. "The role of the social sci-
        entist in the medicolegal certification of death from
        suicide," in Farberow, N. L. and Shneidman, E. S.
        (eds.), The Cry for Help (New York: McGraw-Hill,
        1961), Chapter 7, pp. 110-117.

212)   Curphey, Theodore J., Shneidman, Edwin S., and
        Farberow, Norman L. "Drugs, deaths and suicides--
        Problems of the coroner," in Clark, William G. and
        del Guidice, Joseph (eds.), Principles of Psychopharm-
        acology (New York/London: Academic Press, 1970),
        pp. 523-536.

213)   Cutter, F. and Farberow, N. L. "Consensus Ror-
        schach theory and clinical application," in Klopfer,
        B. and Meyer, M. (eds.), Developments in the Ror-
        schach Technique. Vol. III. (New York: Harcourt,
        Brace, Jovanovich, 1970), pp. 209-261.

214) Cutter, Fred, Farberow, Norman L., and Cutter,
      Dorothy. "Suicide in art," in Farberow, Norman L.
      (ed.), Proceedings: Fourth International Conference
      for Suicide Prevention (Los Angeles: Suicide Preven-
      tion Center, 1968), pp. 208-215.

215) Danon-Boileau, H., Lab, P., and Levy, Eliane "A
      special type of chronic suicidal case," in Fox, Rich-
      ard (ed.), Proceedings of the Fifth International Con-
      ference for Suicide Prevention, London, Sept. 24-27,
      1969 (Vienna: International Association for Suicide Pre-
      vention, 1970), p. 267.

216) Davis, Joseph H. and Spelman, Joseph W. "The role
      of the medical examiner or coroner," in Resnik,
      H. L. P. (ed.), Suicidal Behaviors: Diagnosis and
      Management (Boston: Little, Brown & Co., 1968),
      pp. 453-461.

217) De Rosis, Louis. "Suicide: The Horney point of view,"
      in Farberow, N. L. and Shneidman, E. S. (eds.), The
      Cry for Help (New York: McGraw-Hill, 1961), Chapter
      17, pp. 236-254.

218) De Vos, George A. "Suicide in cross-cultural per-
      spective," in Resnik, H. L. P. (ed.), Suicidal Be-
      haviors: Diagnosis and Management (Boston: Little,
      Brown & Co., 1968), pp. 105-134.

219) Deniker, Pierre. "The chemotherapy of depressions
      and the risk of suicide," in Fox, Richard (ed.), Pro-
      ceedings of the Fifth International Conference for Sui-
      cide Prevention, London, Sept. 24-27, 1969, (Vienna:
      Intern. Assoc. for Suicide Prevention, 1970), pp. 260-267.

220) Devries, Alcon. "Prediction of suicide by means of
      psychological tests," in Farberow, Norman L. (ed.),
      Proceedings: Fourth International Conference for Sui-
      cide Prevention (Los Angeles: Suicide Prevention Cen-
      ter, 1968), pp. 252-265.

221) Diamond, Solomon. "The nondirective handling of
      suicidal behavior," in Farberow, N. L. and Shneid-
      man, E. S. (eds.), The Cry for Help (New York:
      McGraw-Hill, 1961), Chapter 19, pp. 281-289.

222) Diggory, James C. "Suicide and value," in Resnik,

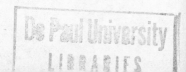

H. L. P. (ed.), Suicidal Behaviors: Diagnosis and
Management (Boston: Little, Brown & Co., 1968),
pp. 3-18.

223)   Dizmang, Larry. "Self-destructive behavior in children: A suicidal equivalent, " in Farberow, Norman L.
(ed.), Proceedings: Fourth International Conference for
Suicide Prevention (Los Angeles: Suicide Prevention
Center, 1968), pp. 316-320.

224)   Dominian, J. "Suicide as a gesture in marital break-
down, " in Fox, Richard (ed.), Proceedings of the
Fifth International Conference for Suicide Prevention,
London, Sept. 24-27, 1969 (Vienna: International Association for Suicide Prevention, 1970), pp. 167-169.

225)   Dorpat, Theodore L., Anderson, William F., and
Ripley, Herbert S. "The relationship of physical ill-
ness to suicide, " in Resnik, H. L. P. (ed.), Suicidal
Behaviors: Diagnosis and Management (Boston: Little,
Brown & Co., 1968), pp. 209-219.

226)   Ettlinger, Ruth W. "Certification of suicide in Sweden, " in Farberow, Norman L. (ed.), Proceedings:
Fourth International Conference for Suicide Prevention
(Los Angeles: Suicide Prevention Center, 1968), pp.
36-38.

227)   Ettlinger, Ruth and Wistrand, Marianne. "Suicide
prevention at a general hospital, " in Fox, Richard
(ed.), Proceedings of the Fifth International Conference
for Suicide Prevention, London, Sept. 24-27, 1969
(Vienna: International Association for Suicide Prevention, 1970), pp. 243-245.

228)   Farber, Maurice L. "Suicide and hope: a theoretical
analysis, " in Farberow, Norman L. (ed.), Proceedings: Fourth International Conference for Suicide Pre-
tion (Los Angeles: Suicide Prevention Center, 1968),
pp. 297-306.

229)   Farberow, N. L. "Crisis, disaster and suicide: Theory
and therapy, " in Shneidman, E. S. (ed.), Essays in
Self-Destruction (New York: Science House, 1967).

230)   Farberow, N. L. "Group psychotherapy with suicidal
persons, " in Resnik, H. L. P. (ed.), Suicidal Be-

haviors: Diagnosis and Management (Boston: Little, Brown & Co., 1968), pp. 328-340.

231) Farberow, Norman L. "The suicidal patient in medical practice," in Tice's Practice of Medicine. Vol. X. Hagerstown, Md. (New York: Harper & Row, 1970), Chapter 42.

232) Farberow, Norman L. "Suicide: psychological aspects," in International Encyclopedia of the Social Sciences (New York: Macmillan Co. and the Free Press, 1968), pp. 390-394.

233) Farberow, Norman L. and Shneidman, Edwin S. "A survey of agencies for the prevention of suicide," in Farberow, N. L. and Shneidman, E. S. (eds.), The Cry for Help (New York: McGraw-Hill, 1961), Chapter 10, pp. 136-149.

234) Farberow, Norman L., Schneidman, Edwin S., and Leonard, Calista V. "Suicide among schizophrenic mental hospital patients," in Farberow, N. L. and Shneidman, E. S. (eds.), The Cry for Help (New York: McGraw-Hill, 1961), Chapter 6, pp. 78-109.

235) Farberow, Norman L.; Stein, Kenneth; Hirsch, Sophie; Darbonne, Allen; and Cutter, Fred. "Indirect self-destructive behavior in patients with diagnoses of diabetes," in Farberow, Norman L. (ed.), Proceedings: Fourth International Conference for Suicide Prevention (Los Angeles: Suicide Prevention Center, 1968), pp. 345-355.

236) Finlay, S. E. "Suicide and self-injury in Leeds University students," in Fox, Richard (ed.), Proceedings of the Fifth International Conference for Suicide Prevention, London, Sept. 24-27, 1969 (Vienna: International Association for Suicide Prevention, 1970), pp. 202-205.

237) Follinsbee, Marjory C. "Time passes--a history of two suicidally oriented adolescents," in Farberow, Norman L. (ed.), Proceedings: Fourth International Conference for Suicide Prevention (Los Angeles: Suicide Prevention Center, 1968), pp. 391-395.

238) Fox, Richard. "Samaritans and the medical profes-

sion, " in Fox, Richard (ed.), Proceedings of the Fifth
International Conference for Suicide Prevention, London, Sept. 24-27, 1969 (Vienna: International Association for Suicide Prevention, 1970), pp. 152-156.

239)   Fox, Richard. "The Samaritans, " in Resnik, H. L. P.
       (ed.), Suicidal Behaviors: Diagnosis and Management
       (Boston: Little, Brown & Co. , 1968), pp. 405-417.

240)   Frederick, Calvin J. "Treatment considerations in
       suicidal patients, " in Fox, Richard (ed.), Proceed-
       ings of the Fifth International Conference for Suicide
       Prevention, London, Sept. 24-27, 1969 (Vienna: Inter-
       national Association for Suicide Prevention, 1970),
       pp. 229-232. [Abstract.]

241)   Friedman, Paul. "The history of the Zilboorg Ar-
       chives, " in Farberow, Norman L. (ed.), Proceed-
       ings: Fourth International Conference for Suicide Pre-
       vention (Los Angeles: Suicide Prevention Center,
       1968), pp. 307-315.

242)   Friedman, Paul. "Suicide, " in Deutsch, A. (ed.),
       The Encyclopedia of Mental Health (New York: Frank-
       lin Watts, 1963), pp. 1983-1991.
       (Reprinted--Metuchen, N. J. : Scarecrow Press, 1970.)

243)   Futterman, S. "Suicide: Psychoanalytic point of view,"
       in Farberow, N. L. and Shneidman, E. S. (eds.), The
       Cry for Help (New York: McGraw-Hill, 1961), pp.
       167-180.

244)   Garrard, R. L. "Community suicide prevention activ-
       ities: Greensboro, North Carolina, " in Resnik, H. L.
       P. (ed.), Suicidal Behaviors: Diagnosis and Manage-
       ment (Boston: Little, Brown & Co. , 1968), pp. 399-
       404.

245)   Gershman, Andrew P. "A critical period in attempted
       suicide: the first contact following the act, " in Fox,
       Richard (ed.), Proceedings of the Fifth International
       Conference for Suicide Prevention, London, Sept. 24-
       27, 1969 (Vienna: International Association for Suicide
       Prevention, 1970), pp. 94-95.

246)   Gibbs, J. P. "Suicide, " in Merton, R. K. and Nisbet,
       R. A. (eds.), Contemporary Social Problems (New

York: Harcourt, Brace, and World, 1961).

247) Glaser, Kurt. "Suicide in children and adolescents, "
      in Weissman, S. L. and Abt, L. E. (eds.), Acting
      Out: Theoretical and Clinical Aspects (New York:
      Grune & Stratton, 1965).

248) Glaser, Kurt. "Suicide prevention in the young--whose
      role?", in Farberow, Norman L. (ed.), Proceedings:
      Fourth International Conference for Suicide Prevention
      (Los Angeles: Suicide Prevention Center, 1968), pp.
      368-371.

249) Goldberg, Martin and Mudd, Emily H. "The effects
      of suicidal behavior upon marriage and the family, " in
      Resnik, H. L. P. (ed.), Suicidal Behaviors: Diagnosis
      and Management (Boston: Little, Brown & Co. , 1968),
      pp. 348-356.

250) Gorceix, Antone L. "First clinical encounters with the
      survivor, " in Fox, Richard (ed.), Proceedings of the
      Fifth International Conference for Suicide Prevention,
      London, Sept. 24-27, 1969 (Vienna: International Asso-
      ciation for Suicide Prevention, 1970), pp. 36-37.

251) Gorceix, Antone and Zimbacca, Nicole. "The useful-
      ness of psychological tests with attempted suicides, "
      in Farberow, Norman L. (ed.), Proceedings: Fourth
      International Conference for Suicide Prevention (Los
      Angeles: Suicide Prevention Center, 1968), pp. 166-190.

252) Green, Maurice R. "Suicide: The Sullivanian point of
      view, " in Farberow, N. L. and Shneidman, E. S.
      (eds.), The Cry for Help (New York: McGraw-Hill,
      1961), pp. 220-235.

253) Gutbrodt, Erika J. , Lyman, Roger C. , and Jerry,
      Marian B. "Suicide attempts and suicide in psychiatric
      patients, a risk assessment with psychological tech-
      niques, " in Proceedings of the Annual Convention of
      the American Psychological Association, 1970, pp. 559-
      560.

254) Hamburger, Ernst. "Homicidal behavior as a suicidal
      equivalent, " in Farberow, Norman L. (ed.), Proceed-
      ings: Fourth International Conference for Suicide Pre-
      vention (Los Angeles: Suicide Prevention Center), pp.
      340-344.

255)   Hankoff, Leon D. and Waltzer, Herbert. "A suicide-
        prevention service in a psychiatric receiving hospital
        setting, " in Resnik, H. L. P. (ed.), Suicidal Behav-
        iors: Diagnosis and Management (Boston: Little,
        Brown & Co., 1968), pp. 391-398.

256)   Harris, James R. and Myers, J. Martin. "Hospital
        management of the suicidal patient, " in Resnik, H.
        L. P. (ed.), Suicidal Behaviors: Diagnosis and Man-
        agement (Boston: Little, Brown & Co., 1968), pp.
        297-305.

257)   Heilig, S. M. "The Los Angeles Suicide Prevention
        Center, " in Farberow, Norman L. (ed.), Proceed-
        ings: Fourth International Conference for Suicide Pre-
        vention (Los Angeles: Suicide Prevention Center, 1968),
        pp. 117-120.

258)   Heilig, S. M. and Klugman, D. J. "The social
        worker in a suicide prevention center, " in Parad,
        H. J. (ed.), Crisis Intervention: Selected Readings
        (New York: Family Service Association of America,
        1965), pp. 274-283.

259)   Hendin, Herbert. "Suicide: Psychoanalytic point of
        view, " in Farberow, N. L. and Shneidman, E. S.
        (eds.), The Cry for Help (New York: McGraw-Hill,
        1961), Chapter 13, pp. 181-192.

260)   Herzog, Alfred and Resnik, H. L. P. "A clinical
        study of parental response to adolescent death by sui-
        cide with recommendations for approaching the survi-
        vors, " in Farberow, Norman L. (ed.), Proceedings:
        Fourth International Conference for Suicide Prevention
        (Los Angeles: Suicide Prevention Center, 1968), pp.
        381-390.

261)   Heyse, H., Kockott, G., and Feuerlein, W. "The
        serious suicidal attempt: A biometric investigation of
        100 patients, " in Fox, Richard (ed.), Proceedings of
        the Fifth International Conference for Suicide Preven-
        tion, London, Sept. 24-27, 1969 (Vienna: International
        Association for Suicide Prevention, 1970), pp. 42-45.

262)   Hole, Günter P. "Correlations between guilt feelings,
        religion and suicidal tendencies in depressed patients,"
        in Fox, Richard (ed.), Proceedings of the Fifth Inter-

national Conference for Suicide Prevention, London,
Sept. 24-27, 1969 (Vienna: International Association
for Suicide Prevention, 1970), pp. 59-61.

263) Hunter, Richard C. "The role of the mental health
association, " in Resnik, H. L. P. (ed.), Suicidal Behaviors: Diagnosis and Management (Boston: Little
Brown & Co., 1968), pp. 479-485.

264) Iga, M. "Japanese adolescent suicide and social
structure, " in Shneidman, E. S. (ed.), Essays in
Self-Destruction (New York: Science House, 1967).

265) Ironside, Wallace and Kehoe, Michael. "Studies in
the experimental induction of depression using hypnosis: the depressive responses with fantasies of being
killed, suicide, and sleep, " in Proceedings of the
Third World Congress of Psychiatry (Toronto: Univer-
sities of Toronto and McGill Presses, 1962).

266) Jackson, D. D. "Theories of suicide, " in Shneidman, E. S. and Farberow, N. L. (eds.), Clues to
Suicide (New York: McGraw-Hill, 1957), pp. 11-21.

267) Jacobson, Helmuth. "The dialogue of a world-weary
man with his Ba, " in Hillman, J. (ed.), Studies in
Jungian Thought: Timeless Documents of the Soul
(Evanston, Ill.: Northwestern University Press, 1968),
pp. 5-54.

268) Jones, Keith E. "Some social and personal factors in
twenty attempted suicides, " in Fox, Richard (ed.),
Proceedings of the Fifth International Conference for
Suicide Prevention, London, Sept. 24-27, 1969 (Vienna:
International Association for Suicide Prevention, 1970),
pp. 235-236.

269) Kalinowsky, Lothar B. "Somatotherapy of suicidal
patients, " in Resnik, H. L. P. (ed.), Suicidal Behaviors: Diagnosis and Management (Boston: Little,
Brown & Co., 1968), pp. 306-312.

270) Kearney, T. R. "Aetiology of attempted suicide--a
preliminary report, " in Fox, Richard (ed.), Proceedings of the Fifth International Conference for Suicide
Prevention, London, Sept. 24-27, 1969 (Vienna: International Association for Suicide Prevention, 1970), pp.
190-194.

271)   Kelly, George A.   "Suicide: The personal construct
       point of view, " in Farberow, N. L. and Shneidman,
       E. S. (eds.), The Cry for Help (New York: McGraw-
       Hill, 1961), Chapter 18, pp. 255-280.

272)   Kiev, Ari and Slavin, Jane.   "The natural history of
       attempted suicide, " in Fox, Richard (ed.), Proceed-
       ings of the Fifth International Conference for Suicide
       Prevention, London, Sept. 24-27, 1969 (Vienna: Inter-
       national Association for Suicide Prevention, 1970),
       pp. 106-108.

273)   Klebba, Joan.   "Mortality trends in the United States:
       1954-1963, "   P. H. S. Publication No. 1000-series
       20(2), June 1966 (Washington, D. C. : National Center
       for Health Statistics), pp. 50-53.

274)   Kleiner, George J. and Hirsh, Joseph.   "Suicide in
       pregnancy, " in Fox, Richard (ed.), Proceedings of
       the Fifth International Conference for Suicide Preven-
       tion, London, Sept. 24-27, 1969 (Vienna: International
       Association for Suicide Prevention, 1970), pp. 170-171.

275)   Kline, Nathan S.   "Lithium as a prophylactic against
       recurrence of affective disorders, " in Fox, Richard
       (ed.), Proceedings of the Fifth International Conference
       for Suicide Prevention, London, Sept. 24-27, 1969
       (Vienna: International Association for Suicide Preven-
       tion, 1970), pp. 256-259.

276)   Kline, Nathan S.   "Pharmacotherapy of the depressed
       and suicidal patient, " in Resnik, H. L. P. (ed.),
       Suicidal Behaviors: Diagnosis and Management (Boston:
       Little, Brown & Co. , 1968), pp. 313-327.

277)   Kloes, Karen K.   "The suicidal patient in the com-
       munity: A challenge for nurses, " in A. N. A. Clinical
       Sessions, Dallas (Dallas: Appleton-Century-Crofts,
       1968).

278)   Klopfer, Bruno.   "Suicide: The Jungian point of view,"
       in Farberow, N. L. and Shneidman, E. S. (eds.), The
       Cry for Help (New York: McGraw-Hill, 1961), Chapter
       14, pp. 193-203.

279)   Knight, James A.   "Suicide among students, " in
       Resnik, H. L. P. (ed.), Suicidal Behaviors: Diagnosis

and Management (Boston: Little, Brown & Co., 1968), pp. 228-240.

280) Kockott, Goetz and Feuerlein, Wilhelm. "The relationship between suicidal attempt and delirium tremens," in Farberow, Norman L. (ed.), Proceedings: Fourth International Conference for Suicide Prevention (Los Angeles: Suicide Prevention Center, 1968), pp. 71-74.

281) Kockott, G., Heyse, H., and Feuerlein, W. "The repeated suicidal attempt," in Fox, Richard (ed.), Proceedings of the Fifth International Conference for Suicide Prevention, London, Sept. 24-27, 1969 (Vienna: Intern. Assoc. for Suicide Prevention, 1970), pp. 45-52.

282) Kornmaaler, Ole and Sørensen, B. Florian. "Suicide among alcoholics," in Fox, Richard (ed.), Proceedings of the Fifth International Conference for Suicide Prevention, London, Sept. 24-27, 1969 (Vienna: International Association for Suicide Prevention, 1970), pp. 150-151.

283) Kreeger, Irving S. "Problems of transference and counter-transference in the psychological treatment of suicidal patients," in Fox, Richard (ed.), Proceedings of the Fifth International Conference for Suicide Prevention, London, Sept. 24-27, 1969 (Vienna: International Association for Suicide Prevention, 1970), pp. 104-106.

284) Laufer, Moses. "Suicide attempts in adolescence," in Fox, Richard (ed.), Proceedings of the Fifth International Conference for Suicide Prevention, London, Sept. 24-27, 1969 (Vienna: International Association for Suicide Prevention, 1970), pp. 102-103.

285) Lieberman, Daniel. "Suicide among adolescents," in Wolff, Kurt (ed.), Patterns of Self-Destruction (Springfield, Ill.: Charles C. Thomas, 1970), pp. 18-28.

286) Lin, T-Y. "Some epidemiological findings of suicides in youth," in Caplan, G. and Lebovici, S. (eds.), Adolescents in a Period of Change (New York: Basic Books, 1967).

287) Linden, Joachim. "Attempted suicide--a statistical and sociological analysis," in Fox, Richard (ed.),

Proceedings of the Fifth International Conference for
Suicide Prevention, London, Sept. 24-27, 1969 (Vienna:
International Association for Suicide Prevention, 1970),
pp. 245-246.

288)   Litman, R. E.   "Eroticism, aggression and suicide in
         depressions, " in Masserman, J. H. (ed.), Science
         and Psychoanalysis.   Vol. 17 (New York: Grune &
         Stratton, 1970).

289)   Litman, R. E.   "Evaluation and management of the
         suicidal patient, " in Enelow, A. (ed.), Depression in
         Medical Practice (Rahway, N. J.: Merck, Sharp &
         Dohme, 1969.

290)   Litman, Robert E.   "Psychotherapists' orientations
         toward suicide, " in Resnik, H. L. P. (ed.), Suicidal
         Behaviors: Diagnosis and Management (Boston: Little,
         Brown & Co., 1968), Chapter 27.

291)   Litman, R. E.   "Suicide: A clinical manifestation of
         acting out, " in Abt, L. E. and Weissman, S. L.
         (eds.), Acting Out (New York: Grune & Stratton, 1965).

292)   Litman, R. E.   "The suicidal patient, " in Fink, P. J.
         and Oaks, W. W. (eds.), Psychiatry and the Internist
         (New York: Grune & Stratton, 1970).

293)   Litman, Robert E. and Farberow, Norman L.   "Emer-
         gency evaluation of self-destructive potentiality, " in
         Farberow, N. L. and Shneidman, E. S. (eds.), The
         Cry for Help (New York: McGraw-Hill, 1961), Chapter
         4, pp. 48-59.

294)   Litman, Robert E. and Farberow, Norman L.   "Eval-
         uating the effectiveness of suicide prevention, " in Fox,
         Richard (ed.), Proceedings of the Fifth International
         Conference for Suicide Prevention, London, Sept. 24-
         27, 1969 (Vienna: International Association for Suicide
         Prevention, 1970), pp. 246-250.

295)   Litman, Robert E. and Tabachnick, Norman.   "Psy-
         choanalytic theories of suicide, " in Farberow, Norman
         L, (ed.), Proceedings: Fourth International Conference
         for Suicide Prevention (Los Angeles: Suicide Preven-
         tion Center, 1968), pp. 277-285.

296)   Lonsdorf, Richard G.   "Legal aspects of suicide, " in
       Resnik, H. L. P. (ed.), Suicidal Behaviors: Diagnosis
       and Management (Boston: Little, Brown & Co. , 1968),
       pp. 135-143.

297)   McClelland, D.   "The Harlequin complex, " in White,
       R. W. (ed.), The Study of Lives (Englewood Cliffs,
       N. J. : Prentice-Hall, Inc. , 1963), pp. 94-119.

298)   McGee, L. I. and Holtner, Seward.   "The role of the
       clergy, " in Resnik, H. L. P. (ed.), Suicidal Behaviors:
       Diagnosis and Management (Boston: Little, Brown &
       Co. , 1968), pp. 441-452.

299)   McGee, Richard K.   "The manpower problem in suicide
       prevention, " in Farberow, Norman L. (ed.), Pro-
       ceedings: Fourth International Conference for Suicide
       Prevention (Los Angeles: Suicide Prevention Center,
       1968), pp. 98-103.

300)   McGee, Richard K. and McGee, Jean P.   "A total
       community response to the cry for help: We Care, Inc. ,
       of Orlando, Florida, " in Resnik, H. L. P. (ed.), Sui-
       cidal Behaviors: Diagnosis and Management (Boston:
       Little, Brown & Co. , 1968), pp. 441-452.

301)   Matilda S. and Angle, Carol R.   " 'Suicide' as seen in
       Poison Control Centres, in those aged 6-18, " in Fox,
       Richard (ed.), Proceedings of the Fifth International
       Conference for Suicide Prevention, London, Sept. 24-
       27, 1969 (Vienna: International Association for Suicide
       Prevention, 1970), pp. 146-150.

302)   Mayer, Doris Y.   "An approach to the psychotherapy
       of suicidal people, " in Fox, Richard (ed.), Proceed-
       ings of the Fifth International Conference for Suicide
       Prevention, London, Sept. 24-27, 1969 (Vienna: Inter-
       national Association for Suicide Prevention, 1970), pp.
       236-239.

303)   Meerloo, Joost A.   "Hidden suicide, " in Resnik, H.
       L. P. , (ed.), Suicidal Behaviors: Diagnosis and Man-
       agement (Boston: Little, Brown and Co. , 1968), pp.
       82-89.

304)   Menard, Bernard S. and Thibodeau, Suzanne.   "Suicide
       amongst French Canadians, " in Fox, Richard (ed.),

Proceedings of the Fifth International Conference for
Suicide Prevention, London, Sept. 24-27, 1969 (Vienna:
International Association for Suicide Prevention, 1970),
pp. 212-213.

305)   Mintz, Ronald S. "Psychotherapy of the suicidal
        patient, " in Resnik, H. L. P. (ed.), Suicidal Behav-
        iors: Diagnosis and Management (Boston: Little, Brown
        & Co., 1968).

306)   Moran, E. "Gambling and suicide, " in Fox, Richard
        (ed.), Proceedings of the Fifth International Conference
        for Suicide Prevention, London, Sept. 24-27, 1969
        (Vienna: International Association for Suicide Preven-
        tion, 1970), pp. 93-94.

307)   Moriyama, Iwao M. and Israel, Robert A. "Problems
        in compilation of statistics on suicide in the United
        States, " in Farberow, Norman L. (ed.), Proceedings:
        Fourth International Conference for Suicide Prevention
        (Los Angeles: Suicide Prevention Center, 1968), pp.
        16-21.

308)   Motto, Jerome A. "An approach to research in suicide
        prevention, " in Farberow, Norman L. (ed.), Proceed-
        ings: Fourth International   Conference for Suicide Pre-
        vention (Los Angeles, Suicide Prevention Center, 1968),
        pp. 191-194.

309)   Motto, Jerome A. "Newspaper influence on suicide--
        a controlled study, " in Fox, Richard (ed.), Proceed-
        ings of the Fifth International Conference for Suicide
        Prevention, London, Sept. 24-27, 1969 (Vienna: Inter-
        national Association for Suicide Prevention, 1970), pp.
        85-92.

310)   Munter, P. K. "Depression and suicide in college
        students, " in McNeer, Lenore (ed.), Proceedings of
        the Conference on Depression and Suicide in Adoles-
        cents and Young Adults, Fairlee, Vermont, 1966, pp.
        20-25.

311)   Murphy, George, Clendenin, William, Walbran, Bonnie,
        and Robins, Eli. "The role of the police in suicide
        prevention: Analysis of 380 consecutive cases involving
        police, " in Fox, Richard (ed.), Proceedings of the
        Fifth International Conference for Suicide Prevention,

London, Sept. 24-27, 1969 (Vienna: International Association for Suicide Prevention, 1970), p. 269.
[Abstract.]

312)   Murphy, George E. and Robins, Eli.   "The communication of suicide ideas," in Resnik, H. L. P. (ed.), Suicidal Behaviors: Diagnosis and Management (Boston: Little, Brown & Co., 1968), pp. 163-170.

313)   Murphy, George E., Wetzel, Richard D., Swallow, Carolyn S., and McClure, James N., Jr.   "Who calls the suicide prevention center: A study of 55 self-callers," in Farberow, Norman L. (ed.), Proceedings: Fourth International Conference for Suicide Prevention (Los Angeles: Suicide Prevention Center, 1968), pp. 266-267.   [Abstract.]

314)   Neuringer, Charles.   "Suicide certification as a diagnostic method," in Farberow, Norman L. (ed.), Proceedings: Fourth International Conference for Suicide Prevention (Los Angeles: Suicide Prevention Center, 1968), pp. 34-35.

315)   O'Connor, George W.   "The role of law-enforcement agencies," in Resnik, H. L. P. (ed.), Suicidal Behaviors: Diagnosis and Management (Boston: Little Brown & Co., 1968), pp. 475-478.

316)   Palola, E. G., Dorpat, T. L., and Larson, W. R. "Alcoholism and suicidal behavior," in Pittman, D. J. and Snyder, C. R. (eds.), Society, Culture, and Drinking Patterns (New York: John Wiley & Sons, Inc., 1962), Chapter 29, pp. 511-534.

317)   Peck, Michael and Schrut, Albert.   "Suicide among college students," in Farberow, Norman L. (ed.), Proceedings: Fourth International Conference for Suicide Prevention (Los Angeles: Suicide Prevention Center, 1968), pp. 356-360.

318)   Piotrowski, Zygmunt A.   "Psychological test prediction of suicide," in Resnik, H. L. P. (ed.), Suidical Behaviors: Diagnosis and Management (Boston: Little, Brown & Co., 1968), pp. 198-208.

319)   Piotrowski, Zygmunt A.   "Test differentiation between effected and attempted suicides," in Wolff, Kurt (ed.),

Patterns of Self-Destruction: Depression and Suicide
(Springfield, Ill.: Charles C. Thomas, 1970), pp. 67-
81.

320)   Pokorny, Alex D.   "Myths about suicide, " in Resnik,
H. L. P. (ed.), Suicidal Behaviors: Diagnosis and
Management (Boston: Little, Brown & Co. , 1968), pp.
57-72.

321)   Pöldinger, W. J. , Gehring, A. , and Blaser, P.
"Anxiety, depression and suicidal risk, " in Fox, Richard (ed.), Proceedings of the Fifth International Conference for Suicide Prevention, London, Sept. 24-27,
1969 (Vienna: International Association for Suicide Prevention, 1970), pp. 181-185.

322)   Pöldinger, Walter.   "Psychopharmaceuticals and the
prevention of suicide, " in Farberow, Norman L. (ed.),
Proceedings: Fourth International Conference for Suicide
Prevention (Los Angeles: Suicide Prevention Center,
1968), pp. 39-53.

323)   Prokupek, J.   "Certification of suicides in Czechoslo-
vakia, " in Farberow, Norman L. (ed.), Proceedings:
Fourth International Conference for Suicide Prevention
(Los Angeles: Suicide Prevention Center, 1968), pp.
31-33.

324)   Prokupek, Josef.   "Suicide recording in Czechoslo-
vakia: 1963-1968, " in Fox, Richard (ed.), Proceedings of the Fifth International Conference for Suicide
Prevention, London, Sept. 24-27, 1969 (Vienna: International Association for Suicide Prevention, 1970), pp.
77-83.

325)   Proudfoot, A. T. , and Aitken, R. C. B.   "The myth
of barbiturate automatism, " in Fox, Richard (ed.),
Proceedings of the Fifth International Conference for
Suicide Prevention, London, Sept. 24-27, 1969 (Vienna:
International Association for Suicide Prevention, 1970),
pp. 144-145.

326)   Quidu, M.   "Suicide attempts in adolescents and the
elderly: a comparative study, " in Fox, Richard (ed.),
Proceedings of the Fifth International Conference for
Suicide Prevention, London, Sept. 24-27, 1969 (Vienna:
International Association for Suicide Prevention, 1970),
pp. 37-40.

327)   Rees, W. Linford. "The drug treatment of depressive
       illness, " in Fox, Richard (ed.), Proceedings of the
       Fifth International Conference for Suicide Prevention,
       London, Sept. 24-27, 1969 (Vienna: International Asso-
       ciation for Suicide Prevention, 1970), pp. 251-256.

328)   Reimer, Fritz. "Classification of attempted suicide, "
       in Farberow, Norman L. (ed.), Proceedings: Fourth
       International Conference for Suicide Prevention (Los
       Angeles: Suicide Prevention Center, 1968), pp. 140-
       142.

329)   Resnik, H. L. P. "A community antisuicide organiza-
       tion: The FRIENDS of Dade County, Florida, " in
       Resnik, H. L. P. (ed.), Suicidal Behaviors: Diagnosis
       and Management (Boston: Little, Brown & Co., 1968),
       pp. 418-440.

330)   Resnik, H. L. P. "A community antisuicide organiza-
       tion, " in Masserman, J. H. (ed.), Current Psychiatric
       Therapies. Vol. IV (New York: Grune & Stratton,
       1964).

331)   Resnik, H. L. P. "Suicide and the American Indian, "
       in Fox, Richard (ed.), Proceedings of the Fifth Inter-
       national Conference for Suicide Prevention, London,
       Sept. 24-27, 1969 (Vienna: International Association
       for Suicide Prevention, 1970), p. 268. [Abstract.]

332)   Retterstøl, Nils. "Long-term prognosis in suicidal
       attempts, " in Fox, Richard (ed.), Proceedings of the
       Fifth International Conference for Suicide Prevention,
       London, Sept. 24-27, 1969 (Vienna: International Asso-
       ciation for Suicide Prevention, 1970), pp. 108-110.

333)   Richman, Joseph and Rosenbaum, Milton. "A clinical
       study of role relationships in suicidal and non-suicidal
       psychiatric patients, " in Fox, Richard (ed.), Proceed-
       ings of the Fifth International Conference for Suicide
       Prevention, London, Sept. 24-27, 1969 (Vienna: Inter-
       national Association for Suicide Prevention, 1970), pp.
       116-120.

334)   Richman, Joseph. "Family determinants of attempted
       suicide, " in Farberow, Norman L. (ed.), Proceedings:
       Fourth International Conference for Suicide Prevention
       (Los Angeles: Suicide Prevention Center, 1968), pp.
       372-380.

335)   Ringel, Erwin. "Suicide prevention in Vienna," in
       Farberow, Norman L. (ed.), Proceedings: Fourth In-
       ternational Conference for Suicide Prevention (Los
       Angeles: Suicide Prevention Center, 1968), pp. 96-97.

336)   Ringel, Erwin. "Suicide prevention in Vienna," in
       Resnik, H. L. P. (ed.), Suicidal Behaviors: Diagnosis
       and Management (Boston: Little, Brown & Co., 1968),
       pp. 381-390.

337)   Rome, Howard P. "Motives for suicide," in Wolff,
       Kurt (ed.), Patterns of Self-Destruction (Springfield,
       Ill.: Charles C. Thomas, 1970), pp. 43-55.

338)   Ropschitz, D. H. "Rationale and scope of the Halifax
       Psychiatric Unit for self-aggressors," in Fox, Richard
       (ed.), Proceedings of the Fifth International Conference
       for Suicide Prevention, London, Sept. 24-27, 1969
       (Vienna: International Association for Suicide Preven-
       tion, 1970), pp. 217-218.

339)   Rosenbaum, Milton and Richman, Joseph. "The role
       of hostility and rejection by society in suicidal be-
       haviour," in Fox, Richard (ed.), Proceedings of the
       Fifth International Conference for Suicide Prevention,
       London, Sept. 24-27, 1969 (Vienna: International Asso-
       ciation for Suicide Prevention, 1970), pp. 228-229.

340)   Ross, Charlotte P. and Motto, Jerome A. "Imple-
       mentation of standards for suicide prevention centers,"
       in Fox, Richard (ed.), Proceedings of the Fifth Inter-
       national Conference for Suicide Prevention, London,
       Sept. 24-27, 1969 (Vienna: International Association
       for Suicide Prevention, 1970), pp. 67-76.

341)   Ross, Mathew. "Suicide among university students: A
       cross-cultural survey," in Fox, Richard (ed.), Pro-
       ceedings of the Fifth International Conference for Sui-
       cide Prevention, London, Sept. 24-27, 1969 (Vienna:
       International Association for Suicide Prevention, 1970),
       pp. 207-210.

342)   Rueda, Theresa. "A clinical approach to attempted
       suicide in adolescents and young adults," in Fox,
       Richard (ed.), Proceedings of the Fifth International
       Conference for Suicide Prevention, London, Sept. 24-
       27, 1969 (Vienna: International Association for Suicide

Prevention, 1970), pp. 40-42.

343) Rushing, W. A. "Individual behaviour and suicide, " in Gibbs, J. P. (ed.), Suicide (New York: Macmillan, 1967).

344) Sainsbury, Peter and Barraclough, Brian. "National suicide statistics, " in Fox, Richard (ed.), Proceedings of the Fifth International Conference for Suicide Prevention, London, Sept. 24-27, 1969 (Vienna: International Association for Suicide Prevention, 1970), pp. 176-179.

345) St. John-Stevas, Norman. "Suicide, " in Life, Death and the Law (Bloomington: Indiana University Press, 1961), Chapter 6, pp. 232-261.

346) Schiff, Samuel B. and Dickey, Brenda. "A suicide prevention program for a state mental health center, " in Farberow, Norman L. (ed.), Proceedings: Fourth International Conference for Suicide Prevention (Los Angeles: Suicide Prevention Center, 1968), pp. 143-150.

347) Schneer, Henry I. and Kay, Paul. "The suicidal adolescent, " in Lorand, Sandor and Schneer, Henry I. (eds.), Adolescents: Psychoanalytic Approach to Problems and Therapy (New York: P. B. Hoeber, 1961), pp. 180-201.

348) Seiden, Richard H. "Suicidal behavior contagion on a college campus, " in Farberow, Norman L. (ed.), Proceedings: Fourth International Conference for Suicide Prevention (Los Angeles: Suicide Prevention Center, 1968), pp. 360-367.

349) Seiden, Richard H. and Tauber, Ronald K. "Pseudocides vs. suicides, " in Fox, Richard (ed.), Proceedings of the Fifth International Conference for Suicide Prevention, London, Sept. 24-27, 1969 (Vienna: International Association for Suicide Prevention, 1970), pp. 219-222.

350) Shabshin, M. "The treatment of depression--the major suicidal illness, " in Yochelson, L. (ed.), Symposium on Suicide (Washington, D. C.: George Washington University School of Medicine, 1965).

351)   Shaw, David Murray. "Biochemical changes in the
        brain in depressive suicides, " in Fox, Richard (ed.),
        Proceedings of the Fifth International Conference for
        Suicide Prevention, London, Sept. 24-27, 1969 (Vienna:
        International Association for Suicide Prevention, 1970),
        pp. 132-134.

352)   Shea, Marian and Barraclough, Brian. "A study of
        Samaritan clients who subsequently commit suicide, "
        in Fox, Richard (ed.), Proceedings of the Fifth Inter-
        national Conference for Suicide Prevention, London,
        Sept. 24-27, 1969 (Vienna: International Association
        for Suicide Prevention, 1970), pp. 232-234.

353)   Shneidman, Edwin S. "Orientations toward death: A
        vital aspect of the study of lives, " in Resnik, H. L. P.
        (ed.), Suicidal Behaviors: Diagnosis and Management
        (Boston: Little, Brown & Co., 1968), pp. 19-48.

354)   Shneidman, E. S. "Suicide, " in Farberow, N. L. (ed.),
        Taboo Topics (New York: Atherton Press, 1963), pp. 33-43.

355)   Shneidman, Edwin S. "Suicide prevention: A current
        national view, " in Farberow, Norman L. (ed.), Pro-
        ceedings: Fourth International Conference for Suicide
        Prevention (Los Angeles: Suicide Prevention Center,
        1968, pp. 83-89.

356)   Shneidman, E. S. "Suicide: symptom of lethality, "
        in Costello, C. (ed.), Symptoms of Psychopathology
        (New York: John Wiley & Sons, 1970).

357)   Shneidman, E. S. and Farberow, N. L. "Sample in-
        vestigations of equivocal suicidal deaths, " in Farberow,
        N. L. and Shneidman, E. S. (eds.), The Cry for Help
        (New York: McGraw-Hill, 1961), Chapter 8, pp. 118-
        128.

358)   Shneidman, E. S. "Suicide of children and adoles-
        cents: A national problem, " in McNeer, Lenore (ed.),
        Proceedings of the Conference on Depression and Suicide
        in Adolescents and Young Adults, Fairlee, Vermont,
        1966, pp. 5-8.

359)   Shneidman, E. S. and Farberow, N. L. "The Suicide
        Prevention Center of Los Angeles, " in Resnik, H. L. P.
        (ed.), Suicidal Behaviors: Diagnosis and Management

(Boston: Little, Brown & Co., 1968).

360)   Shneidman, Edwin S., Farberow, Norman L., and
       Litman, Robert E. "The Suicide Prevention Center,"
       in Farberow, N. L. and Shneidman, E. S. (eds.), The
       Cry for Help (New York: McGraw-Hill, 1961), Chapter
       2, pp. 6-18.

361)   Shneidman, Edwin S., Farberow, Norman L., and Lit-
       man, Robert E. "A taxonomy of death--a psycholog-
       ical point of view," in Farberow, N. L. and Shneid-
       man, E. S. (eds.), The Cry for Help (New York:
       McGraw-Hill, 1961), Chapter 9, pp. 129-135.

362)   Shneidman, Edwin S. and Farberow, Norman L. "Sta-
       tistical comparisons between attempted and committed
       suicides," in Farberow, N. L. and Shneidman, E. S.
       (eds.), The Cry for Help (New York: McGraw-Hill,
       1961), Chapter 3, pp. 19-47.

363)   Sim, Myre. "Suicide and attempted suicide," in Sim,
       Myre, Guide to Psychiatry (Edinburgh & London: E. &
       S. Livingstone Ltd., 1968), Chapter 15.

364)   Simon, Werner and Lumry, Gayle K. "Suicide among
       physician-patients," in Farberow, Norman L. (ed.),
       Proceedings: Fourth International Conference for Sui-
       cide Prevention (Los Angeles: Suicide Prevention Cen-
       ter, 1968), pp. 195-207.

365)   Simon, Werner and Lumry, Gayle K. "Suicide of the
       spouse as a divorce substitute," in Fox, Richard (ed.),
       Proceedings of the Fifth International Conference for
       Suicide Prevention, London, Sept. 24-27, 1969 (Vienna:
       International Association for Suicide Prevention, 1970),
       pp. 172-173.

366)   Slater, Eliot. "Choosing the time to die," in Fox,
       Richard (ed.), Proceedings of the Fifth International
       Conference for Suicide Prevention, London, Sept. 24-
       27, 1969 (Vienna: International Association for Suicide
       Prevention, 1970), pp. 269-272.

367)   Soubrier, Jean-Pierre. "Psychiatric problems in
       poisoning treatment centres," in Fox, Richard (ed.),
       Proceedings of the Fifth International Conference for
       Suicide Prevention, London, Sept. 24-27, 1969 (Vienna:

International Association for Suicide Prevention, 1970), pp. 151-152.

368) Soubrier, Jean-Pierre. "Use, misuse of drugs, and the problem of self-poisoning, " in Farberow, Norman L. (ed.), Proceedings: Fourth International Conference for Suicide Prevention (Los Angeles: Suicide Prevention Center, 1968), pp. 67-70.

369) Speck, Ross V. "Family therapy of the suicidal patient, " in Resnik, H. L. P. (ed.), Suicidal Behaviors: Diagnosis and Management (Boston: Little, Brown & Co., 1968), pp. 341-347.

370) Spencer, Seymour. "Four suicides in Oxford and their implication, " in Fox, Richard (ed.), Proceedings of the Fifth International Conference for Suicide Prevention, London, Sept. 24-27, 1969 (Vienna: International Association for Suicide Prevention, 1970), pp. 206-207. [Abstract.]

371   Stengel, Erwin. "Attempted suicides, " in Resnik, H. L. P. (ed.), Suicidal Behaviors: Diagnosis and Management (Boston: Little, Brown & Co., 1968), pp. 171-189.

372) Stengel, Erwin. "Euthanasia and suicide prevention, " in Fox, Richard (ed.), Proceedings of the Fifth International Conference for Suicide Prevention, London, Sept. 24-27, 1969 (Vienna: International Conference for Suicide Prevention, 1970), pp. 273-277.

373) Stengel, Erwin and Farberow, Norman L. "Certification of suicide around the world, " in Farberow, Norman L. (ed.), Proceedings: Fourth International Conference for Suicide Prevention (Los Angeles: Suicide Prevention Center, 1968), pp. 8-15.

374) Swenson, David D. "Publication problems, " in Farberow, Norman L. (ed.), Proceedings: Fourth International Conference for Suicide Prevention (Los Angeles: Suicide Prevention Center, 1968), pp. 151-155.

375) Tabachnick, Norman D. and Farberow, Norman L. "The assessment of self-destructive potentiality, " in Farberow, N. L. and Shneidman, E. S. (eds.), The Cry for Help (New York: McGraw-Hill, 1961), Chapter

5, pp. 60-77.

376) Tabachnick, Norman and Litman, Robert E.   "Self-
      destructiveness in accident, " in Farberow, Norman
      L. (ed.), Proceedings: Fourth International Conference
      for Suicide Prevention (Los Angeles: Suicide Preven-
      tion Center, 1968), pp. 321-327.

377) Temby, W. D.   "Suicide, " in Blaine, G. B. and
      McArthur, C. C. (eds.), Emotional Problems of the
      Student (New York: Appleton-Century-Crofts, 1961),
      pp. 133-152.

378) Thilges, R. and Battegay, R.   "Attempted suicide
      treated in a psychiatric out-patient clinic, " in Fox,
      Richard (ed.), Proceedings of the Fifth International
      Conference for Suicide Prevention, London, Sept. 24-
      27, 1969 (Vienna: International Association for Suicide
      Prevention, 1970), pp. 127-128.

379) Thomas, Klaus.   "The computer in suicide preven-
      tion, " in Fox, Richard (ed.), Proceedings of the Fifth
      International Conference for Suicide Prevention, Lon-
      don, Sept. 24-27, 1969 (Vienna: International Associ-
      ation for Suicide Prevention, 1970), pp. 61-63.

380) Thomson, Captane P.   "Suicide prevention in a rural
      area, " in Farberow, Norman L. (ed.), Proceedings:
      Fourth International Conference for Suicide Prevention
      (Los Angeles: Suicide Prevention Center, 1968), pp.
      123-127.

381) Thomson, I. G.   "Suicide and mortality in depression,"
      in Fox, Richard (ed.), Proceedings of the Fifth Inter-
      national Conference for Suicide Prevention, London,
      Sept. 24-27, 1969 (Vienna: International Association
      for Suicide Prevention, 1970), pp. 140-143.

382) Tomorug, E.   "Biological crises and suicide, " in Fox,
      Richard (ed.), Proceedings of the Fifth International
      Conference for Suicide Prevention, London, Sept. 24-
      27, 1969 (Vienna: International Association for Suicide
      Prevention, 1970), pp. 194-195.   [Abstract.]

383) Tomorug, E. and Pirozynski, T.   "Suicide attempts
      and their prevention, " in Farberow, Norman L. (ed.),
      Proceedings: Fourth International Conference for

Suicide Prevention (Los Angeles: Suicide Prevention
Center, 1968), pp. 216-226.

384)   Toolan, James M.   "Suicide in childhood and adoles-
        cence, " in Resnik, H. L. P. (ed.), Suicidal Behaviors:
        Diagnosis and Management (Boston: Little, Brown &
        Co. , 1968), pp. 220-227.

385)   Topp, D. O.   "Self-destructive behaviour in English
        prisons, " in Fox, Richard (ed.), Proceedings of the
        Fifth International Conference for Suicide Prevention,
        London, Sept. 24-27, 1969 (Vienna: International Asso-
        ciation for Suicide Prevention, 1970), pp. 179-181.

386)   Tuckman, Jacob.   "Suicide and the suicide prevention
        center, " in Wolff, Kurt (ed.), Patterns of Self-
        Destruction (Springfield, Ill. : Charles C. Thomas, 1970),
        pp. 3-17.

387)   Tuckman, Jacob and Youngman, William F.   "Assess-
        ment of suicide risk in attempted suicides, " in Resnik,
        H. L. P. (ed.), Suicidal Behaviors: Diagnosis and Man-
        agement (Boston: Little, Brown & Co. , 1968), pp. 190-
        197.

388)   van de Loo, K. J. M. and Diekstra, R. W. F.   "A
        questionnaire for the prediction of subsequent suicidal
        attempts, a preliminary research study, " in Fox,
        Richard (ed.), Proceedings of the Fifth International
        Conference for Suicide Prevention, London, Sept. 24-
        27, 1969 (Vienna: International Association for Suicide
        Prevention, 1970), pp. 111-114.

389)   Varah, Chad.   "The use of lay volunteers in suicide
        prevention, " in Farberow, Norman L. (ed.), Proceed-
        ings: Fourth International Conference for Suicide Pre-
        vention (Los Angeles: Suicide Prevention Center, 1968),
        pp. 90-95.

390)   Védrinne, Jacques.   "Prospects of clinical assistance
        for suicide cases, " in Farberow, Norman L. (ed.),
        Proceedings: Fourth International Conference for Suicide
        Prevention (Los Angeles: Suicide Prevention Center,
        1968), pp. 77-82.

391)   Vining, Roy M.   "The role of the lay volunteer in
        suicide prevention, " in Fox, Richard (ed.), Proceed-

ings of the Fifth International Conference for Suicide
Prevention, London, Sept. 24-27, 1969 (Vienna: International Association for Suicide Prevention, 1970),
pp. 156-159.

392)   Waltzer, Herbert. "Depersonalization and self-con-
       struction, " in Farberow, Norman L. (ed.), Proceed-
       ings: Fourth International Conference for Suicide Pre-
       vention (Los Angeles: Suicide Prevention Center, 1968),
       pp. 292-296.

393)   Weinstein, George J. "Introduction to film suicide
       prevention in hospitals, " in Wolff, Kurt (ed.), Patterns
       of Self-Destruction (Springfield, Ill.: Charles C.
       Thomas, 1970), pp. 29-32.

394)   Weiss, J. M. A. "The suicidal patient, " in Arieti, S.
       (ed.), American Handbook of Psychiatry. Vol. III
       (New York: Basic Books, 1966).

395)   Weiss, James M. A. "Suicide in the aged, " in
       Resnik, H. L. P. (ed.), Suicidal Behaviors: Diagnosis
       and Management (Boston: Little, Brown & Co. , 1968),
       pp. 255-267.

396)   Weiss, J. M. A. , Nunez, N. , and Schaie, N. W.
       "Quantification of certain trends in attempted suicide,"
       Proceedings Third World Congress of Psychiatry,
       2:1236-1240, 1961.

397)   Weisz, Alfred E. , Staight, Donald C. , Houts, Peter,
       and Voten, Michael P. "Suicide threats, suicide at-
       tempts and the emergency psychiatrist, " in Farberow,
       Norman L. (ed.), Proceedings: Fourth International
       Conference for Suicide Prevention (Los Angeles: Suicide
       Prevention Center, 1968), pp. 227-251.

398)   Weyl, H. H. "A poisoning advisory service, " in Fox,
       Richard (ed.), Proceedings of the Fifth International
       Conference for Suicide Prevention, London, Sept. 24-
       27, 1969 (Vienna: International Association for Suicide
       Prevention, 1970), pp. 195-196.

399)   Wiendieck, Gerd. "Social determinants of suicide in
       old age, " in Fox, Richard (ed.), Proceedings of the
       Fifth International Conference for Suicide Prevention,
       London, Sept. 24-27, 1969 (Vienna: International

Association for Suicide Prevention, 1970), pp. 196-197.

400)   Wolff, Kurt. "Observations on depression and suicide
        in the geriatric patient, " in Wolff, Kurt (ed.), Patterns
        of Self-Destruction (Springfield, Ill. : Charles C.
        Thomas, 1970), pp. 33-42.

401)   Wolfgang, Marvin E. "Suicide by means of victim-
        precipitated homicide, " in Resnik, H. L. P. (ed.),
        Suicidal Behaviors: Diagnosis and Management (Boston:
        Little, Brown & Co. , 1968), pp. 90-104.

402)   Yamamoto, Joe, Lipson, Leslie, and Litman, Robert
        E. "A comparison of committed suicides in Los
        Angeles County in 1963 and 1966 previously treated at
        the Los Angeles County General Hospital, " in Farberow,
        Norman L. (ed.), Proceedings: Fourth International
        Conference for Suicide Prevention (Los Angeles: Suicide
        Prevention Center, 1968), pp. 156-165.

403)   Yessler, Paul G. "Suicide in the military, " in
        Resnik, H. L. P. (ed.), Suicidal Behaviors: Diagnosis
        and Management (Boston: Little, Brown & Co. , 1968),
        pp. 241-254.

404)   Yolles, Stanley F. "Suicide: A public health prob-
        lem, " in Resnik, H. L. P. (ed.), Suicidal Behaviors:
        Diagnosis and Management (Boston: Little, Brown &
        Co. , 1968), pp. 49-56.

405)   Zimbacca, Nicole. "The subjective relational field of
        the suicide survivor, " in Fox, Richard (ed.), Proceed-
        ings of the Fifth International Conference for Suicide
        Prevention, London, Sept. 24-27, 1969 (Vienna: Inter-
        national Association for Suicide Prevention, 1970), pp.
        120-123.

IV. ARTICLES FROM THE POPULAR PRESS

406) "Adolescent suicide: results of a study by P. Cantor," Time, 99:57, Jan. 3, 1972.

407) Alexander, S. "Decision to die," Life, 56:74-6+, May 29, 1964.

408) Alvarez, A. "The savage God: art, suicide, and mourning," Listener, 86:297-99, Sept. 2, 1971.

409) Alvarez, A. "The savage God: suicide as an art," Listener, 86:264-66, Aug. 26, 1971.

410) AMHI Reports on Suicide Rates. Amer. Mental Health Inst. report on world suicide rates; Protestants 7 times as high as Jews or Catholics; West Berlin highest rate, etc. New York Times, 1963, My 5, 2:4.

411) Ardley, R. Article on suicidal instinct in animals (spec. lemmings) to control overpopulation; compares man's impending situation..., Suicidal instinct in animals. New York Times, 1971, S 28, 39:3. S. C. Woods disputes - O 13, 44:3.

412) "Autocide: question of road fatalities," Time, 89:23, Mar. 10, 1967.

413) Baden, M. M. NYC medical examiner, Dr. M. M. Baden, notes adverse position of men concerning suicide; disputes claims that female hormone imbalances disqualify women for leadership. Suicide rates show males weaker sex, New York Times, 1970, Ag 2, 13:7.

414) Balikci, A. "Suicidal behavior among the Netsilik Eskimos," North, 8:12-19, July-Aug. 1961.

415) Banks, L. "Black suicide," Ebony, 25:76-8+, May 1970.

416)   Bell, J. N. "Lifeline for would-be suicides: with list
        of suicide-prevention centers, " Today's Health, 45:30-
        3+, June 1967.

417)   Bell, J. N. "Special report on a growing social
        problem: when the cry for help comes: suicide pre-
        vention centers. " Good Housekeeping, 162:108-9+,
        June 1966.

418)   Berczeller, R. "Morphinist: incident at hospital of
        the city of Vienna, 1928, " New Yorker, 42:141-2+,
        April 16, 1966.

419)   Blatt, G. Poverty major cause of suicide among eld-
        erly. OE official cites poverty as major cause of
        suicide among older Americans; reports rate of men
        over 55 four times that of younger men, etc. New
        York Times, 1968, N 24, 116:6.

420)   Bogard, H. M. More psychiatric care for suicidals
        needed. Dr. Bogard urges more psychiatric care to
        attempters; two-thirds get none. Also discussion by
        Drs. J. Fawcett, E. S. Shneidman, and Dr. S. Palmer,
        various aspects. New York Times, 1969, Mr 30, 48:3.

421)   Brown, D. "Hopes, heartaches and hara-kiri, "
        Senior Scholastic, 76:17T-19T, Feb. 3, 1960.

422)   "Causes of suicide" [Depression & alcohol lead],
        Financial Post, 61:30, March 4, 1967.

423)   "Child suicides: Can these tragedies be prevented?",
        Good Housekeeping, 169:207-9, Oct. 1969.

424)   Clark, Marguerite. "Children in the dark, " PTA
        Magazine, 55:10-13, 1966.

425)   "Concerning suicide: Anglican committee report, "
        Time, 74:74+, Nov. 2, 1959.

426)   Cresswell, Peter. "Interpretations of 'Suicide, '"
        British Journal of Sociology, 23:133-145, June 1972.

427)   Curphey, T. J. Team approach to suicide treatment
        valuable. Dr. Curphey cites value of teams of psy-
        chiatrists, sociologists, and psychiatric social workers
        in probing suspected suicides; medico-legal conf. on

murder and suicide, Boston. New York Times, 1962, N4, 130:2.

428)   "Death of a Playwright, " Time, 90:40, Sept. 15, 1967.

429)   "Do not try to jolly a suicidal person, " Science News Letter, 78:93, Aug. 6, 1960.

430)   Dorac, R. "Learning to live, " [London] Times Educational Supplement, Jan. 5, 2433:18, 1962.

431)   Evans, J. C. "Meaningful death, " Christian Century, 82:1598, Dec. 29, 1965.

432)   "Examination hell: Japan's student suicides, " [London] Times Educational Supplement, Oct. 26, 1972; 2475-2533.

433)   "Fake suicide calls, " Science News, 89:278, April 16, 1966.

434)   Faux, E. J. and Crawford, B. "Deaths in a youth program, " Mental Hygiene, 54:569-71, Oct. 1970.

435)   "Fiery rebellion: self-immolations in South Vietnam, " Newsweek, 67:48-9, June 13, 1966.

436)   Friedman, P. "Psychiatrist examines suicide, questions and answers; excerpts from Encyclopedia of mental health, " Today's Health, 41:56-9+, Dec. 1963; correction 42:87, Jan. 1964.

437)   "Giving and taking one's life: case of N. R. Morrison, " Christian Century, 82:1404, Nov. 17, 1965; Discussion 83:84, Jan. 19, 1966.

438)   Gould, Donald. "The suicide scare, " New Statesman, Oct. 1, 1971, pp. 430-431.

439)   Gould, R. E. and Baden, M. M. More suicides can be prevented. Drs. Gould and Baden talk about suicide; how most are preventable, but treatment facilities are inadequate; say data is unreliable; etc., New York Times, 1971, S 26, 60:1.

440)   Grigson, Geoffrey. "The extremists of Al Alvarez. Suicide, chaos, violence, " Encounter, 39:59-60, Aug. 1972.

441)   Gunther, M. "Why children commit suicide," Satur-
        day Evening Post, 240:86-9, June 17, 1967.

442)   Hackney, S. "Southern violence," American His-
        torical Review, 74:906-25, Feb. 1969.

443)   Halloran, Richard. "In Japan, a sober, thoughtful
        approach to suicide," New York Times, April 30,
        1973, p. 10.

444)   Halloran, Richard T. "Politics of suicide: Mishima's
        seppuku," Commonweal, 94:34-6, Mar. 19, 1971.

445)   Hamilton, A. "I'm going to kill myself," Science
        Digest, 54:57-63, Sept. 1963.

446)   Hansen, Joseph. "Suicide and the Homosexual,"
        One [Tangents], 13:5-7, May 1965.

447)   Hartley, W. and Hartley, E. "New test helps make
        suicide predictable: Index of potential suicide," Sci-
        ence Digest, 72:25-31, Nov. 1972.

448)   Heilig, S. "Increase in suicide rate among young,
        especially women," New York Times, April 3, 1972,
        p. 1. (Discussed by exec. dir., L.A. Suicide Prev.
        Ctr.)

449)   Hendin, H. NIMH study of suicide among young blacks.
        Prof. Hendin's study of 25 Negroes, NYC, who at-
        tempted suicide. Why is especially common among
        young blacks, effect of slums, etc. Natl. Inst. Mental
        Health sponsored research. New York Times, 1969,
        Je 21, 28:2.

450)   Herzog, A. "Suicide can't be eliminated," New York
        Times Magazine, Mar. 20, 1966, pp. 32-3+.

451)   "His canon 'gainst self-slaughter; spies and self-
        destruction," America, 103:371, June 18, 1960.

452)   Hoffer, W. "What's being done about campus sui-
        cide?", Education Digest, 38:54-6, Oct. 1972.

453)   Holland, R. F. "Suicide as a social problem; some
        reflections on Durkheim," Ratio, 12:116-24, Dec. 1970.

454)   "How to keep patients from jumping out of the win-
       dow, " Trans-Action, 7:13, Feb. 1970.

455)   Huxley, M. "Incompleat suicide; concerning Sympo-
       sium on suicide held in Washington, D. C. , " Nation,
       201:414-17, Nov. 29, 1965.

456)   Kettle, J. "Charting the future: graphs, " Executive,
       13:38, Jan. 1971.

457)   Kettle, J. "Violence in North America, " Executive,
       13:55-6, Jan. 1971.

458)   Kobler, -- --. Hopelessness key factor in suicide.
       Dr. Kobler finds atmosphere of anxiety or hopeless-
       ness can stimulate potential suicides. New York
       Times, 1960, S 3, 18:1.

459)   Lawson, Herbert G. "Focus on suicide, " Wall Street
       Journal, Sept. 20, 1963, p. 1+.

460)   Levin, R. J. "When listening means life: the Samar-
       itans and other suicide prevention groups, " Saturday
       Review, 49:65, Oct. 1, 1966.

461)   Levinson, H. "What killed Bob Lyons? Executive's
       emotional problems, " Harvard Business Review, 41:
       127-42+, Jan. 1963.

462)   Litman, R. E. , et al. Many auto accidents linked to
       suicide. Drs. Litman, Ross, and Schneidman see link
       between suicide tendencies and many auto accidents.
       New York Times, 1968, Apr 1, 35:5.

463)   Mailer, N. "Big bite, " Esquire, 58:168, Dec. 1962.

464)   Mano, K. Should suicide be called a crime? Mano
       questions right of society to make suicide a crime.
       New York Times, 1970, D 17, 47:1.

465)   Meerloo, J. A. M. "Freedom to choose one's death,"
       Nation, 200:344-5, Mar. 29, 1965.

466)   Murphy, K. B. "Do they really want to die?", To-
       day's Health, 43:48-9+, Apr. 1965.

467)   Myrdal, G. Sweden's high suicide rate not due to

welfare state. Prof. Myrdal rebuts theories linking
Sweden's welfare state to high suicide rate. New York
Times, 1966, Ja 30, VI, p. 14. Tables Ja 30, VI,
p. 17.

468)   Nelson, B. "Suicide prevention: NIMH wants more
        attention for taboo subject, " Science, 161:766-7, Aug.
        23, 1968.

469)   NJ State Educ. Dept. reports loneliness major factor
        in suicides of 41 school children, Sept '60-June '63;
        other findings. New York Times, 1965, F 17, 88:1.

470)   "No one cares: suicides at Rikers Island penitentiary,"
        Newsweek, 75:51-2, Mar. 2, 1970.

471)   Nott, K. "Mortal statistics, " Commentary, 38:64-8,
        Oct. 1964.

472)   O'Dell, B. Y. "Suicide in children, " Parents Maga-
        zine, 44:58-9+, Jan. 1969.

473)   O'Hara, J. D. "Elementary sin, " New Republic,
        166:29-32, Apr. 22, 1972.

474)   O'Neill, M. E. "Desperate people, " Guardian, April
        21, 1964, p. 10.

475)   "On suicide: 'Time' essay, " Time, 88:48-9, Nov. 25,
        1966.

476)   "Opening of SPC at Yeshiva University Graduate Cen-
        ter, " New York Times, March 28, 1971, p. 61.

477)   Page, Campbell. "Getting away from it all, " Guard-
        ian, Nov. 9, 1971, p. 12.

478)   Patel, Nat. "Suicide, " Guardian, July 22, 1972, p. 9.

479)   Peck, M. L. Study of suicide among college students.
        Dr. Peck reports on conclusions of 2-year study of
        suicidal behavior among college students conducted at
        52 colleges and universities in L. A. County; report
        presented at American Association of Suicidology meet-
        ing. New York Times, 1970, Mar. 23, 1:1.

480)   Pinkerton, W. Stewart, Jr. "The lethal impulse:

climbing suicide toll spurs intensive study and prevention, " Wall Street Journal, March 6, 1969, p. 1.

481)   "Playboy Forum. " Playboy, 14; 174, June 1967.
       ("Suicide and homosexuality. ")

482)   Pollack, J. H.   "I want out: teens who threaten sui-
       cide, " Today's Health, 49:32-4+, Jan. 1971.

483)   Roldan, Julio.   Death of Julio Roldan termed suicide.
       NYC Correction Board reports term death suicide; list
       detailed account of last days.   New York Times, 1970,
       N 18, 1:7.

484)   Rose, Ben.   "A new way to rescue suicides, "   Mac-
       lean's, October 2, 1965, p. 20+.

485)   Rosenbaum, Milton and Richman, Joseph.   "Therapy
       may prevent some suicide. "   Drs. Rosenbaum and
       Richman report on studies aimed at use of possible
       therapy treatment for preventing suicides.   Many find-
       ings.   London.   New York Times, 1969, S 27, 17:1.

486)   Ross, M.   Suicide second greatest cause of death
       among college youth.   Dr. Ross says suicide is second
       greatest death cause among college students and third
       among high school youth; report to Amer. Coll. of
       Physicians, breakdown by age groups.   New York
       Times, 1967, Ap 26, 39:1.

487)   Rushing, William A.   "Deviance, interpersonal rela-
       tions and suicide, " Human Relations, 22:61-76, Feb.
       1969.

488)   Rutherford, Marjory.   "Suicide: Unanswered SOS, "
       Atlanta Constitution, April 1966.   [Series of news-
       paper articles.]

489)   Schreiber, F. R. and Herman, M.   "How to cure
       depression, " Science Digest, 61:12-15, Feb. 1967.

490)   Schreiber, F. R. and Herman, M.   "Why people can't
       take it. " Science Digest, 56:66-9, Sept. 1964.

491)   "Sensitivity toward suicide, " Christianity Today, 13:
       21-2, July 18, 1969.

492)   Shepherd, J.   "When college students crack up, "
        Look, 31(12):23-25, 1967.

493)   Shields, Robert.   "Why girls are driven to suicide, "
        Observer, Sept. 21, 1969, p. 11.

494)   "Should suicide be called a crime?   English law, "
        Christian Century, 77:1078, Sept. 21, 1960.

495)   Smith, V. E.   "Tragedy at Beecher high; P. L.
        Cabell's suicide, "   Ebony, 27:154-6+, Oct. 1972.

496)   "Special Commission for reform of Canon Law sug-
        gested Roman Catholic Church lift ban on religious
        burial of suicides, "   New York Times, March 4, 1971,
        p. 20.

497)   Strachan, J. C. G.   "Who did forbid suicide at Phaedo
        626?",   Classical Quarterly,   20:216-20, Nov. 1970.

498)   "Student suicides, "   Science News,   91:45, Jan. 14, 1967.

499)   "Study probes youngsters' suicidal signs, "   Today's
        Health, 47:82, April 1969.

500)   "Suicidal tendencies, "   Science News,   90:513, Dec. 17,
        1966.

501)   "Suicidal tendencies, "   Time,   88:114, Oct. 14, 1966.

502)   "Suicide among top ten causes of death in U. S. , "
        Science Digest, 49:24-5, Feb. 1961.

503)   "Suicide and jobless rates closely related, "   Science
        News Letter, 83:296, May 11, 1963.

504)   "Suicide research shows facts versus fables, "   Science
        News Letter, 80:384, Dec. 9, 1961.

505)   "Symbolic suicide: Nguyen Tuong Tam, "   Newsweek,
        62:43-4, July 22, 1963.

506)   Toolan, James.   "Alarming rise in suicide among
        young. "   Dr. Toolan reports startling incidence of
        attempts among children and adolescents, Bellevue
        Hosp. study, 1960.   New York Times, 1961, My 9,
        52:7.

507) U. S. PHS. "Tranquilizers major factor in many suicides." PHS survey reports tranquilizing drugs now
rival barbiturates as suicide pills. New York Times,
1963, Ag 10, 13:7.

508) Warren, Michael. "Is suicide a crime in North Carolina?", Popular Government, 37: 12-16, June 1971.

509) Watson, Peter. "Samaritans and suicide," New Society, Sept. 10, 1970, p. 456.

510) Weikel, C. P. "Life you can save," Harvest Years,
10:6-11, Jan. 1970.

511) "Welfare, suicide linked?", Science News Letter, 88:
11, Aug. 14, 1965.

512) "Western civilization vs. Japanese view of suicide,"
(editorial) New York Times, April 29, 1972, p. 44.

513) Winegarten, R. "On the love of suicide," Commentary, 54:29-34, Aug. 1972.

514) Winickoff, S. A. and Resnik, H. L. P. "Student suicide," Today's Education, 60:30-2+, April 1971.

515) "Women suicides increase due to social pressures,"
Science News Letter, 85:271, April 25, 1964.

516) Woodford, J. N. "Why Negro suicides are increasing," Ebony, 20:89-90+, July 1965.

517) "Youthful suicides," Newsweek, 77:70-1, Feb. 15,
1971.

V. ARTICLES FROM RELIGIOUS JOURNALS

518) Anderson, D. A. "Resurrection model for suicide prevention through the church," Pastoral Psychology 23:33-40, Feb. 1972.

519) Baelz, P. R. "Voluntary euthanasia; some theological reflections," Theology, 75:238-51, May 1972.

520) Benningfield, M. F. "Review of suicide prevention centers in the United States," Pastoral Psychology, 16:41-5, Jan. 1966.

521) Clinebell, H. J. "First aid in counselling; the suicidal emergency," Expository Times, 77:328-32, Aug. 1966.

522) Close, Henry T. "Forgiveness and responsibility: a case study," Pastoral Psychology, 21:19-25, June 1970.

523) Culver, E. T. "Suicide: Need for a significant other," Christian Century, 86:100-2, Jan. 15, 1969.

524) Daube, D. "Death as a release in the Bible," Novum Testamentum, 5:82-104, July 1962.

525) Derrett, J. D. M. "St. Thomas More and the would-be suicide," Downside Review, 88:372-7, Oct. 1970.

526) Douglas, Jack D. "The moral meanings of suicide," New Society, July 13, 1967, pp. 44-6.

527) Edwards, D. L. "Twentieth century sickness," Frontier, 3:37-41, Spring 1960.

528) Grollman, E. A. "Pastoral counseling of the potential suicidal person," Pastoral Psychology, 16:46-52, Jan. 1966.

529) Jacobson, Gerald F. "Crisis intervention from the viewpoint of the mental health professional, " Pastoral Psychology, April 1970.

530) Jensen, J. S. "Reaction of a church to a suicide, " Journal of Pastoral Care, 21:229-32, Dec. 1967.

531) Levani, M. "Suicide in the League of Nations, " cond. Jewish Digest, 11:16-20, Nov. 1966.

532) McCall, D. D. "Anomie my enemy, " Christian Century, 85:941-943, July 24, 1968.

533) McCaughley, J. Davis. "Suicide: Some theological considerations, " Theology, 70:63-8, Feb. 1967.

534) McConnell, T. A. "Suicide ethics in cross-disciplinary perspective, " Journal of Religion and Health, 7:7-25, Jan. 1968.

535) Myra, H. "Teenage suicides, " Youth for Christ, Aug. 1965, p. 9.

536) Nott, K. "Mortal statistics, " Commentary, 38:64-8, Oct. 1964.

537) Okamoto, M. "Suicide of Arishima Takeo; the failure of a Christian intellectual, " Japan Christian Quarterly, 29:181-91, July 1963.

538) Pretzel, P. W. "Role of the clergyman in suicide prevention, " Pastoral Psychology, 21:47-52, Apr. 1970.

539) Pretzel, Paul W. "Suicide as a failure of trust, " Journal of Pastoral Care, 21:94-9, June 1967.

540) Pretzel, Paul W. "The clergy in suicide prevention, " American Rabbi, 2:45-66, 1967.

541) Rabinowicz, H. "Judaism on suicide, " Hebrew Medical Journal, 2:239-241, 1961.

542) Reines, C. W. "Jewish attitude toward suicide, " Judaism, 160-170, Spring 1961.

543) Rose, M. C. "Religious functions of suffering, " Anglican Theological Review, 43:186-95, April 1966.

544)   Rosner, F.   "Suicide in Biblical, Talmudic and Rab-
        binic writings, "   Tradition, 11:25-40, Summer 1970.

545)   Smith, G. B.   "Suicide is Not the Way Out, "   War
        Cry, Feb. 19, 1966, p. 3.

546)   Stalter, D.   "We can do something about suicide, "
        Christianity Today, 4:3-4, June 18, 1960.

547)   Stein, E. V.   "Clergyman's role with the suicidal
        person, "   Journal of Pastoral Care, 19:74-83, Sum-
        mer 1965.

548)   Stein, E. V.   "Faith, hope and suicide, "   Journal of
        Religion and Health, 10:214-25, July 1971.

549)   Strunk, O. and Jordan, M. R.   "Experimental course
        for clergymen in suicidology and crisis intervention, "
        Journal of Pastoral Care, 26:50-4, March 1972.

550)   "Suicide prevention centers, "   Pastoral Psychology,
        18:48-9, Feb. 1967.

551)   Tabachnick, Norman.   "Suicide and the clergy, "   Bul-
        letin: The Council for Social Service, No. 194, June
        1966, pp. 1-7.

552)   Towne, A.   "Immolations and consensus: the justifica-
        tion of innocence, "   (Discussion) Christian Century,
        83:276, March 2, 1966.

553)   "Ultimately sorrowful, "   Christian Century, 84:1415,
        Nov. 1967.

554)   van der Horst, P. W.   "Pagan Platonist and a
        Christian Platonist on suicide, "   Vigiliae Christianae,
        4:282-8, 1971.

555)   Vincent, M. O.   "Suicide and how to prevent it, "
        Christianity Today, 14:10-12, Jan. 16, 1970.

556)   Whalley, Elsa A.   "Religion and suicide, "   Review of
        Religious Research, Vol. 4, No. 5, 1964.

557)   Whalley, Elsa A.   "Values and the suicide threat, "
        Journal of Religion and Health, 3(3):241-249, 1964.

558)   Winklemann, R. R.   "Texas plane crash: nonviolent
       man's final act brings destruction and death, "   The
       Christian Century,   88:26+, Jan. 6, 1971.

559)   Zahn, Gordon.   "Saint or suicide?   The ethics of
       martyrdom, "   Listener, 75:833-4, June 9, 1966.

560)   Zeitlin, S.   "The Sicarii and Masada, "   Jewish Quart-
       erly Review, 57:251-70, April 1967.

VI. ARTICLES FROM LEGAL JOURNALS

561) "Attempted suicide as evidence of guilt in criminal cases: the legal and psychological views, " Washington University Law Quarterly, 1964:204, April 1964.

562) Barry, J. V. "Suicide and the law, " Melbourne University Law Review, 5:1, May 1965.

563) "California court permits wrongful death action for suicide resulting from tortions infliction of mental disturbance, " [Tate v. Canonica, 5 Cal Rptr 28], Columbia Law Review, 60:1047, Nov. 1960.

564) "Causation of suicide actionable under New York wrongful death statute, " Buffalo Law Review, 9:370, Winter 1960.

565) Conway, J. V. P. "Investigation of suicide notes, " Journal of Forensic Sciences, 5:48, Jan. 1960.

566) "Criminal law-attempted suicide, " [State v. Willis (NC) 121 SE 2d 854], North Carolina Law Review, 40: 323, Feb. 1962.

567) Daube, D. "Josephus on suicide and liability of depositee, " Juridical Review, 1964:212, Dec. 1964.

568) Downey, B. W. M. "Statutes, Suicide Act, 1961, " Modern Law Review, 25: 60-3, Jan. 1962.

569) Edland, J. F. "Suicide by automobile, " Albany Law Review, 36:536, Spring 1972.

570) Goldberg, F. D. "Suicide and physician liability, " Medical Legal Bulletin, 205:1-3, 1970.

571) Hails, F. G. "Attempted suicide, " Justice of the Peace, 124:405, June 18, 1960.

572) Hindman, W. P., Jr. "Presumption against suicide
      in disappearance cases," American Bar Association
      Section of Insurance, Negligence and Compensation
      Law, 1965:109, 1965; Insurance Law Journal, 1965:645,
      Nov. 1965.

573) "Ill treatment as the cause of suicide," Cleveland-
      Marshall Law Review, 16:86, Jan. 1967.

574) Joling, R. J. "Legal commentaries on suicide by
      fire," Journal of Forensic Sciences, 7:397, Oct. 1962.

575) Lalli, M. and Turner, S. H. "Suicide and homicide:
      a comparative analysis by race and occupational
      levels," Journal of Criminal Law, Criminology and
      Police Science, 59:191, June 1968.

576) "Law revision--attempted suicide," Justice of the
      Peace, 125:240, Apr. 22, 1961.

577) Litman, Robert E. "Medical-legal aspects of suicide,"
      Washburn Law Journal, 6:395, Winter 1967.

578) Litman, Robert E. "Police aspects of suicide: legal
      aspects of suicide; handling suicidal persons; suicide
      prevention services," Police, 10:14-18, Jan./Feb.1966.

579) McBay, A. J. "Toxicologic studies in suicide inves-
      tigation," Journal of Forensic Sciences, 5:72, Jan.
      1960.

580) Markson, David S. "The punishment of suicide--a
      need for change," Villanova Law Review, 14(3):463-
      483, 1969.

581) Milner, A. "Suicide statistics," Law Journal, 111:
      118, Feb. 24, 1961.

582) Mitrovich, P. "Workmen's compensation for suicide
      after traumatic injury," Cleveland-Marshall Law Re-
      view, 15:116, Jan. 1966.

583) Muhr, E. "Life insurance and suicide--history and
      the Colorado statute," Denver Law Center Journal,
      41:51, Jan.-Feb. 1964.

584) "New York's mistreatment of burden of proof and the

presumption against suicide, " Fordham Law Review, 34:305, Dec. 1965.

585)   Page, J. A.   "Suicide and workmen's compensation," Plaintiff's Advocate, 6:28, July 1962.

586)   Palmer, D. M.   "Psycho-dynamics of suicide, " Journal of Forensic Sciences, 5:39, Jan. 1960.

587)   Palmer, Stuart.   "Murder and suicide in 40 non-literate societies, " Journal of Criminal Law, Criminology and Police Science, 56(3): 320-324, 1965.

588)   Perr, I. N.   "Suicide responsibility of hospital and psychiatrist, " Cleveland-Marshall Law Review, 9:427, Sept. 1960.

589)   "Punishment of suicide--a need for change, " Villanova Law Review, 14:463, Spring 1969.

590)   Regan, W. A.   "Law forum, " Hospital Progress, 46: 19-24, 1965.

591)   Rheingold, P. D.   "Negligence liability for suicide: the contribution of dynamic psychiatry, " Plaintiff's Advocate, 7:50, Oct. 1963.

592)   "Right to die, " Houston Law Review, 7:564, May 1970.

593)   Samuels, A.   "Two recent acts, " Criminal Law Review, 1961:582, Sept. 1961.

594)   Scanlon, T. J.   "Suicide under workmen's compensation laws, " Cleveland-Marshall Law Review, 12:26, Jan. 1963.

595)   Schulman, R. E.   "Suicide and suicide prevention: a legal analysis, " American Bar Association Journal, 54:855, Sept. 1968.

596)   Schwartz, V. E.   "Civil liability for causing suicide: a synthesis of law and psychiatry, " Vanderbilt Law Review, 24:217, March 1971.

597)   "Suicide and the fatal accidents act, " Solicitors' Journal, 104:817, Oct. 14, 1960.

598)   "Suicide or attempted suicide, " Justice of the Peace, 124:733, Nov. 12, 1960.

598a)   Thurston, G. "Remedying a misidentification, " Med. Leg. Journal, 39:31, 1971.

599)   Timperman, J. and Maes, R. "Suicidal poisoning by sodium chorate: a report of three cases, " Journal of Forensic Medicine, 13:123, Oct. -Dec. 1966.

600)   Topp, D. O. "The stepping-stones to current knowledge on suicide, " Medicine, Science and the Law, 11: 131-4, July 1971.

601)   "Tortious inducement to suicide: a study of the judicial ostrich, " Washington University Law Quarterly, 1970: 166, Spring 1970.

602)   "Torts--action for suicide under wrongful death statute, " [Tate v. Canonica, 5 Cal Rptr 28], Georgia Bar Journal, 23:275, Nov. 1960.

603)   "Torts--cause of action for inducing suicide, " [Cauverien v. De Metz, 188 NYS 2d 627], Louisiana Law Review, 20:791, June 1960.

604)   "Torts--cause of action for wrongful death may be based upon a suicide arising out of intentional or negligent mental harassment, " [Tate v. Canonica 5 Cal Rptr 28], Syracuse Law Review, 12:125, Fall 1960.

605)   "Torts--intentional and negligent harms--intervening suicide--relevance of proximate cause, " [Tate v. Canonica, 5 Cal Rptr 28], Wayne Law Review, 7:386, Winter 1960.

606)   "Torts--liability for causing suicide, " [Cauverien v. De Metz, 188 NYS 2d 627), Oklahoma Law Review, 13:459, Nov. 1960.

607)   "Torts--liability for suicide--guidance counselor held not responsible for the suicide-death of his counselee, " [Bogust v. Iverson (Wis.) 102 NW 2d 228], Wisconsin Law Review, 1961:517, May 1961.

608)   "Torts--proximate cause--liability for suicide, " [Cauverien v. De Metz, 188 NYS 2d 627], South Carolina

Law Quarterly, 12:482, Spring 1960.

609) "Torts--suicide while insane as result of conversion held actionable in wrongful death, " [Cauverien v. De Metz, 188 NYS 2d 627], St. John's Law Review, 34: 361, May 1960.

610) "Torts--wrongful death--civil liability for suicide resulting from either the intentional or negligent infliction of mental distress, " [Tate v. Canonica, 5 Cal Rptr 28], Rutgers Law Review, 15:134, Fall 1960.

611) Usher, A. "Murder or suicide, " Medicine, Science and the Law, 8:260-1, Oct. 1968.

612) Wilkerson, R. C. "The physician's liability in suicide and homicide, " Medico-Legal Bulletin, 157:1-5, 1966.

613) Wood, Arthur L. "A socio-structural analysis of murder, suicide and economic crime in Ceylon, " American Sociological Review, 26:744-753, 1961.

614) "Workmen's compensation; compensability of suicide of mentally ill employee, " [Burnight v. Industrial Acc. Comm'n, 5 Cal Rptr 786], UCLA Law Review, 8:673, May 1961.

615) "Workmen's compensation--compensation injury causing insanity--death by suicide as compensable, " [Harper v. Industrial Commission (Illinois) 180 NE 2d 480], Arkansas Law Review, 16:312, Spring 1962.

616) "Workmen's compensation--suicide compensable where causal connection to injury, " [Harper v. Industrial Commission (Ill.) 18 NE 2d 480], University of Cincinnati Law Review, 31:188, Spring 1962.

617) "Workmen's compensation: suicide resulting from mental disorder caused by work-connected injury held compensable, " [Harper v. Industrial Commission (Ill.) 180 NE 2d 480], Duke Law Journal, 1962:618, Autumn 1962.

618) Zamcheck, N. and Geisler, M. A. "Homicides and suicides of World War II: a critical analysis of 656 homicides and 1179 suicides, " Journal of Forensic Sciences, 5:84, January 1960.

619)   "Aetna Life Ins. Co. v. McLaughlin (Tex) 380 SW 2d
       101, " Houston Law Review, 2:396, Winter 1965; North
       Dakota Law Review, 41:372, March 1965.

620)   "Bill v. Farm Bureau Life Insurance Co. (Iowa), 119
       NW 2d 768, " Kansas Law Review, 12:458, March 1964.

621)   "Erikson v. Dilgard, 252 NYS 2d 705, " Fordham Law
       Review, 33:513, March 1965.

622)   "Lancaster v. Montesi (Tenn.) 390 SW 2d 217, " Ten-
       nessee Law Review, 33:540, Summer 1966.

623)   "Life and Casualty Insurance Co. v. Daniel (Va.) 163
       SE 2d 1577, " University of Richmond Law Review, 3:
       338, Spring 1969.

624)   "Little v. Chicago Hoist & Body Co. (Ill.) 203 NE 2d
       902, " De Paul Law Review, 15:219, Autumn-Winter,
       1965.

VII. SUICIDE AND STATE LEGISLATION

Once there were severe social and moral sanctions against suicide in this country, and the penalties for committing such an act were severe. According to Massachusetts law, "...By the act of 1660, suicides were denied the privilege of Christian burial, and were directed to be buried in the highway, with a cartload of stones laid upon the grave 'as a brand of infamy,'" Later, in 1877, we read, "...By the common law of England suicide was considered a crime against the laws of God and man, the lands and chattels of the criminal were forfeited to the king, his body had an ignominious burial in the highway, and he was deemed a murderer of himself and a felon, felo de se." (Commonwealth v. Mink, 1877.)

Committing suicide, or attempting to commit suicide, is no longer in itself a crime in Massachusetts, nor is it in most states. Interestingly enough, the majority of states have simply neglected to make any laws regarding suicide, save rules for coroners' inquests, inheritance, and the like. Such states as Colorado, Delaware, Georgia, Idaho, Illinois, Kansas, Kentucky, Louisiana, Maine, and Maryland, to go only partially through the list, have no criminal statutes regarding suicide on the books. Others, Iowa and Texas for example, have laws clearly stating that suicide is not a crime. An Iowa decision reads, "Attempt to commit suicide, not being made unlawful by statute, is not an 'unlawful act.'" (State v. Campbell, 1934.) In the Texas statutes we find, "It is not a violation of any law in Texas for a person to take his own life, and it is specifically provided by law that the estates of those who destroy their own lives shall descend or vest as in case of natural death." This law removes even the economic, though non-criminal, sanctions which often exist against suicides in that suicide often complicates inheritance procedures.

Generally, in states where there are criminal statutes concerning suicide, they involve penalties for aiding another person to commit the act, rather than penalties for taking

one's own life (or making the attempt).   Section 11. 15. 050 of
the Alaska Criminal Law reads, "A person who purposely and
deliberately procures another to commit self-murder or
assists another in the commission of self-murder is guilty of
manslaughter, and is punishable accordingly. "   There is a
similar law with the penalty of manslaughter involved in Florida.

In New York, there are three felony charges that can
be brought against anyone aiding or abetting a suicide: Class
A felony, murder; Class C felony, manslaughter; and Class
E felony, "promoting a suicide attempt. "   There is, however,
no law to prosecute the actual victim of a suicide attempt.

There are a few laws in this country, however, that
provide criminal penalties for the actual act of attempting
suicide.   The State of Washington provides the best example.
Washington statute 9. 80. 020, "Attempting suicide, " states,
"Every person who, with intent to take his own life, shall
commit upon himself any act dangerous to human life, or
which, if committed upon or toward another person, and followed by death as a consequence, would render the perpetra-
tor chargeable with homicide, shall be punished by imprisonment in the State penitentiary for not more than two years,
or by a fine of not more than one thousand dollars. "   It
apparently matters a great deal in some cases where a would-
be suicide makes the attempt, particularly if the attempt fails.
One can only hope that the law is not often enforced.

Laws against aiding and abetting suicide are also
severe in Washington.   Statute 9. 80. 030, "Aiding suicide, "
states, "Every person who, in any manner, shall willfully
advise, encourage, abet or assist another in taking his own
life, shall be guilty of manslaughter. "   Further, "Every person who, in any manner, shall willfully advise, encourage,
abet or assist another person in attempting to take the lat-
ter's life shall be punished by imprisonment in the state penitentiary for not more than ten years. "

Apparently, some states feel that suicide is somehow
a crime against society, while most feel it is a personal
matter.   There does not seem to be any discernible pattern.
States often thought to have the most repressive or antiquated
laws are often most liberal on this question, while supposedly
liberal states take a hard-line stand.   Persons interested in
pursuing the subject will have a tangled web to unweave as
they search the primary sources to determine the ramifica-

tions of legislation dealing with suicide.   Legal experts who
were consulted on this subject deplored the variations in attitude and penalties relating to suicide.   Suicide is one of the
oldest acts of violence and the fact that it has moral and religious as well as legal aspects is the reason cited for the
complex maze one encounters when tracing the law in this
area.

VIII. ARTICLES FROM MEDICAL
AND SCIENTIFIC JOURNALS

625) Abram, Harry S., Moore, Gordon L., and Westervelt, Frederic B. "Suicidal behavior in chronic dialy-
sis patients," American Journal of Psychiatry, 127:
1199-1204, Mar. 1971.

626) Abrams, R. "Suicide and ECT," American Journal
of Psychiatry, 126:272, 1969.

627) Achté, K. and Ginman, L. "Suicidal attempts with
narcotics and poisons," Acta Psychiatrica Scandinavica, 42:214-32, 1966.

628) Achté, K. A., Hillbom, E., and Lonnqvist, J. "Suicides following war brain injuries," Scandinavian
Journal of Clinical and Laboratory Investigation, 23
(108, Suppl.):84, 1969.

629) Achté, K A., Lonnqvist, J., and Hillbom, E. "Suicides of war brain-injured veterans," Finnish Psychiatry. Yearbook of the Psychiatric Clinic of the Helsinki University Central Hospital, 1970, pp. 231-239.

630) Achté, K. A., Stenback, A., and Teravainen, H.
"On suicides committed during treatment in psychiatric
hospitals," Acta Psychiatrica Scandinavica, 42(3):272-
284, 1966.

631) Ackerly, W. C. "Latency-age children who threaten
or attempt to kill themselves," Journal of the American Academy of Child Psychiatry, 6:242-261, 1967.

632) Adam, Kenneth S. "Suicide: A critical review of the
literature," Canadian Psychiatric Association Journal,
12(4):413-420, 1967.

633) Adam, K. S., Lohrenz, J. G., and Harper, D. "Sui-

cidal ideation and parental loss. A preliminary research report...," Canadian Psychiatric Association
Journal, 18:95-100, April 1973.

634) Aitken, R. C., Daly, R. J., Kreitman, N., Matthew,
H. and Proudfoot, A. T. "Coal gas and the brain,"
British Medical Journal, 1:706-707, 1968.

635) Aitken, R. C. and Proudfoot, A. T. "Barbiturate
automatism--myth or malady?", Postgraduate Medical
Journal, 45:612-616, 1969.

636) Alleman, S. A. "Psychotherapeutic aspects of unsuccessful suicide attempts," J. American Coll. Health
Assn., 13:390-8, Feb. 1965.

637) Allen, Thomas E. "Suicidal impulse in depression
and paranoia," International Journal of Psycho-Analysis, 48:433-438, 1967.

638) Altman, Harold, Sletten, Ivan W., Eaton, Mary E.,
and Lolett, George A. "Demographic and mental status
profiles: Patients with homicidal, assaultive, suicidal,
persecutory, and homosexual ideation," Psychiatric
Quarterly, 45:57-64, 1971.

639) Anastassopoulos, G. and Kokkini, D. "Suicidal attempts in psychomotor epilepsy," Behavioral Neuropsychiatry, 1:11-16, 1969.

640) Anderson, Camilla M. "Depression and suicide re-
assessed," Journal of the American Medical Women's
Association, 19:457-471, 1964.

641) Anderson, Camilla M. "Depression and suicide re-
assessed," Rational Living, 1(2):31-36, 1966.

642) Ansbacher, Heinz L. "Adler and the 1910 Vienna
symposium on suicide; a special review," Journal of
Individual Psychology, 24:181-191, 1968.

643) Ansbacher, Heinz L. "Alfred Adler, individual psychology, and Marilyn Monroe," Psychology Today,
3:42-44, Feb. 1970.

644) Ansbacher, Heinz L. "Suicide as communication:
Adler's concept and current applications," Journal of

Individual Psychology, 25(2):174-180, 1969.

645)   Anstice, E. "Dial MANsion House 9000. The Samar-
       itans," Nursing Times, 63:123-124, 1967.

646)   APHA conference report, 1968. "Mental health,"
       Public Health Reports, 84:223-226, 1969.

647)   Applebaum, S. A. "The problem solving aspect of
       suicide," Journal of Projective Techniques and Per-
       sonality Assessment, 27(3):259-68, 1963.

648)   Applebaum, S. A. and Holzman, P. S. "The color-
       shading response and suicide," Journal of Projective
       Techniques and Personality Assessment, 26(2):155-61,
       1962.

649)   Applebaum, Stephen A. and Colson, Donald B. "A
       reexamination of the color-shading Rorschach test re-
       sponse and suicide attempts," Journal of Projective
       Techniques and Personality Assessment, 32(2):160-164,
       1968.

650)   Arlen, M. S. "Emergency assessment and manage-
       ment of the potentially suicidal patient," Clinical
       Medicine, 69:1101-1118, 1962.

651)   Asensio, J. "Suicide among doctors," British Med-
       ical Journal, 5386:789-790, 1964. [Editorial]

652)   Asensio, J. "Attempted suicide with cheese," Bri-
       tish Medical Journal, 5387:907, 1964.

653)   Assael, M. I. "Thanatophilia," Diseases of the
       Nervous System, 26:777-781, 1965.

654)   Atkinson, Eulalia. "Four hours on the suicide phones,"
       Bulletin of Suicidology, No. 7:38-51, Fall 1970.

655)   Atkinson, J. M. "On the sociology of suicide,"
       Sociological Review, 16:83-92, 1968.

656)   Atkinson, J. M. "Suicide and the student," Univer-
       sities Quarterly, September 1968.

657)   Atkinson, Maxwell. "The Samaritans and the elderly:
       some problems in communication between a suicide

prevention scheme and a group with a high suicide rate, " Social Science and Medicine, 5:483-490, Oct. 1971.

658) Attkisson, C. Clifford. "Suicide in San Francisco's skid row, " Archives of General Psychiatry, 23(2): 149-157, 1970.

659) Aurerly, W. C. "Latency age children who threaten or attempt to kill themselves, " Journal of the American Academy of Child Psychiatry, 6:242-261, 1967.

660) Austin, R. G. "Suicide as catharsis, " Lancet, 2:757, Oct. 7, 1972.

661) Avella, A. N. "Prevention of suicide, " New York State Journal of Medicine, 66:3023-3025, 1966.

662) Ayd, F. J., Jr. "Drug-induced depression: fact or fallacy, " New York State Journal of Medicine, 58:354-356, 1958.

663) Ayd, F. J., Jr. "Suicide, a hazard in depression, " Journal of Neuropsychiatry, 2:52-54, 1961.

664) Bab, W. "Suicide and the ophthalmologist, " Eye, Ear, Nose and Throat Monthly, 47:147-149, 1968.

665) Baden, M. M. "Homicide, suicide and accidental death among narcotic addicts, " Human Pathology, 3:91-5, March 1972.

666) Bagley, Christopher and Greer, Steven. "'Black suicide': a report of 25 English cases and controls, " Journal of Social Psychology, 86:175-79, April 1972.

667) Bagley, Christopher. "Causes and prevention of repeated attempted suicide, " Social and Economic Admin., 4:322-30, Oct. 1970.

668) Bagley, Christopher and Greer, Steven. "Clinical and social predictors of repeated attempted suicide: a multivariate analysis, " British Journal of Psychiatry, 119:515-21, Nov. 1971.

669) Bagley, Christopher. "The evaluation of a suicide prevention scheme by an ecological method, " Social

Science and Medicine, 2(1):1-14, 1968.

670)   Bakan, David. "Suicide and immortality," Humanitas,
       6(1):15-21, 1970.

671)   Baker, J. "Survey on suicides and accidental poison-
       ing," Nursing Times, 67:258-61, March 4, 1971.

672)   Bakwin, H. "Suicide in children and adolescents,"
       Journal of the American Medical Women's Association,
       19:489-491, 1964.

673)   Banen, David M. and Gordon, Nancy. "Suicide among
       psychotic patients," Bedford Research, 8:3, 1962.

674)   Banks, L. J. "Black suicide," Ebony, 25(7):76-84,
       1970.

675)   Barakat, Halim. "Alienation: a process of encounter
       between utopia and reality," British Journal of So-
       ciology, 20(1):1-10, 1969.

676)   Barlow, S. M. "Suicide and Samaritan clients,"
       Lancet, 2(7682):1091, 1970.

677)   Barno, A. "Criminal abortion--deaths and suicides in
       pregnancy in Minnesota, 1950-1964," Minnesota Med-
       icine, 50:11-16, 1967.

678)   Barno, A. "Criminal abortion deaths, illegitimate
       pregnancy deaths, and suicides in pregnancy, Minne-
       sota, 1950-1965," American Journal of Obstetrics
       and Gynecology, 98:346-367, 1967.

679)   Barr, A. M. "Further experience in the treatment of
       severe organic phosphate poisoning," Medical Journal
       of Australia, 1:490-492, 1966.

680)   Barr, John. "Death in cherry blossom time: Tokyo
       report," New Society, Apr. 8, 1965, p. 21.

681)   Barraclough, B. "A medical approach to suicide pre-
       vention," Soc. Sci. Med., 6:661-7, Dec. 1972.

682)   Barraclough, B. "Suicide prevention, recurrent affec-
       tive disorder and lithium," British Journal of Psy-
       chiatry, 121:391-2, Oct. 1972.

683)   Barraclough, B. M.   "Suicide rate, " British Medical
        Journal, 3:590, Sept. 2, 1972.

684)   Barraclough, B. M.   "Suicide rate, " British Medical
        Journal, 1:293, Feb. 3, 1973.

685)   Barraclough, B. M. , Nelson, B. , Bunch, J. , and
        Sainsbury, P.   "Suicide and barbiturate prescribing, "
        J. R. Coll. Gen. Pract. , 21:645-53, Nov. 1971.

686)   Barraclough, B. M. and Shea, Marian.   "A compari-
        son between 'Samaritan suicides' and living Samaritan
        clients, " British Journal of Psychiatry, 120:79-84,
        Jan. 1972.

687)   Barraclough, B. M. and Shea, Marian.   "Suicide and
        Samaritan clients, " Lancet, 2(7678):868-870, 1970.

688)   Barraclough, B. M. and Shea, M.   "Suicide preven-
        tion, " Lancet, 2:365, Aug. 15, 1970.

689)   Barrett, Gerald V. and Franke, Richard H.   "'Psy-
        chogenic' death: A reappraisal, " Science, 167 (3916):
        304-306, 1970.

690)   Barter, James T. , Swaback, Dwight A. , and Todd,
        Dorothy.   "Adolescent suicide attempts: A follow-up
        study of hospitalized patients, " Archives of General
        Psychiatry, 19:523-27, 1968.

691)   Bartholomew, Allen A. and Kelley, M. F.   "An analy-
        sis of 500 consecutive patients (other than alcoholics)
        in an out-patient clinic largely concerned with psycho-
        social problems, " Medical Journal of Australia, 2:
        825-7, November 21, 1964.

692)   Bartholomew, Allen A. and Olijnyk, E.   "An analysis
        of suicide calls received by a personal emergency tele-
        phone advisory service after ten years of operation, "
        Medical Journal of Australia, 2:929-32, Oct. 21, 1972.

693)   Bartholomew, Allen A.   "The survivor of a suicide
        pact, " R. V. Arnold, Australian & New Zealand
        Journal of Psychiatry, 3(3):145-151, 1969.

694)   Bartholomew, A. A. and Kelley, Margaret F.   "Sui-
        cidal intentions expressed in telephone calls to the per-

sonal emergency advisory service, " Australian Journal of Social Work, 15:3-11, 1962.

695) Bartholomew, A. A. and Kelley, Margaret F. "The personal emergency advisory service, " Mental Hygiene, 46:382-392, 1962.

696) Bartholomew, A. A. and Kelley, Margaret F. "An analysis of suicide calls received by a personal emergency advisory (telephone) service, " Medical Journal of Australia, 2(12):488-492, 1963.

697) Bartholomew, A. A., Kelley, Margaret F., and Staley, E. M. "An analysis of 'night calls' received by a personal emergency (telephone) service, " Social Service, 14(5):13, 1963.

698) Barwin, H. "Suicide in children and adolescents, " Journal of the American Medical Women's Association, 19(6):489-491, 1964.

699) Barwin, H. "Teenage suicide, " Archives of Environmental Health, 12(3):276-278, 1966.

700) Basescu, S. "The threat of suicide in psychotherapy," American Journal of Psychotherapy, 19:99-105, Jan. 1965.

701) Beach, G. O., Fitzgerald, R. P., Holmes, R., Phibbs, B., and Struckenhoff, H. "Scopolamine poisoning, " New England Journal of Medicine, 270:1354-1355, 1964.

702) Beall, Lynnette. "The dynamics of suicide: a review of the literature, 1897-1965, " Bulletin of Suicidology, Mar. 1969, pp. 2-16.

703) Beall, Lynnette. "The psychopathology of suicide in Japan, " International Journal of Social Psychiatry, 14(3):213-225, 1968.

704) Beighton, P., MacFarlane, A., and Wasseg, C. "Medico-social aspects of attempted suicide, " British Journal of Clinical Practice, 21:593-97, 1967.

705) Beisser, Arnold R. and Blanchette, James E. "A study of suicides in a mental hospital, " Diseases of

the Nervous System, 22:365-369, 1961.

706) Bell, Karen K. "The nurse's role in suicide prevention," Bulletin of Suicidology, 6:60-65, Spring 1970.

707) Bender, Lauretta L. and Schilder, P. "Suicidal pre-
occupations and attempts in children," American
Journal of Orthopsychiatry, 7:225-243, 1957.

708) Benensohn, H. S. and Resnik, H. L. "Guidelines for
'Suicide-proofing' a psychiatric unit," American
Journal of Psychotherapy, 27:204-12, Apr. 1973.

709) Bennett, A. E. "Prevention of suicide," Post-graduate Medical Journal, 32:160-164, 1962.

710) Bennett, A. E. "Recognizing the potential suicide,"
Geriatrics, 22(5):175-81, 1967.

711) Bennett, A. E. and Evans, P. J. "Suicide prevention
on psychiatric wards," Mental Hospitals, 16(3):105-
108, 1965.

712) Benostrand, C. G. and Otto, V. "Suicidal attempts in
adolescence and childhood," Acta Paediatrica, 51(1):
17-26, 1962.

713) Benson, M. "Doctors' wives tackle suicide problem,"
Today's Health, 42:60-63, 1964.

714) Berardo, Felix, M. "Widowhood status in the United
States: perspective on a neglected aspect of the family
life-cycle," Family Coordinator, 17(3):191-203, 1968.

715) Berblinger, K. W. "Suicide as a message," Psychosomatics, 5:144-146, 1964.

716) Berenson, G. "Critical incidents in the context of
family therapy," Critical incident no. 1, International
Psychiatry Clinics, 7:261-272, 1970.

717) Berg, Donald E. "Crisis intervention concepts for
emergency telephones," Crisis Intervention, 2(4,
Suppl.):11-20, 1970.

718) Berger, F. M. "Drugs and suicide in the United
States," Clinical Pharmacology and Therapeutics,

8(2):219-223, 1967.

719)   Berger, J. C.   "Suicide attempts related to congenital
       facial deformities.   Two unusual case reports, " Plas-
       tic Reconstructive Surgery, 51:323-5, March, 1973.

720)   Bergstrand, C. G. and Otto, U.   "Suicidal attempts
       in adolescence and childhood, " Acta Paediatrica, 51
       (1):17-26, 1962.

721)   Berliner, Beverly S.   "Nursing a patient in crisis, "
       American Journal of Nursing, 70(10):2154-57, Oct. 1970.

722)   Beswick, David G.   "Attitudes to taking human life, "
       Australian and New Zealand Journal of Sociology, 6
       (2):120-130, Oct. 1970.

723)   Beukenkamp, C.   "Parental suicide as a source of
       resistance to marriage, " International Journal of
       Group Psychotherapy, 11:204-208, 1961.

724)   Bigras, Julien, Gauthier, Yvon, Bouchard, Colette,
       and Tassé, Yolande.   "Suicidal attempts in adolescent
       girls: a preliminary study, " Canadian Psychiatric
       Association Journal, 11:275-282, 1966.

725)   Binns, W. A. , Kerkman, D. , and Schroeder, S. O.
       "Destructive group dynamics: an account of some pe-
       culiar interrelated incidents of suicide and suicidal
       attempts in a university dormitory, " Journal of the
       American College Health Association, 14(4):250-256,
       1966.

726)   Bioras, J. , Gauthier, Y. , Bouchard, Colette, and
       Taber, Yolande.   "Suicidal attempts in adolescent
       girls: a preliminary study, " Canadian Psychiatric
       Association Journal, (Suppl):275-282, 1966.

727)   Birtchnell, John and Alarcon, Jose.   "The motivation
       and emotional state of 91 cases of attempted suicide,"
       British Journal of Medical Psychology, 44(1):45-52,
       Mar. 1971.

728)   Birtchnell, John.   "The relationship between attempted
       suicide, depression and parent death, " British Journal
       of Psychiatry, 116(532):307-13, Mar. 1970.

729)   Blachly, P. H.   "Suicide as seduction: a concept for
        evaluation of suicidal risk, " Hospital Medicine, 5(9):
        117-118, 1969.

730)   Blachly, P. H. , Disher, William, and Roduner,
        Gregory. "Suicide by physicians, " Bulletin of Sui-
        cidology, December 1969, pp. 1-18.

731)   Blachly, P. H. and Fairley, N.   "Market analysis for
        suicide prevention. Relationship of age to suicide on
        holidays, day of the week and month, " Northwest
        Medicine, 68:232-238, 1969.

732)   Blachly, P. H. , Osterud, H. T. , and Josslin, R.
        "Suicide in professional groups, " New England Journal
        of Medicine, 268:1278-1282, 1963.

733)   Blaine, Graham B. , Jr. and Carmen, Lida R.   "Causal
        factors in suicide attempts by male and female college
        students, " American Journal of Psychiatry, 125(6):834-
        37, 1968.

734)   Blair, A. A. , Hallpike, J. F. , Lascelles, P. T. , and
        Wingate, D. L.   "Acute diphenylhydantoin and primi-
        done poisoning treated by peritoneal dialysis, " Journal
        of Neurology, Neurosurgery and Psychiatry, 31(5):520-
        523, 1968.

735)   Blaker, K.   "Crisis maintenance, " Nursing Forum,
        8:42-49, 1969.

736)   Blaker, K. P.   "Systems theory and self-destructive
        behavior--a new theoretical base, " Perspectives in
        Psychiatric Care, 10:168-72, 1972.

737)   Blanton, Williams C. and Niclels, J. B.   "Internal-
        external control dimension as related to accident and
        suicide proneness, " Journal of Consulting & Clinical
        Psychology, 33(4):485-494, 1969.

738)   Blath, R. A. , McClure, J. N. J. , and Wetzel, R. D.
        "Familial factors in suicide, " Diseases of the Ner-
        vous System, 34:90-3, Feb. 1973.

739)   Block, Jeanne and Christiansen, Bjorn.   "A test of
        Hendin's hypotheses relating suicide in Scandinavia to
        child-rearing orientations, " Scandinavian Journal of
        Psychology, 7(4):267-286, 1966.

740)   Bloom, Victor. "An analysis of suicide at a training
       center, " American Journal of Psychiatry, 123(8):918-
       925, 1967.

741)   Bloom, V. "Prevention of suicide, " Current Psychi-
       atric Therapies, 10:105-109, 1970.

742)   Bloomberg, S. G. "The present state of suicide pre-
       vention--an African survey, " International Journal of
       Social Psychiatry, 18:104-8, Summer 1972.

743)   Blumenthal, S. and Bergner, L. "Suicide and news-
       papers--a replicated study, " American Journal of
       Psychiatry, 130:458-71, April 1973.

744)   Bock, E. Wilbur. "Aging and suicide: the signifi-
       cance of marital, kinship, and alternative relations, "
       Family Coordinator, 21(1):71-79, Jan. 1972.

745)   Bock, H. B. and Digon, E. "Suicides and climatol-
       ogy, " Archives of Environmental Health, 12:279-286,
       1966.

746)   Bodie, M. K. "When a patient threatens suicide, "
       Perspectives in Psychiatric Care, 6:76-79, 1968.

747)   Bogard, H. M. "Primary and secondary gain in a
       general hospital suicide prevention program, " Journal
       of the Hillside Hospital, 18(1):40-47, 1969.

748)   Bogard, Howard M. "Follow-up study of suicidal
       patients seen in emergency room consultation, "
       American Journal of Psychiatry, 126(7):1017-1020, 1970.

749)   Bolin, Robert K. , Wright, Robert E. , Wilkinson, Mary
       N. , and Linder, Clare K. "Survey of suicide among
       patients on home leave from a mental hospital, " Psy-
       chiatric Quarterly, 42(1):81-89, 1968.

750)   Bollea, G. and Mayer, K. "Psychopathology of suicide
       in the formative years, " Acta Paedopsychiatrica, 35
       (11-12):336-344, 1968.

751)   Boreham, John. "The prediction of suicide, " Ror-
       schach Newsletter, 12(2):5-7, 1967.

752)   Bowlby, John. "Disruption of affectional bonds and

its effects on behavior, " Canada's Mental Health Supplement, 1969, No. 59, 12p.

753)   Bowlby, John. "Disruption of affectional bonds and
       its effects on behavior, " Journal of Contemporary
       Psychotherapy, Vol. 2(2):75-86, Winter 1970.

754)   Braaten, L. J. "Some reflections on suicidal tenden-
       cies among college students, " Mental Hygiene, 47(4):
       562-568, 1963.

755)   Braaten, L. J. and Darling, C. D. "Suicidal tenden-
       cies among college students, " The Psychiatric Quart-
       erly, 36(4):665-692, 1962.

756)   Braatz, Gordon A. and Lumry, Gayle K. "The young
       veteran as a psychiatric patient, " Military Medicine,
       134(12):1434-1439, 1969.

757)   Braceland, Francis J. "Changes in the treatment of
       involutional melancholia, " Hospital and Community
       Psychiatry, 20(5):136-140, May 1969.

758)   Branch, C. H. "Management of depression and sui-
       cide attempts, " Northwest Medicine, 65:1060-1064,
       1966.

759)   Brandwin, Marvin A. and Blunt, Lynn W. "Suicidal
       emergencies in a university medical center: a five-
       and ten-year comparison, " Comprehensive Psychiatry,
       9(6):551-562, 1968.

760)   Branzei, P., Pirozynski, T., and Avramovici, J. A.
       "Considerations upon the attempts of suicide during
       infant-juvenile growth period, " Acta Psychiatrica Belg.,
       72:413-23, May 1972.

761)   Bratfos, O. "Attempted suicide--a comparative study
       of patients who have attempted suicide and psychiatric
       patients in general, " Acta Psychiatrica Scandinavia,
       47:38-56, 1971.

762)   Braucht, G. Nicholas and Wilson, Lowell T. "Pre-
       dictive utility of the Revised Suicide Potential Scale,"
       Journal of Consulting and Clinical Psychology, 35(3):
       426, Dec. 1970.

763) Braun, M. "Suicide in psychiatrists," Journal of
      the American Medical Association, 223:81, Jan. 1, 1973.

764) Breed, Warren. "Male suicide: Los Angeles and New
      Orleans compared," Bulletin of Suicidology, Dec. 11-
      14, Dec. 1967.

765) Breed, Warren. "Occupational mobility and suicide
      among white males," American Sociological Review,
      28(2):179-188, 1963.

766) Breed, Warren. "Suicide, migration and race: a study
      of cases in New Orleans," Journal of Social Issues,
      22(1):30-43, 1966.

767) Breed, Warren. "The Negro and fatalistic suicide,"
      Pacific Sociological Review, 13(3):156-162, 1970.

768) Brenner, B. "Alcoholism and fatal accidents,"
      Quarterly Journal of Studies on Alcohol, 28:517-528,
      1967.

769) Bridges, P. K. and Koller, K. M. "Attempted sui-
      cide: a comparative study," Comprehensive Psychi-
      atry, 7(4):240-247, 1966.

770) Brockopp, Gene W. and Lester, David. "Time com-
      petence and suicidal history," Psychological Reports,
      28(1):80, Feb. 1971.

771) Brockopp, Gene W. and Lester, David. "Time per-
      spective in suicidal and nonsuicidal individuals,"
      Crisis Intervention, 2(4):98-100, 1970.

772) Brockopp, Gene W. "A note on the telephone handling
      of the obscene caller," Crisis Intervention, 2(4):96-
      98, 1970.

773) Brockopp, G. W. "Assessment of suicide," Penn.
      Nurse, 25(6):2-4, 21, 1970.

774) Brockopp, Gene W. and Yasser, Allen. "Training the
      volunteer telephone therapist," Crisis Intervention,
      2(3):65-72, 1970.

775) Brockopp, Gene W. "Crisis theory and suicide pre-
      vention," Crisis Intervention, 2 (2, Suppl.):38-41, 1970.

776)   Brockopp, Gene W.   "The telephone call: Conversation
       or therapy, " Crisis Intervention, 2(3):73-75, 1970.

777)   "Broken homes and suicide, " Journal of the American
       Medical Association, 191:494, Feb. 8, 1965.

778)   Brooke, E. M. and Glatt, M. M.   "More and more
       barbiturates, " Med. Sci. Law, 4:277-82, Oct. 1964.

779)   Brophy, James J.   "Suicide attempts with psychothera-
       peutic drugs, " Archives of General Psychiatry, 17(6):
       652-657, 1967.

780)   Brown, J. H.   "Suicide--the deserted field, " Canadian
       Psychiatric Association Journal, 18:93-4, Apr. 1973.

781)   Brown, William and Pisetsky, Joseph.   "Suicidal be-
       havior in a general hospital, " American Journal of
       Medicine, 29:307-315, 1960.

782)   Browne, N. J.   "Attempted suicide, " Medical Journal
       of Australia, 2:1309, 18 Dec. 1971.

783)   Browning, Charles H., Tyson, Robert L., and Miller,
       Sheldon I.   "A study of psychiatric emergencies: Sui-
       cide, " Psychiatry in Medicine, 1(4):359-366, Oct.
       1970.   (15 ref.)

784)   Bruhn, John G.   "Broken homes among attempted sui-
       cides and psychiatric out-patients: A comparative
       study, " Journal of Mental Science (now British Journal
       of Psychiatry), 108:772-779, 1962.

785)   Bruhn, J. G.   "Comparative study of attempted sui-
       cides and psychiatric out-patients, " British Journal
       of Preventive and Social Medicine, 17(4):197-201, 1963.

786)   Bruhn, J. G. and McCulloch, J. W.   "Paternal de-
       privation among attempted suicides, " British Journal
       of Psychiatric Social Work, 6:186-191, 1962.

787)   Brüll, F.   "The treatment of two patients after serious
       attempts at suicide, " Israel Annals of Psychiatry and
       Related Disciplines, 6:30-39, 1968.

788)   Brunt, H. H.   "Organization of a suicide prevention
       center, " Journal of the Medical Society of New Jersey,

66:62-65, 1969.

789) Brunt, Harry H., Rotov, Michail, and Glenn, Trevor. "A suicide prevention center in a public mental hospital," Mental Hygiene, 52(2):254-262, 1968.

790) Bruyn, H. and Seiden, R. H. "Student suicide: fact or fancy?" Journal of the American College Health Association, 14(2):69-77, 1965.

791) Bryan, William J. "Survival today, tomorrow and forever," Journal of the American Institute of Hypnosis, 12(3):135-138, 142, July 1971.

792) Buglass, Dorothy and McCulloch, J. W. "Further suicidal behavior: The development and validation of predictive scales," British Journal of Psychiatry, 116(534):483-491, May 1970.

793) Bunch, J., Barraclough, B., Nelson, B., and Sainsbury, P. "Early parental bereavement and suicide," Social Psychiatry, 6(4):200-202, Dec. 1971.

794) Bunch, J. "Recent bereavement in relation to suicide," Journal of Psychosomatic Research, 16:361-6, Aug. 1972.

795) Bunch, J., Barraclough, B., Nelson, B., and Sainsbury, P. "Suicide following bereavement of parents," Social Psychiatry, 6(4):193-199, Dec. 1971.

796) Bunch, J. and Barraclough, B. "The influence of parental death anniversaries upon suicide rates," British Journal of Psychiatry, 118(547):621-626, Jan. 1971.

797) Bunney, W. E., Jr. and Fawcett, J. A. "Possibility of a biochemical test for suicidal potential," Archives of General Psychiatry, 13:232-239, 1965.

798) Burston, G. R. "Self-poisoning in elderly patients," Gerontologia Clinica (Basel), 11:279-289, 1969.

799) Burvill, P. W. "Analysis of rates in selected countries specific for age and sex," International Journal of Social Psychiatry, 18:137-9, Summer 1972.

800)   Butler, G. C. "Incidence of suicide among the ethnic
       groups of the Northwest Territories and Yukon Terri-
       tory, " Medical Services Journal (Canada), 21:252-256,
       1965.

801)   Cain, Albert C. and Fast, Irene. "Children's dis-
       turbed reactions to parent suicides, " American Journal
       of Orthopsychiatry, 36(5):873-880, 1966.

802)   Cain, Albert C. and Fast, Irene. "The legacy of sui-
       cide: observations on the pathogenic impact of suicide
       upon marital partners, " Psychiatry, 29(4):406-411,
       1966.

803)   Capstick, A. "Recognition of emotional disturbance
       and the prevention of suicide, " British Medical Journal,
       1:1179-1182, 1960.

804)   Capstick, A. "Urban and rural suicide, " Journal of
       Mental Science, 106:1327-1336, 1960.

805)   Capstick, A. "The methods of suicide, " Medico-
       Legal Journal, 29:33-38, 1961.

806)   Carmen, Lida R. and Blaine, Graham B., Jr. "A
       study of suicidal attempts by male and female univer-
       sity students, " International Psychiatry Clinics, 7(3):
       181-199, 1970.

807)   Carstairs, G. M. "Characteristics of the suicide
       prone, " Proceedings of the Royal Society of Medicine,
       54:262-264, 1961.

808)   Carstairs, G. M. "Preventable deaths, " Lancet,
       2:248, 1962.

809)   Cash, Larry M. and Kooker, Earl W. "Attitudes
       toward death of NP patients who have attempted sui-
       cide, " Psychological Reports, 26(3):879-882, June 1970.

810)   Cashion, Barbara G. "Durkheim's concept of anomie
       and its relationship to divorce, " Sociology and Social
       Research, 55(1):72-81, Oct. 1970.

811)   Cassidy, W. J. "Assessing attempted suicide, " Henry
       Ford Hospital Medical Journal, 18:205-210, 1970.

812)   Cassidy, W. J. "Psychiatric emergencies," Henry
       Ford Hospital Medical Journal, 15(2):119-131, 1967.

813)   Cazzulo, C. L., Balestri, L., and Generali, L.
       "Some remarks on the attempted suicide in the period
       of adolescence," Acta Paedopsychiatrica, 35(11-12):
       373-375, 1968.

814)   Cerbus, George. "Seasonal variation in some mental
       health statistics: suicides, homicides, psychiatric ad-
       missions, and institutional placement of the retarded,"
       Journal of Clinical Psychology, 26(1): 61-63, 1970.

815)   Chambliss, W. J. and Steele, M. F. "Status integra-
       tion and suicide: an assessment," American Socio-
       logical Review, 31(4):524-532, 1966.

816)   "Changing concepts of suicide," Journal of the Ameri-
       can Medical Association, 199(10):752, 1967. [Editorial]

817)   Chapman, Richard F. "Suicide during psychiatric hos-
       pitalization," Bulletin of the Menninger Clinic, 29(2):
       35-43, 1965.

818)   Chasin, R. M. "Special clinical problems in day hos-
       pitalization," American Journal of Psychiatry, 123(7):
       779-785, 1967.

819)   Chodorkoff, B. "Alcoholism and ego function," Quart-
       erly Journal of Studies on Alcohol, 25:292-299, 1964.

820)   Choron, Jacques. "Notes on suicide prevention in
       antiquity," Bulletin of Suicidology, July 1968, pp. 46-
       48.

821)   Choron, Jacques. "Concerning suicide in Soviet Rus-
       sia," Bulletin of Suicidology, Dec. 1968, pp. 31-36.

822)   Chowdhury, Nilima and Kreitman, Norman. "The
       clientele of the Telephone Samaritan organization,"
       Applied Social Studies, 2:123-135, 1970.

823)   Clark, Marguerite. "Let's talk sense about suicide,"
       RN, Nov. 1960, pp. 58-88.

824)   Clement, J. A. and Holloway, A. M. "Suicidal strych-
       nine poisoning," Lancet, 1:983, 1964.

825)   Clemmons, Phyllis K.   "The role of the nurse in
        suicide prevention, " Journal of Psychiatric Nursing
        and Mental Health Services, 9(1):27-30, Jan. 1971.

826)   Clifton, B. S., Mackey, K. H., and McLeod, J. G.
        "Barbiturate poisoning, " Medical Journal of Aus-
        tralia, 1:63, 1965.

827)   Cline, D. W.   "Management of adolescent suicide
        attempts, " Minnesota Medicine, 56:111-3, Feb. 1973.

828)   Clinebell, Howard J.   "First aid in counselling: the
        suicidal emergency, " Expository Times, 77:328-32,
        Aug. 1966.

829)   Coe, J.   "Suicide: a statistical and pathological re-
        port, " Minnesota Medical Journal, 46:22-30, 1963.

830)   Cohen, E.   "Melancholy and suicide, " Journal of the
        American Medical Association, 212:2121, 1970.

831)   Cohen, Earl, Motto, Jerome A., and Seiden, Richard
        H.   "An instrument for evaluating suicide potential: a
        preliminary study, " American Journal of Psychiatry,
        122(8):886-891, 1966.

832)   Cohen, E.   "Suicide in physicians, " Journal of the
        American Medical Association, 222:489, Oct. 1972.

833)   Cohen, J.   "Forms of suicide and their significance, "
        Triangle, 6:280-6, Dec. 1964.

834)   Cohen, John.   "A study of suicide pacts, " Medico-
        Legal Journal, 29:114-151, 1961.

835)   Cohen, S.   "Suicide following morning glory seed in-
        gestion, " American Journal of Psychiatry, 120:1024-
        1025, 1964.

836)   Cohen, Sidney.   "The incurables, " Journal of Reha-
        bilitation, 33(5):16-18, 1967.

837)   Cohen, Sidney, Leonard, Calista V., Farberow, Nor-
        man L., and Shneidman, Edwin S.   "Tranquilizers
        and suicide in the schizophrenic patient, " Archives of
        General Psychiatry, 11(3):312-321, 1964.

838)   Colson, C. E.   "Effects of different explanations of
       disordered behavior on treatment referrals, " Journal
       of Consult. Clinical Psychology, 34:432-5, June 1970.

839)   Colson, C. E.   "Neuroticism, extraversion and re-
       pression--sensitization in suicidal college students, "
       British Journal of Social Clinical Psychology, 11:88-9,
       Feb. 1972.

840)   Colson, D. B. and Hurwitz, B. A.   "A new experi-
       mental approach to the relationship between color-
       shading and suicide attempts, " Journal of Pers.
       Assess., 37:237-41, June 1973.

841)   Connell, H. M.   "Attempted suicide in schoolchildren,"
       Medical Journal of Australia, 1:686-90, April 1, 1972.

842)   Cooper, George W., Jr., Bernstein, Lewis, and Hart,
       Cynthia.   "Predicting suicidal ideation from the Ror-
       schach: An attempt to cross-validate, " Journal of
       Projective Techniques and Personality Assessment, 29
       (2):168-170, 1965.

843)   Copas, J. B., Freeman-Browne, D. L., and Rosin,
       A. A.   "Danger periods for suicide in patients under
       treatment, " Psychological Medicine, 1:400-404, Nov.
       1971.

844)   Corbett, J. and Meier, G.   "Suicide attempted by
       rectal administration of drug, " Journal of the Ameri-
       can Medical Association, 206(10):2320-2321, 1968.

845)   Coulter, Elizabeth J.   "A demographic study of the
       suicide problem among Ohio residents, " Ohio's Health,
       17(2):8-26, 1965.

846)   Cowen, J.   "Depression or disappointment, " American
       Family Physician, 3:99-103, Feb. 1971.

847)   Craig, Alan G. and Pitts, Ferris N.   "Suicide by phy-
       sicians, " Diseases of the Nervous System, 29(11):763-
       772, 1968.

848)   Crawford, J. P. and Perinpanayogam, M. A.   "At-
       tempted suicide, " Lancet, 1:499, March 6, 1971.

849)   Crawford, J. P. and Willis, J. H.   "Double suicide

in psychiatric hospital patients, " British Journal of
Psychiatry, 112(493):1231-1235, 1966.

850)   Cresswell, P. "Interpretations of suicide, " British
       Journal of Sociology, 23:133-45, June 1972.

851)   Crown, D. A. and Crim, M. "Historical research,
       document examination and Crown Prince Rudolph of
       Austria, " Journal of Forensic Sciences, 11:330-57,
       July 1966.

852)   Cunningham, E. "Suicide in today's society, " Medi-
       cal Journal of Australia, 2:1197-1200, 1968.

853)   Curlee, Joan. "A comparison of male and female
       patients at an alcoholism treatment center, " Journal of
       Psychology, 74(2):239-247, 1970.

854)   Curphey, Theodore J. "The psychological autopsy: the
       role of the forensic pathologist in the multi-disciplinary
       approach to death, " Bulletin of Suicidology, July 1968,
       pp. 39-45.

855)   Curran, W. J. "Public health and the law. Suicide:
       civil right or punishable crime?", American Journal
       of Public Health, 60:163-164, 1970.

856)   Cutter, Fred and Farberow, Norman L. "Serial ad-
       ministration of consensus Rorschachs to one patient, "
       Journal of Projective Techniques & Personality Assess-
       ment, 32(4):358-374, 1968.

857)   Cutter, F. , Jorgensen, Mary, and Farberow, N. L.
       "Replicability of Rorschach signs with known degrees
       of suicidal intent, " Journal of Projective Techniques
       & Personality Assessment, 32:428-434, 1968.

858)   Cutter, F. , Cantor, J. , and Potter, Mary M. "Sui-
       cidal intent, alcoholism and syndrome related con-
       cepts, " Quarterly Journal of Studies on Alcohol, 31A
       (4):861-867, 1970.

859)   Cutter, F. , Jorgensen, Mary, Farberow, N. L. , and
       Ganzler, S. "Ratings of intention of suicidal behav-
       ior, " Newsletter for Research in Psychology (Vet-
       erans Administration Center, Hampton, Virginia), 10
       (2):36-37, 1968.

860)   Cutter, Fred.   "Role complements and changes on
       consensus Rorschachs, " Journal of Projective Tech-
       niques & Personality Assessment, 32(4):339-347, 1968.

861)   Dale, J.   "Psychiatric factors in barbiturate intoxica-
       tion, " International Anesthesiology Clinics, 4:389-398,
       1966.

862)   Dancey, T. E.   "Prevention of suicide, " Canadian
       Nurse, 62:29-32, 1966.

863)   Danto, B. L.   "How to start a suicide prevention
       center without really trying, " Michigan Medicine, 69:
       119-121, 1970.

864)   Danto, Bruce L.   "The relationship of suicides to
       riots, " Archives of the Foundation of Thanatology,
       2(1):25-26, 1970.

865)   Daston, Paul G.   "Applicability of a Rorschach sign
       approach to a British suicide, " Rorschach Newsletter,
       12(1):19-20, 1967.

866)   Daston, P. G. and Sakheim, G. A.   "Prediction of
       suicide from the Rorschach test using a sign approach,"
       Journal of Projective Techniques, 4:355-361, 1960.

867)   Davidson, H. A.   "Suicide in the hospital, " Hospitals,
       43:55-59, 1969.

868)   Davies, A. Michael and Kaplan-Dinur, Atara.   "Suicide
       in Israel: an epidemiological study, " International
       Journal of Social Psychiatry, 8:32-44, 1961/62.

869)   Davis, Frederick B.   "Sex differences in suicide and
       attempted suicide, " Diseases of the Nervous System,
       29(3):193-194, 1968.

870)   Davis, Frederick B.   "The relationship between suicide
       and attempted suicide: a review of the literature, "
       Psychiatric Quarterly, 41(4):752-765, 1967.

871)   Davis, J. M.   "Efficacy of tranquilizing and antide-
       pressant drugs, " Archives of General Psychiatry, 13:
       552-566, 1965.

872)   Davis, John M., Bartlett, Edward, and Termini, Bene-

dict A.   "Overdosage of psychotropic drugs: a review:
II. Antidepressants and other psychotropic agents, "
Diseases of the Nervous System, 29(4):246-256, 1968.

873)   Davis, John M. and Termini, Benedict A.   "Attempted
       suicide with psychotropic drugs: diagnosis and treat-
       ment (Part 2), "   Medical Counterpoint, 6:59-63, 1969.

874)   Dax, E. C.   "Suicide in today's society, "   Medical
       Journal of Australia, 1:425, 1969.

875)   Dax, E. C.   "The prevention of suicide, "   Medical
       Journal of Australia, 1(1):46-49, 1961.

876)   Dax, E. C.   "The termination of depression, "   Medi-
       cal Journal of Australia, 1:177-182, Feb. 8, 1964.

877)   Day, George.   "Suicide: English Style, "   Perspectives
       in Biology and Medicine, 14(2):290-300, Winter 1971.

878)   Day, G. H.   "Suicide--a need for sympathy, "   Nursing
       Times, 67:1235-6, Oct. 7, 1971.

879)   Dean, R. A., Miskimins, W., De Cook, R., Wilson,
       L. T., and Maley, R. F.   "Prediction of suicide in a
       psychiatric hospital, "   Journal of Clinical Psychology,
       23(3):296-301, 1967.

880)   De Busk, Robert F. and Seidl, Larry G.   "Attempted
       suicide by cyanide, "   California Medicine, 110(5):394-
       396, 1969.

881)   Dek, S., Nandi, D. N., and Basumaltil, T.   "A study
       on the relationship between suicidal thoughts and other
       symptoms in depressive illness, "   Journal of the Indian
       Medical Association, 59:507-8, Dec. 16, 1972.

882)   De La Torre, J. I. and Abram, H. S.   "Twenty-three
       cases of attempted suicide with firearms, "   Virginia
       Medical Monthly, 94(3):165-169, 1967.

883)   Delong, W. Bradford and Robins, Eli.   "The com-
       munication of suicidal intent prior to psychiatric hos-
       pitalization: a study of 87 patients, "   American Journal
       of Psychiatry, 117:695-705, 1961.

884)   Denner, J. Lee.   "Management of suicide attempt, "

New York State Journal of Medicine, 70(12):1666-1667,
June 1970.

885) De Sole, Daniel E. , Singer, Philip, and Aronson,
Samuel.   "Suicide and role strain among physicians, "
International Journal of Social Psychiatry, 15(4):294-
301, Fall 1969.

886) Detre, T.   "Sleep disorder and psychosis, " Canadian
Psychiatric Association Journal, II (Supplement):169-
177, 1966.

887) Devries, A. G.   "Control variables in the identification of suicidal behavior, " Psychological Reports, 29
(3, Part 2):1131-1135, 1967.

888) Devries, A. G.   "A potential suicide personality inventory, " Psychological Reports, 18(3):731-738, 1966.

889) Devries, Alcon G. "Definition of suicidal behaviors,"
Psychological Reports, 22(3, Pt. 2):1093-1098, 1968.

890) Devries, Alcon G. and Farberow, Norman L.   "A
multivariate profile analysis of MMPIs of suicidal and
nonsuicidal neuropsychiatric hospital patients, " Journal
of Projective Techniques and Personality Assessment,
31(5):81-84, 1967.

891) Devries, Alcon G.   "Identification of suicidal behavior
by means of the MMPI, " Psychological Reports, 19
(2):415-419, 1966.

892) Devries, Alcon G.   "Model for prediction of suicidal
behavior, " Psychological Reports, 22(3, Pt. 2):1285-
1302, 1968.

893) Devries, Alcon G. and Shneidman, Edwin S.   "Multiple MMPI profiles of suicidal persons, " Psychological
Reports, 21(2):401-405, 1967.

894) Dewey, E. T.   "Suicides--a look at the statistics, "
Trans. Ass. Life Insur. Med. Dir. Amer., 47:54-69,
1964.

895) Dickenson, William B. , Jr.   "Anatomy of suicide, "
Editorial Research Reports, Sept. 25, 1963, pp. 705-
22.

896)   Dicter, R. M.   "Suicidal patients among admissions
        to Louisville General Hospital (1961-1970)--incidence
        and diagnostic conclusion," Journal of the Kentucky
        Medical Association, 70:773-6, Oct. 1972.

897)   Diggory, James C.   "Calculation of some costs of
        suicide prevention using certain predictors of suicidal
        behavior," Psychological Bulletin, 1969, 71(5), 373-
        386.

898)   Diggory, James C.   "Taking accountability seriously,"
        Crisis Intervention, 2(4):84-85, 1970.   [Editorial]

899)   Dinitz, Simon.   "A sociologist looks at suicide,"
        Ohio's Health, 17(2):1-7, 1965.

900)   Directory of suicide prevention facilities, June 1967,
        Bulletin of Suicidology, July 1967, pp. 14-18.

901)   Directory of suicide prevention facilities, March 1969,
        Bulletin of Suicidology, March 1969, pp. 47-58.

902)   Dizmang, L. H.   "Suicide among the Cheyenne Indians,"
        Bulletin of Suicidology, July, 1967, pp. 9-11.

903)   Dodds, A.   "Attempted suicide: nomenclature,"
        British Journal of Psychiatry, 117:121, 1970.

904)   Dohrenwend, Bruce P.   "The social psychological na-
        ture of stress: a framework for causal inquiry,"
        Journal of Abnormal and Social Psychology, 62(2):294-
        302, 1961.

905)   Doig, R. J.   "Self-poisoning and relationships with
        medical practitioners," Practitioner, 210:268-70,
        Feb. 1973.

906)   Dole, Vincent P.   "Detoxification of sick addicts in
        prison," Journal of the American Medical Association,
        220(3):366-369, Apr. 1972.

907)   Donovan, W. B. and Nash, G.   "Suicide rate, a prob-
        lem of validity and comparability," Marquette Medical
        Review, 27:150-158, 1962.

908)   Dorfman, Wilfred.   "The recognition and management
        of depression," Psychosomatics, 11(5):416-419, 1970.

909)   Dorpat, T. L.   "Evaluation and management of suicide
        reactions, "   Medical Times,   913:1212-1218,   1963.

910)   Dorpat, T. L.   "Loss of control over suicidal im-
        pulses, "   Bulletin of Suicidology,   Dec. 1968, 26-30.

911)   Dorpat, T. L.   "Suicide in murderers, "   Psychiatric
        Digest,   27:51-55, 1966.

912)   Dorpat, T. L. and Boswell, J. W.   "An evaluation of
        suicidal intent in suicide attempts, "   Comprehensive
        Psychiatry,   4(2):117-125, 1963.

913)   Dorpat, T. L., Jackson, J. J., and Ripley, H. S.
        "Broken homes and attempted and completed suicide,"
        Archives of General Psychiatry,   12(2):213-216, 1965.

914)   Dorpat, Theodore L., and Ripley, Herbert S.   "The
        relationship between attempted suicide and committed
        suicide, "   Comprehensive Psychiatry,   8(2):74-79, 1967.

915)   Douglas, J. D.   "The sociological analysis of social
        meanings of suicide, "   European Journal of Sociology,
        7:249-275, 1966.

916)   Drake, Ann K. and Rusnak, Alan W.   "An indicator of
        suicidal ideation on the Rorschach: a replication, "
        Journal of Projective Techniques and Personality
        Assessment,   30(6):543-544, 1966.

917)   Drapkin, Israel S.   "Aspects of suicide in Israel, "
        Israel Annals of Psychiatry and Related Disciplines,
        3(1):35-50, 1965.

918)   Drye, R. C., Goulding, R. L., and Goulding, M. E.
        "No-suicide decisions--patient monitoring of suicidal
        risk, "   American Journal of Psychiatry,   130:171-4,
        Feb. 1973.

919)   Dublin, L. I.   "Suicide--a public health problem, "
        American Journal of Public Health,   55:12-5, Jan. 1965.

920)   Dublin, Louis I.   "Suicide: an overview of a health
        and social problem, "   Bulletin of Suicidology,   Dec.
        1967, 25-30.

921)   Duffy, J. E.   "Suicides by physicians in training, "

Journal of Medical Education, 43:1196, 1968.

922)   Eastwood, M. R., Henderson, A. S., and Montgomery,
        I. M.   "Personality and parasuicide--methodological
        problems," Medical Journal of Australia, 1:170-75,
        Jan. 22, 1972.

923)   Eckert, W. G.   "The college death," Journal of the
        Florida Medical Association, 53:891, Sept. 1966.

924)   Edgell, P. G.   "Depression--the commonest disease.
        (2) Suicide," Canadian Medical Association Journal,
        106:175-9, Jan. 22, 1972.

925)   Efron, H. Y.   "An attempt to employ a sentence-
        completion test for the detection of psychiatric patients
        with suicidal ideas," Journal of Consulting Psychology,
        24:156-160, 1960.

926)   Eggertsen, P. F.   "Psychodynamic relationships: sui-
        cide and flying phobia," International Psychiatry
        Clinics, 4:155-175, 1967.

927)   Eggertsen, P. F.   "Suicide, the opaque act," Mili-
        tary Medicine, 132:9-17, 1967.

928)   Eggertsen, P. F. and Goldstein, S. M.   "Suicide by
        Air Force personnel 1958 to 1964," Military Medicine,
        133(1):26-32, 1968.

929)   Eisenthal, Sherman.   "Death ideation in suicidal pati-
        ents," Journal of Abnormal Psychology, 73(2):162-
        167, 1968.

930)   Eisenthal, Sherman, Farberow, Norman L., and
        Shneidman, Edwin S.   "Follow-up of neuropsychiatric
        patients in suicide observation status," Public Health
        Reports, 81(11):977-990, 1966.

931)   Eisenthal, Sherman.   "Suicide and aggression," Psy-
        chological Reports, 21(3):745-751, 1967.

932)   Elliott, T. N., Smith, R. D., and Wildman, R.
        "Suicide and systematic desensitization--a case study,"
        Journal of Clinical Psychology, 28:420-3, July 1972.

933)   Epstein, L. C., Thomas, C. B., Schaffer, J. W.,

and Perlin, S. "Clinical prediction of physician suicide based on medical student data," Journal of Nervous Mental Diseases, 156:19-29, Jan. 1973.

934) Ettlinger, Ruth W. "Suicides in a group of patients
who had previously attempted suicide," Acta Psychiatrica Scandinavica, 40(4):363-378, 1964.

935) "Examination hell: Japan's student suicides," London
Times Educational Supplement, October 26, 1962, pp.
2475-2533.

936) Faber, M. D. "The adolescent suicides of Romeo and
Juliet," Psychoanalytic Review, 59:169-81, Summer
1972.

937) Faber, M. D. "Suicide and the 'Ajax' of Sophocles,"
Psychoanalytic Review, 54(3):49-60, 1967.

938) Fahy, T. J., Brocklebank, J. T., and Ashby, D. W.
"Syndromes of self-poisoning. A factor analysis,"
Irish Journal of Medical Science, 3(11):497-503, 1970.

939) Faigel, H. C. "Suicide among young persons. A review for its incidence and causes, and methods of its
prevention," Clinical Pediatrics, 5:187-190, 1966.

940) Fallon B. "And certain thoughts through my head...,"
American Journal of Nursing, 72:1257-9, July 1972.

941) Farber, L. H. "Despair and the life of suicide,"
Review of Existential Psychology and Psychiatry, 2:125-
139, 1962.

942) Farber, M. L. "Suicide and the welfare state,"
Mental Hygiene, 49:371-3, July 1965.

943) Farberow, Norman L. "Crisis prevention," International Journal of Psychiatry, 6(5):382-384, 1968.

944) Farberow, Norman L. "Self-destruction and identity,"
Humanitas, 6(1):45-68, 1970.

945) Farberow, Norman L. "Suicide prevention: a view
from the bridge," Community Mental Health Journal,
4(6):469-474, 1968.

946) Farberow, Norman L.   "Ten years of suicide preven-
      tion--past and future, "   Bulletin of Suicidology, No. 6:
      6-11, Spring 1970.

947) Farberow, Norman L.   "Training in suicide prevention
      for professional and community agents, " American
      Journal of Psychiatry, 125(12):1702-1705, 1969.

948) Farberow, Norman L., et al.   "Suicide prevention
      around the clock, " American Journal of Orthopsychi-
      atry, 36(3):551-558, 1966.

949) Farberow, Norman L. and Devries, Alcon G.   "An
      item differentiation analysis of MMPIs of suicidal
      neuropsychiatric hospital patients, " Psychological Re-
      ports, 29(2):607-617, 1967.

950) Farberow, N. L. and McEvoy, T. L.   "Suicide among
      patients with diagnosis of anxiety reaction or depres-
      sive reaction in general medical and surgical hos-
      pitals, " Journal of Abnormal Psychology, 71(4):287-
      299, 1966.

951) Farberow, Norman L. and Simon, Maria D.   "Suicides
      in Los Angeles [Cal.] and Vienna [Austria]: an inter-
      cultural study of two cities, " Public Health Reports,
      84:389-403, May 1969.

952) Farberow, N. L., McKelligott, J. W., Cohen, S.,
      and Darbonne, A.   "Suicide among patients with cardi-
      orespiratory illnesses, " Journal of the American
      Medical Association, 195:422-428, 1966.

953) Farberow, N. L. and Palmer, Ruby A.   "The nurse's
      role in the prevention of suicides, " Ohio's Health,
      17(2):37-44, 1965.

954) Farberow, Norman L., Darbonne, Allen R., Stein,
      Kenneth, and Hirsch, Sophie.   "Self-destructive be-
      havior of uncooperative diabetics, " Psychological Re-
      ports, 27:935-946, 1970.

955) Farberow, Norman L. and Reynolds, David K.   "Dyadic
      crisis suicides in mental hospital patients, " Journal of
      Abnormal Psychology, 78(1):77-85, Aug. 1971.

956) Farberow, Norman L., Shneidman, Edwin S., and

Litman, Robert E. "The suicidal patients and the physician, " MIND, 1:69-74, 1963.

957) Farberow, Norman L. , Shneidman, Edwin S. , Litman, Robert E. , Wold, Carl I. , Heilig, S. M. , and Kramer, Jan. "Suicide prevention around the clock, " American Journal of Orthopsychiatry, 36(3):551-558, 1966.

958) Farberow, Norman L. , Shneidman, Edwin S. , and Neuringer, Charles. "Case history and hospitalization factors in suicides of neuropsychiatric hospital patients, " Journal of Nervous and Mental Disease, 142 (1):32-44, 1966.

959) Farberow, Norman L. , Stein, Kenneth, Darbonne, Allen, and Hirsch, Sophie. "Indirect self-destructive behavior in diabetic patients, " Hospital Medicine, 6 (5):123-133, 1970.

960) Farnham-Diggory, S. "Self-evaluation and subjective life expectancy among suicidal and nonsuicidal psychotic males, " Journal of Abnormal and Social Psychology, 69(6):628-634, 1964.

961) Fatteh, A. "Murder or suicide--a case report, " Journal of Forensic Medicine, 18:122-3, July-Sept. 1971.

962) Faux, E. J. and Crawford, B. "Deaths in a youth program, " Mental Hygiene, 54:569-571, 1970.

963) Fawcett, Jan. "Suicidal depression and physical illness, " Journal of the American Medical Association, 219(10):1303-1306, Mar. 1972.

964) Fawcett, Jan, Leff, Melitta, and Bunney, William E., Jr. "Suicide. Clues from interpersonal communication, " Archives of General Psychiatry, 21(2):129-137, 1969.

965) Feiden, Elaine S. "One year's experience with a suicide prevention service, " Social Work, 15(3):26-32, July 1970.

966) Feinstein, Howard M. "Suicide, " Community Mental Health Journal, 3(3):259-261, 1967.

967)   Felix, R. H. "Suicide--a neglected problem, " Ameri-
        can Journal of Public Health, 55:16-20, Jan. 1965.

968)   Fellner, Carl H. "Provocation of suicidal attempts,"
        Journal of Nervous and Mental Disease, 133:55-58,
        1961.

969)   Fellner, C. H. "Suicide: a neglected medical prob-
        lem, " American Practitioner, 12:883-885, 1961.

970)   Ferguson, R. K. and Boutros, A. R. "Death follow-
        ing self-poisoning with aspirin, " Journal of the
        American Medical Association, 213(7):1186-1188, 1970.

971)   Finck, P. A. "Case for diagnosis, " Military Medi-
        cine, 135:409-410, 1970.

972)   Firth, Raymond. "Suicide and risk-taking in Tikopia
        society, " Psychiatry, 24(1):1-17, 1961.

973)   Fishbein, M. "Suicidology, " Post-graduate Medicine,
        45:229, 1969.

974)   Fitzgerald, Roy G. "Reactions to blindness: An ex-
        ploratory study of adults with recent loss of sight, "
        Archives of General Psychiatry, 22(4):370-379, 1970.

975)   Flanagan, T. A. and Murphy, G. E. "Body donation
        and suicide. Is there a relationship?", Archives of
        General Psychiatry, 28:732-4, May 1973.

976)   Fleetwood, J. "An analysis of 563 accidents to per-
        sons over the age of 65, " Journal of the Irish Medi-
        cal Association, 55:79-80, 1964.

977)   Flinn, D. E. and Leonard, C. V. "Prevalence of
        suicidal ideation and behavior among basic trainees
        and college students, " Military Medicine, 137:317-20,
        Aug. 1972.

978)   Flood, R. A. and Seager, C. P. "A retrospective
        examination of psychiatric case records of patients who
        subsequently committed suicide, " British Journal of
        Psychiatry, 114(509):443-450, 1968.

979)   Ford, R. and Moseley, A. L. "Motor vehicular sui-
        cides, " Journal of Criminal Law, Criminology, and

Police Science, 54:257-259, 1963.

980)   Fox, R.   "Help for the despairing: the work of the
        Samaritans," Lancet, 2:1102-1105, 1962.

981)   Fox, R.   "Today's students: suicide among students
        and its prevention," Royal Social Health Journal, 91:
        181-5, July-Aug. 1971.

982)   Frank, M. G.   "Suicide in automobile accidents,"
        Medi. College Bulletin, 147:1-4, July 1965.

983)   Frankel, F. H.   "Emotional first aid," Archives of
        Environmental Health, 11:824-827, 1965.

984)   Frederick, Calvin J.   "An investigation of handwriting
        of suicide persons through suicide notes," Journal of
        Abnormal Psychology, 72(3, Pt. 1):263-267, 1968.

985)   Frederick, Calvin J.   "Drug abuse--a self-destructive
        enigma," Maryland State Medical Journal, 22:19-21,
        May 1973.

986)   Frederick, Calvin J.   "Organizing and funding suicide
        prevention and crisis services," Hospital Community
        Psychiatry, 23:346-8, Nov. 1972.

987)   Frederick, Calvin J.   "The present suicide taboo in
        the United States," Mental Hygiene, 55(2):178-183,
        Apr. 1971.

988)   Frederick, Calvin J.   "Suicide Notes: a survey and
        evaluation," Bulletin of Suicidology, Mar. 1969, pp.
        17-26.

989)   Frederick, C. J. and Farberow, N. L.   "Group psy-
        chotherapy with suicidal persons--a comparison with
        standard group methods," International Journal of
        Social Psychiatry, 16:103-11, Spring, 1970.

990)   Frederick, Calvin J. and Resnik, H. L.   "How sui-
        cidal behaviors are learned," American Journal of
        Psychotherapy, 25(1):37-55, Jan. 1971.

991)   Frederick, Calvin J. and Resnick, H. L.   "Interven-
        tions with suicidal patients," Journal of Contemporary
        Psychotherapy, 2(2):103-109, Winter 1970.

992)   Frederick, C. J., Resnik, H. L., and Wittlin, B. J.
       "Self-destructive aspects of hard-core addiction,"
       Archives of General Psychiatry, 28:579-85, April 1973.

993)   Freed, E. D.   "Suicide and attempted suicide,"
       Medical Proceedings, 12(13):286-294, 1966.

994)   Freed, Herbert.   "Occupational hazards of physicians
       --suicide," Pennsylvania Medicine, 72(10):65-66, 1969.

995)   Freeman, Walter.   "Psychiatrists who kill themselves:
       a study in suicide," American Journal of Psychiatry,
       124(6):846-847, 1957.

996)   Friedman, G. A.   "Suicide and the altered prescrip-
       tion," New York State Journal of Medicine, 66:3005-
       3007, 1966.

997)   Friedman, I. S.   "Medical management of suicide
       victim," New York State Journal of Medicine, 66:
       3007-3009, 1966.

998)   Friedman, M., Glasser, M., Laufer, E., Laufer,
       M., and Wohl, M.   "Attempted suicide and self-muti-
       lation in adolescence--some observations from a psy-
       choanalytic research project," International Journal
       of Psychoanalysis, 53:179-83, 1972.

999)   Friedman, P.   "Some considerations on the treatment
       of suicidal depressive patients," American Journal of
       Psychotherapy, 16(3):379-386, 1962.

1000) Friedman, P.   "Trends in suicide--research," Mt.
       Sinai Journal of Medicine, N. Y., 38:135-47, Jan. -
       Feb. 1971.

1001) Fuller, David S.   "Suicide panel discussion," Pro-
       ceedings of the Southwestern Sociological Association,
       14:74-76, 1964.

1002) Furst, S. S. and Ostow, M.   "The psychodynamics of
       suicide," Bulletin of the New York Academy of Medi-
       cine, 41(2):190-204, 1965.

1003) Gabrielson, Ira W.   "Suicide and the teenage mother,"
       Family Planner, 3(4):14, 1970.

1004) Gabrielson, Ira W., Klerman, Lorraine V., Currie, John B., Tyler, Natalie C., and Jekel, James F. "Suicide attempts in a population pregnant as teen- agers," American Journal of Public Health, 60(12): 2289-2301, 1970.

1005) Gage, F. B. "Suicide in the aged," American Journal of Nursing, 71:2153-5, Nov. 1971.

1006) Ganguly, H. R. "Depression and suicide," Journal of the Indian Medical Association, 59:525, Dec. 16, 1972.

1007) Garber, R. S. "Management of the depressed pati- ent," Virginia Medical Monthly, 92:59-64, Feb. 1965.

1008) Gardner, Elmer A., Bahn, Anita K., and Mack, Marjorie. "Suicide and psychiatric care in the aging," Archives of General Psychiatry, 10(6):547-553, 1964.

1009) Garnand, R. B. "Suicide and assessing its risk," Rocky Mountain Medical Journal, 63(11):55-57, 1966.

1010) Garrard, Robert L. "The role of the physician in suicide prevention," North Carolina Medical Journal, 30(12):473-476, 1969.

1011) Gasque, M. R. and Plumb, C. S. "Suicide during productive years," Archives of Environmental Health, 2:457-461, 1961.

1012) Gehrke, S. and Kirschenbaum, M. "Survival patterns in family conjoint therapy," Family Process, 6(1):67- 80, 1967.

1013) Gershman, A. P. "Attempted suicide or inadequate defense mechanism?", British Journal of Social Psy- chiatry, 3(4):255-257, 1969.

1014) Gibbens, T. C., Briscoe, O., and Dell, S. "Psy- chopathic and neurotic offenders in mental hospitals," International Psychiatry Clinics, 5:143-151, 1968.

1015) Gibbons, H. L., Plechus, J. L., and Mohler, S. R. "Consideration of volitional acts in aircraft accident investigations," Aerospace Medicine, 38:1057-9, Oct. 1967.

1016)   Gibbs, J. P.   "Marital status and suicide in the United
        States: a special test of the status integration theory, "
        American Journal of Sociology, 74(5):521-533, 1969.

1017)   Gibbs, J. P. and Martin, W. T.   "On assessing the
        theory of status integration and suicide, " American
        Sociological Review, 31:533-541, 1966.

1018)   Giddens, Anthony.   "Suicide, attempted suicide, and
        the suicidal threat, " Man, July-Aug. 1964, pp. 115-16.

1019)   Giddens, Anthony.   "The suicide problem in French
        sociology, " British Journal of Sociology, 16:3-18,
        Mar. 1965.

1020)   Giddens, Anthony.   "Theoretical problems in the soci-
        ology of suicide, " Advancement of Science, 21:522-6,
        Mar. 1965.

1021)   Giddens, Anthony.   "A typology of suicide, " European
        Journal of Sociology, 7:276-295, 1966.

1022)   Ginsburg, G. P.   "Public conceptions and attitudes
        about suicide, " Journal of Health and Social Behavior,
        12(3):200-207, Sept. 1971.

1023)   "Girls who cut themselves, " Science News, 92(18):
        Nov. 1967.

1024)   Gittleson, N. L.   "The relationship between obsessions
        and suicide attempts in depressive psychosis, " British
        Journal of Psychiatry, 112(440):889-890, 1966.

1025)   Glaser, Kurt.   "Attempted suicide in children and
        adolescents: psychodynamic observations, " American
        Journal of Psychotherapy, 19(2):220-227, 1965.

1026)   Glaser, Kurt.   "Suicidal children-management, "
        American Journal of Psychotherapy, 25(1):27-36, Jan.
        1971.

1027)   Gobar, A. H.   "Suicide in Afghanistan, " British
        Journal of Psychiatry, 116(534):493-496, May 1970.

1028)   Goldfield, Michael D. and Glick, Ira W.   "Self-muti-
        lation of the female genitalia, " Diseases of the
        Nervous System, 31(12):843-845, 1970.

1029) Goldstein, Alan M. and Reznikoff, Marvin. "Suicide
       in chronic hemodialysis patients from an external locus
       of control framework," American Journal of Psychi-
       atry, 127(9):1204-1207, Mar. 1971.

1030) Golin, M. "Anatomy of suicide--by one's own hand.
       (Part one.)," Medico-Legal Digest, 1:17-22, 1960.

1031) Gonsalves, C. T., Baird, A., Rogers, D. R., and
       Sisler, G. C. "A study of attempted suicide," Man-
       itoba Medical Review, 40(1):29-31, 1960.

1032) Goodhart, C. B. "Suicide in pregnancy," British
       Medical Journal, 1:318, 1968.

1033) Goppelt, John W. "Psychiatrists who kill themselves:
       uncertainty of sources," American Journal of Psychi-
       atry, 124:1471, 1968. [Letter]

1034) Goss-Moffitt, N. B. "Attempted suicide: a four-month
       study," Journal of the Kentucky Medical Association,
       61:585-588, 1963.

1035) Gottschalk, L. A. and Gleser, G. C. "An analysis
       of the verbal content of suicide notes," British
       Journal of Medical Psychology, 33:195-204, 1960.

1036) Gould, Robert E. "Suicide problems in children and
       adolescents," American Journal of Psychotherapy,
       19(2):228-246, 1965.

1037) Gourevitch, D. "Suicide among the sick in classical
       antiquity," Bulletin of the History of Medicine, 43:
       501-518, 1969.

1038) Graff, H. "The chronic wrist-slasher," Hospital
       Topics, 45:61-65, 1967.

1039) Graff, H. "The management of self-destructive pati-
       ents," American Journal of Psychiatry, 126:1041-
       1042, 1970. [Letter to the Editor]

1040) Graff, Harold and Mallin, Richard. "The syndrome
       of the wrist cutter," American Journal of Psychiatry,
       124(1):36-42, 1967.

1041) Graham, J. D. P. and Hitchens, R. A. N. "Acute

poisoning and its prevention, " British Journal of Preventive and Social Medicine, 21:108-114, 1967.

1042) Grandis, S. V. "Suicide in children and adolescents,"
Medico-Legal Bulletin, 172:1-5, 1967.

1043) Greaves, George. "Pseudosuicide as a symbolic act,"
Psychological Reports, 31:280, Aug. 1972.

1044) Greaves, George. "Temporal orientation in suicidal
patients, " Perceptual and Motor Skills, 33(3, Pt. 1):
1020, Dec. 1971.

1045) Greaves, George and Ghent, L. "Comparison of accomplished suicides with persons contacting a crisis
intervention clinic, " Psychological Reports, 31:290,
Aug. 1972.

1046) Green, Arthur H. "Self-destructive behavior in physically abused schizophrenic children, " Archives of
General Psychiatry, 19(2):171-179, 1968.

1047) Greenhouse, A. H. "Attempted suicide with clogibrate, " Journal of the American Medical Association,
204:402-3, Apr. 29, 1968.

1048) Greer, Steven. "Parental loss and attempted suicide:
a further report, " British Journal of Psychiatry, 112
(486):465-470, 1966.

1049) Greer, Steven. "The relationship between parental
loss and attempted suicide: a control study, " British
Journal of Psychiatry, 110(468):698-705, 1964.

1050) Greer, Steven and Bagley, Christopher. "Effect of
psychiatric intervention in attempted suicide: a controlled study, " British Medical Journal, 1(5744):310-
312, Feb. 1971.

1051) Greer, Steven and Gunn, J. C. "Attempted suicides
from intact and broken parental homes, " British
Medical Journal, 2:1355-1357, 1966.

1052) Greer, S. , Gunn, J. C. , and Koller, K. M. "Aetiological factors in attempted suicide, " British Medical
Journal, 2:1352-1355, 1966.

1053) Greer, Steven and Lee, H. A. "Subsequent progress of potentially lethal attempted suicides, " Acta Psychiatrica Scandinavica, 43(4):361-371, 1967.

1054) Greiner, T. H. "A case of 'psychosis' from drugs," Texas Journal of Medicine, 60:659-60, Aug. 1964.

1055) Grow, B. K. , Jr. , Schwartz, A. H. , Grinder, D. H., and Lorensen, S. L. "Psychological autopsy in two cases of reported suicide in early adolescence, " American Journal of Orthopsychiatry, 40(2):339-340, 1970.

1056) Guggenheim, F. G. and Weisman, A. D. "Suicide in the subway. Publicly witnessed attempts of 50 cases," Journal of Nervous Mental Disorders, 155:404-9, Dec. 1972.

1057) Guido, J. A. and Payne, D. H. "72-hour psychiatric detention. Clinical observation and treatment in a county general hospital, " Archives of General Psychiatry, 16:233-8, Feb. 1967.

1058) Guile, L. A. "Emergency psychiatry: referrals from a personal advisory service," Australian & New Zealand Journal of Psychiatry, 1:93-97, 1967.

1059) Guralnick, L. and Jackson, A. "An index of unnecessary deaths, " Public Health Reports, 82:180-2, Feb. 1967.

1060) Guze, Samuel B. and Robins, Eli. "Suicide and primary affective disorders, " British Journal of Psychiatry, 117(539):437-438, Oct. 1970.

1061) Gysin, W. "Evaluation of suicide, " Postgraduate Medicine, 30:31-35, 1961.

1062) Haas, Michael. "Toward the study of biopolitics: a cross-sectional analysis of mortality rates, " Behavioral Science, 14(4):257-280, 1969.

1063) Hafner, A. J. and Kaplan, A. M. "Hostility content analysis of the Rorschach and TAT, " Journal of Projective Techniques, 24:137-143, 1960.

1064) Hagedorn, Robert and Labovitz, Sanford. "A note on

status integration and suicide," Social Problems, 14
(1):79-84, 1966.

1065) Haider, Ijaz. "Suicidal attempts in children and adolescents," British Journal of Psychiatry, 114(514):
1133-1134, 1968.

1066) Haight, Frank A. "Some comparisons between traffic
death and suicide," General Systems, 12:117-136, 1967.

1067) Haldane, J. D. and Haider, I. "Attempted suicide in
children and adolescents," British Journal of Clinical
Practice, 21:587-591, 1967.

1068) Halick, J. "Suicides--does our society care?", Michigan Medicine, 71:325-6, Apr. 1972.

1069) Hall, R. C. and Joffe, J. R. "Aberrant response to
diazepam--a new syndrome," American Journal of
Psychiatry, 129:738-42, Dec. 1972.

1070) Hamblin, R. L. and Jacobsen, R. B. "Suicide and
pseudocide--a reanalysis of Maris's data," Journal of
Health Soc. Behav., 13:99-109, Mar. 1972.

1071) Hamburger, Ernest. "Vehicular suicidal ideation,"
Military Medicine, 134(6):441-444, 1969.

1072) Hamm   Max. "Suicide and white reformatory girls'
preference for Negro men," Corrective Psychiatry
and Journal of Social Therapy, 15(3):99-102, 1969.

1073) Hand, M. H. and Meisel, A. M. "Dynamic aspects
of suicide," Diseases of the Nervous System, 27(6):
373-382, 1966.

1074) Hankoff, L. D. "An epidemic of attempted suicide,"
Comprehensive Psychiatry, 2(5):294-298, 1961.

1075) Hankoff, L. D. "(A 24-hour) suicide prevention
service," Medical Tribune, 5:116, October 28, 1964.

1076) Harris, R. A. "Factors related to continued suicidal
behavior in dyadic relationships," Nursing Research,
15:72-75, 1966.

1077) Hartehus, Hans. "A study of suicides in Sweden 1951-

63, including a comparison with 1925-50, " Acta Psychiatrica Scandinavica, 43(2):121-143, 1967.

1078) Haughton, Anson B.   "Planning for the prevention of suicide, " American Journal of Orthopsychiatry, 37 (2):374-375, 1967.

1079) Haughton, Anson B.   "Suicide prevention programs: the current scene, " American Journal of Psychiatry, 124(12):1692-1696, 1968.

1080) Hauschild, T. B.   "Suicide in Europe, " Medical Bulletin of the U. S. Army, Europe, 21:250-254, 1964.

1081) Hauschild, Thomas B.   "Suicidal population of a military psychiatric center: a review of ten years, " Military Medicine, 133(6):425-437, 1968.

1081a) Havens, Leston L.   "The anatomy of a suicide, " New England Journal of Medicine, 272:401-406, 1965.

1082) Havens, Leston L.   "Diagnosis of suicidal intent, " Annual Review of Medicine, 20:419-424, 1969.

1083) Havens, Leston L.   "Recognition of suicidal risks through the psychologic examination, " New England Journal of Medicine, 276:210-215, 1967.

1084) Havighurst, Robert J.   "The extent and significance of suicide among American Indians today, " Mental Hygiene, 55(2):174-177, Apr. 1971.

1085) Heilig, Sam M.   "Training in suicide prevention, " Bulletin of Suicidology, No. 6:41-44, Spring 1970.

1086) Heilig, Sam F., Farberow, Norman L., Robert, E., and Shneidman, Edwin S.   "The role of nonprofessional volunteers in a suicide prevention center, " Community Mental Health Journal, 4(4):287-295, 1968.

1087) Hemphill, R. E. and Thornley, F. I.   "Suicide pacts," South African Medical Journal, 43:1335-1338, 1969.

1088) Henderson, A. A., McCulloch, J. W., and Philip, A. E.   "Survey of mental illness in adolescence, " British Medical Journal, 1(5532):83-84, 1967.

1089) Hendin, Herbert. "Black suicide," Archives of General Psychiatry, 21(4):407-422, 1969.

1090) Hendin, Herbert. "Cross-cultural studies," Psychiatric Digest, 26:25-34, January, 1965.

1091) Hendin, Herbert. "The psychodynamics of suicide," Journal of Nervous and Mental Disorders, 136(3):236-244, 1963.

1092) Hendin, Herbert. "Suicide in Denmark," Psychiatric Quarterly, 1960, pp. 443-460.

1093) Hendin, Herbert. "Suicide in Sweden," Psychiatric Quarterly, 36(1):1-28, 1962.

1094) Hershon, H. I. "Attempted suicide in a largely rural area during an eight-year period," British Journal of Psychiatry, 114(508):279-284, 1968.

1095) Hickman, J. W. "Attempted suicide in the aged," Journal of the Indiana Medical Association, 58:1138-1140, 1965.

1096) Hill, Oscar W. "The association of childhood bereavement with suicidal attempt in depressive illness," British Journal of Psychiatry, 115(520):301-304, 1969.

1097) Hill, O. "Some psychiatric non-sequelae of childhood bereavement," British Journal of Psychiatry, 116:679-80, June 1970.

1098) Hilles, Linda. "Critical incidents precipitating admissions to a psychiatric hospital," Bulletin of the Menninger Clinic, 34(2):89-102, 1970.

1099) Hippler, Arthur E. "Fusion and frustration: dimensions in the cross-cultural ethnopsychology of suicide," American Anthropologist, 71(6):1074-1087, Dec. 1969.

1100) Hirsch, F. G. "Cyanide poisoning," Archives of Environmental Health, 8:622-624, 1964.

1101) Hirsh, Joseph. "Cultural determinants of suicide: the perspective of the Japanese," Mental Hygiene, 50(3):337-339, 1966.

1102) Hirsh, Joseph. "The dimension and dynamics of sui-
       cide, " Archives of Environmental Health, 2:462, 1961.

1103) Hirsh, Joseph. "Methods and fashions of suicide.
       Part II, " Mental Hygiene, 44:3-11, 1960.

1104) Hirsh, Joseph. "Suicide (Part 3: Dynamics of sui-
       cide), " Mental Hygiene, 44:274-180, 1960.

1105) Hirsh, Joseph. "Suicide (Part 4: Predictability and
       prevention), " Mental Hygiene, 44:382-389, 1960.

1106) Hirsh, Joseph. "Suicide (Part 5: The trouble-shooting
       clinic: prototype of a comprehensive community emer-
       gency service), " Mental Hygiene, 44:496-502, 1960.

1107) Hirsh, Joseph. "Suicide as a process: problems, pre-
       dictability and prevention, " Proceedings of the Rudolph
       Virchow Medical Society in the City of New York, 23:
       8-17, 1964.

1108) Hirsh, Joseph, Zauder, H. L., and Drolette, Berna-
       dette M. "Suicide attempts with ingestants, " Ar-
       chives of Environmental Health, 3:212-216, 1961.

1109) Hirsh, S. and Dunsworth, F. A. "The psychiatrist
       and apparently imminent suicide, " Canadian Psychi-
       atric Association Journal, 18:107-11, April 1973.

1110) Hitchcock, John T. "Comments on 'The suicide pre-
       vention contribution to mental health, ' by David Les-
       ter, " Psychological Reports, 28(3):986, June 1971.

1111) Hitchcock, John T. "Fatalistic suicide resulting from
       adaptation to an asymmetrical sex ratio, " Eastern
       Anthropologist, 20(2):133-142, 1967.

1112) Hitchcock, John and Wolford, J. A. "Alternatives to
       the suicide prevention approach to mental health, "
       Archives of General Psychiatry, 22(6):547-549, 1970.

1113) Ho, Young Yoon. "Ecologic survey of attempted sui-
       cide in Korea. A five-year (1963-1967) survey of
       4, 185 consecutive cases (Korean), " Journal of the
       Catholic Medical College (Seoul), 16(4):189-202, 1969.

1114) Hoaken, P. C. "Suicide, " Canadian Medical Association Journal, 106:854, April 22, 1972.

1115) Hoch-Ligeti, C. "Adrenal cholesterol concentration in cases of suicide," British Journal of Experimental Pathology, 47:594-598, 1966.

1116) Hocking, F. D. "Hanging and manual strangulation," Medicine, Science and the Law, 6:49-51, 1966.

1117) Hoff, J. and Chapman, M. "Vertebral fractures associated with suicide attempts," Proceedings of the Veterans Administration Spinal Cord Injury Conference, 18:53-5, 1971.

1118) Hoff, Lee A. "Bismarck's suicide prevention service," Bulletin of Suicidology, Dec. 1968, pp. 44-45.

1119) Hoffer, Abram and Osmond, Humphry. "Schizophrenic physicians: editorial," Journal of Schizophrenia, 2 (2):67-71, 1968.

1120) Homer, L. "Methdilazine intoxication," Journal of the Medical Society of New Jersey, 60:115-6, March 1963.

1121) Hood, Ralph W., Jr. "Effects of foreknowledge of death in the assessment from case history material of intent to die," Journal of Consulting and Clinical Psychology, 34(2):129-133, 1970.

1122) Hood, Ralph W., Jr. "Effects of foreknowledge of manner of death in the assessment from genuine and simulated suicide notes of intent to die," Journal of General Psychology, 82(2):215-221, 1970.

1123) Hood, Ralph W., Jr. "Effect of foreknowledge of sex and manner of death in the assessment from suicide notes of intent to die," Journal of Social Psychology, 84(1):73-80, June 1971.

1124) Hood, W. D. "A note on the incidence and some of the problems of suicide," Health Bulletin (Edinburgh), 20:65-69, 1962.

1125) Hope, Marjorie. "The reluctant way: self-immolation in Vietnam," Antioch Review, 27:149-63, Summer 1967.

1126) Horton, P. C. "The mystical experience as a suicide preventive," American Journal of Psychiatry, 130: 294-6, March, 1973.

1127) Hoskin, John O., Friedman, Michael I., and Cowte, John E. "A high incidence of suicide in a preliterate-primitive society," Psychiatry, 32(2):200-210, 1969.

1128) "Hospital's duty to the suicidal," British Medical Journal, 4:754, 1970.

1129) Howells, L. "Acute poisoning," Proceedings of the Cardiff Medical Society, 3:11, 1967-68.

1130) Hoxworth, D. and Toole, B. "A community's answer to the cry for help," Hospital & Community Psychiatry, 21:296-297, 1970.

1131) Hoyle, James F. "Sylvia Plath: a poetry of suicidal mania," Literature & Psychology, 18(4):187-203, 1968.

1132) Huffman, Robert E. "Which soldiers break down: a survey of 610 psychiatric patients in Vietnam," Bulletin of the Menninger Clinic, 34(6):343-351, Nov. 1970.

1133) Humphrey, J. A., Niswander, G. D., and Casey, T. M. "A comparison of suicidal thinkers and attempters--interim findings," Diseases of the Nervous System, 32:825-36, Dec. 1971.

1134) Humphrey, John A., Puccio, Dominick, Niswander, G. Donald, and Casey, Thomas M. "An analysis of the sequence of selected events in the lives of a suicidal population: a preliminary report," Journal of Nervous and Mental Disease, 154(2):137-140, Feb. 1972.

1135) Ianzito, Benjamin M. "Attempted suicide by drug ingestion," Diseases of the Nervous System, 31(7):453-458, July, 1970.

1136) Iga, Mamoru. "Cultural factors in suicide of Japanese youth with focus on personality," Sociology and Social Research, 46:75-90, 1961.

1137) Iga, Mamoru. "Kyoto and university student suicide," Psychologia: An International Journal of Psychology in the Orient, 14(1):15-23, March, 1971.

1138)   Iga, Mamoru. "Relation of suicide attempt and social
        structure in Kama Kura, Japan," International Journal
        of Social Psychiatry, 12(3):221-232, 1966.

1139)   Iga, Mamoru and Ohara, Kenshiro. "Suicide attempts
        of Japanese youth and Durkheim's concept of anomie:
        an interpretation," Human Organization, 26(1/2):59-
        64, 1967.

1140)   Indin, B. M. "The crisis club: a group experience
        for suicidal patients," Mental Hygiene, 50:280-290,
        1966.

1141)   "An ingenious suicide," Medico-Legal Journal, 35:73-
        74, 1967.

1142)   "Intention--an essential legal ingredient in suicide,"
        Medico-Legal Journal, 35:74-75, 1967.

1143)   "International rise in suicide," Statistical Bulletin of
        the Metropolitan Life Insurance Company, 48:4-7, 1967.

1144)   Inwood, E. R. and Anderson, M. M. "Suicide and
        the family physician," General Practitioner, 30:130-
        3, Oct. 1964.

1145)   Ironside, W. "Iatrogenic contributions to suicide and
        a report on 37 suicide attempts," New Zealand Med-
        ical Journal, 69:207-211, 1969.

1146)   Ironside, W. "The psychopathology of suicide and the
        individual patient," New Zealand Medical Journal, 63:
        763-767, 1964.

1147)   Jacobs, Jerry and Teicher, Joseph D. "Broken homes
        and social isolation in attempted suicides of adoles-
        cents," International Journal of Social Psychiatry, 13
        (2):139-149, 1967.

1148)   Jacobs, Jerry. "A phenomenological study of suicide
        notes," Social Problems, 15(2):60-72, 1967.

1149)   Jacobziner, H. (ed.). "Accidents and attempted sui-
        cide in children and adolescents," Feelings, 6(1):1-4,
        1964.

1150)   Jacobziner, H. "Attempted suicides in adolescence,"

Journal of the American Medical Association, 191(1): 7-11, 1965.

1151) Jacobziner, Harold. "Attempted suicides in adolescents by poisoning," American Journal of Psychotherapy, 19(3):436-444, 1965.

1152) Jacobziner, H. "Attempted suicides in adolescents by poisoning: statistical report," American Journal of Psychotherapy, 19(2):247-252, 1965.

1153) Jacobziner, H. "Attempted suicides in children," Journal of Pediatrics, 56(4):519-525, 1960.

1154) Jacobziner, H. and Raybin, H. W. "Accidental and intentional poisonings," New York State Journal of Medicine, 60(1):100-104, 1960.

1155) Jacobziner, H. and Raybin, H. W. "Modes of occurrence of accidental ingestions in children and a suicide attempt," New York State Journal of Medicine, 60(3): 426-429, 1960.

1156) Jacobziner, H. and Raybin, H. W. "Ingestions with alarming symptoms and suicidal attempts," New York State Journal of Medicine, 60(15):2456-2459, 1960.

1157) Jaffe, G. "Barbiturates for insomnia," Lancet, 1:833-4, Apr. 11, 1964.

1158) Jakab, I. and Howard, M. C. "Art therapy with a 12-year-old girl who witnessed suicide and developed school phobia," Psychotherapy and Psychosomatics, 17(5-6):309, 1969.

1159) James, I. Pierce. "Self-poisoning and alcohol," Lancet, 2:1260-1, Dec. 9, 1972.

1160) James, I. Pierce. "Suicide and mortality amongst heroin addicts in Britain," British Journal of Addiction, 62:391-398, 1967.

1161) James, I. Pierce, Derham, S. P., and Scott-Orr, D. N. "Attempted suicide: a study of 100 patients referred to a general hospital," Medical Journal of Australia, 50(1/11):375-380, 1963.

1162)   James, I. Pierce and Levin, S.   "Suicide following
        discharge from psychiatric hospital, "   Archives of
        General Psychiatry, 10(1):43-46, 1964.

1163)   James, I. Pierce, Scott-Orr, D. N., and Curnow,
        D. H.   "Blood alcohol levels following attempted sui-
        cide, "   Quarterly Journal of Studies on Alcohol, 24
        (1):14-22, 1963.

1164)   James, W. R.   "Suicide by burning, "   Medicine, Sci-
        ence and the Law, 6:48, 1966.

1165)   Jansson, Bengt.   "A catamnestic study of 476 attempted
        suicides, with special regard to the prognosis for
        cases of drug automatism, "   Acta Psychiatrica Scandi-
        navica, 38:183-198, 1962.

1166)   Jansson, Bengt.   "Drug automatism as a cause of
        pseudo suicide, "   Postgraduate Medicine, 30:A34-A40,
        1961.

1167)   Jarmusz, R. T.   "Some considerations in establishing
        a suicide prevention service, "   Mental Hygiene, 53(3):
        351-356, 1969.

1168)   Jensen, Gordon D. and Wallace, John G.   "Family
        mourning process, "   Family Process, 6(1):56-66, 1967.

1169)   Jensen, Leo.   "Nosocomial suicides and suicides among
        discharged patients, "   Acta Psychiatrica Scandinavica,
        42 (Supplement 191):149-170, 1966.

1170)   Jessup, China.   "Films on suicidology, "   Bulletin of
        Suicidology, March 1969, pp. 43-46.

1171)   Johnson, Al.   "An undergraduate essay on suicide, "
        Corrective Psychiatry and Journal of Social Therapy,
        16(1-4):26-31, 1970.

1172)   Johnson, Barclay D.   "Durkheim's one cause of sui-
        cide, "   American Sociological Review, 30(6):875-886,
        1965.

1173)   Johnson, F. G., Terrence, R., and Whitehead, P. C.
        "Self-injury, identification and intervention, "   Canadian
        Psychiatric Association Journal, 18:101-5, Apr. 1973.

1174) Johnson, H. R. "The incidence of unnatural deaths which have been presumed to be natural in coroners' autopsies," Medicine, Science and the Law, 9:102-106, 1969.

1175) Johnson, H. R. "A macabre suicide," Medicine, Science and the Law, 7:210-211, 1967.

1176) Johnson, H. R. and Koumides, O. "Unusual case of mercury poisoning," British Medical Journal, 1:340-341, 1967.

1177) Johnson, P. J., Tucker, E. B., Bradbury, B. A., et al. "Survey of suicide counseling available to students in metropolitan Richmond," Public Health Reports, 84:118-120, 1969.

1178) Johnstone, J. M., Hunt, A. C., and Ward, E. M. "Plastic bag asphyxia in adults," British Medical Journal, 5214:1714-1715, 1960.

1179) Jones, D. I. "Self-poisoning with drugs. A view from a general medical unit," Practitioner, 202:73-78, 1969.

1180) Jones, Kingsley. "Suicide and the hospital service. A study of hospital records of patients who subsequently committed suicide," British Journal of Psychiatry, 111(476):625-630, 1965.

1181) Jourard, Sidney M. "Suicide: an invitation to die," American Journal of Nursing, 70(2):269, 273-275, Feb. 1970.

1182) Kafka, John S. "The body as transitional object: a psychoanalytic study of a self-mutilating patient," British Journal of Medical Psychology, 42:207-212, 1969.

1183) Kahne, Merton, J. "Suicide among patients in mental hospitals: a study of the psychiatrists who conducted their psychotherapy," Psychiatry, 31(1):32-43, 1968.

1184) Kahne, M. J. "Suicide research: a critical review of strategies and potentialities in mental hospitals. Part 1," International Journal of Social Psychiatry, 12:120-129, 1966.

1185)   Kahne, M. J.   "Suicide research: a critical review of
        strategies and potentialities in mental hospitals. Part
        2, " International Journal of Social Psychiatry, 12(3):
        177-186, 1966.

1186)   Kahne, Merton J.   "Suicides in mental hospitals: a
        study of the effects of personnel and patient turnover,"
        Journal of Health and Social Behavior, 9(3):255-266,
        1968.

1187)   Kalish, Richard A.   "Suicide: an ethic comparison in
        Hawaii, " Bulletin of Suicidology, Dec. 1968, pp. 37-
        43.

1188)   Kamano, Dennis K. and Crawford, Carole S.   "Self-
        evaluations of suicidal mental hospital patients, "
        Journal of Clinical Psychology, 22(3):278-279, 1966.

1189)   Kangas, Pamela and Mahrer, Alvin R.   "Suicide
        attempts and threats as goal-directed communications
        in psychotic males, " Psychological Reports, 27(3):
        795-801, 1970.

1190)   Kanzer, Mark.   "An autobiographical legacy of Victor
        Tausk, " International Journal of Psycho-Analysis, 52
        (4):423-430, 1971.

1191)   Kaphan, M. N. and Litman, R. E.   "Suicide consul-
        tation: a psychiatric service to social agencies, "
        American Journal of Psychiatry, 122(12):1357-1361,
        1966.

1192)   Kaphan, M. N. and Litman, R. E.   "Telephone ap-
        praisal of 100 suicidal emergencies, " American
        Journal of Psychotherapy, 16(4):591-599.

1193)   Karhunen, P. and Hartel, G.   "Suicide attempt with
        practolol, " British Medical Journal, 2:178-9, Apr.
        21, 1973.

1194)   Karon, Bertram P.   "Suicidal tendency as the wish to
        hurt someone else, and resulting treatment technique,"
        Journal of Individual Psychology, 20(2):206-212, 1964.

1195)   Kastenbaum, Robert.   "Psychological autopsy: a case
        commentary, " Bulletin of Suicidology, No. 7: 33-35,
        1970.

1196) Kato, Masaaki. "Self-destruction in Japan: a cross-cultural, epidemiological analysis of suicide," Folia Psychiatrica et Neurologica Japonica, 23(4):291-307, 1969.

1197) Kayton, Lawrence and Freed, Harvey. "Effects of a suicide in a psychiatric hospital," Archives of General Psychiatry, 17(2):187-194, 1967.

1198) Kearney, Thomas R. and Taylor, Clarence. "Emotionally disturbed adolescents with alcoholic parents," Acta Paedopsychiatrica, 36(6-7):215-221, 1969.

1199) Kearney, Thomas R. "Psychiatric consultations in a general hospital," British Journal of Psychiatry, 112: 1237-1240, 1966.

1200) Kearney, Thomas R. and Kenyon, J. "Suicidal behavior among Catholics," Excerpta Medica Foundation, International Congress Series No. 150, 1966, pp. 1449-1451.

1201) Keeler, M. H. and Reifler, C. B. "Suicide during an LSD reaction," American Journal of Psychiatry, 123(7):884-885, 1967.

1202) Keith-Spiegel, Patricia and Spiegel, Donald E. "Affective states of patients immediately preceding suicide," Journal of Psychiatric Research, 5(2):89-93, 1967.

1203) Kelly, W. A., Jr. "Suicide and psychiatric education," American Journal of Psychiatry, 130:463-8, Apr. 1973.

1204) Kelman, Harold. "Kairos: the auspicious moment," American Journal of Psychoanalysis, 29(1):59-83, 1969.

1205) Kendall, Robert E. "Relationship between aggression and depression: epidemiological implications of a hypothesis," Archives of General Psychiatry, 22(4): 308-318, 1970.

1206) Kennedy, P. "Efficacy of a regional poisoning treatment center in preventing further suicidal behavior," British Medical Journal, 4:255-7, Nov. 4, 1972.

1207)   Kennedy, P.   "Poisoning treatment centres, " British
        Medical Journal, 4:670, Dec. 16, 1972.

1208)   Kennedy, P. F. , Phanjoo, A. L. , and Shekim, W. O.
        "Risk-taking in the lives of parasuicides (attempted
        suicides), " British Journal of Psychiatry, 119(550):
        281-286, Sept. 1971.

1209)   Kenyon, F. E.   "Emergencies in child psychiatry, "
        Journal of Mental Science, 108(455):419-426, 1962.

1210)   Kessel, Neil.   "Attempted suicide, " Medical World,
        Oct. 1962, pp. 1-6.

1211)   Kessel, Neil.   "The respectability of self-poisoning
        and the fashion of survival, " Journal of Psychosomatic
        Research, 10(1):29-36, 1966.

1212)   Kessel, Neil.   "Self-poisoning. I, " British Medical
        Journal, 5473:1265-1270, 1965.

1213)   Kessel, Neil.   "Self-poisoning. II, " British Medical
        Journal, 5474:1336-1340, 1965.

1214)   Kessel, Neil.   "Suicide by poisoning. 1.   Suicide and
        the survivor, " Nursing Times, 61:960-1, contd. ,
        July 16, 1965.

1215)   Kessel, Neil and Grossman, Gerald.   "Suicide in alco-
        holics, " British Medical Journal, 2:1671-1672, 1961.

1216)   Kessel, Neil and Lee, E. M.   "Attempted suicide in
        Edinburgh, " Scottish Medical Journal, 7:130-135, 1962.

1217)   Kessel, Neil and McCulloch, Wallace.   "Repeated acts
        of self-poisoning and self-injury, " Proceedings of the
        Royal Society of Medicine, 59(2):89-92, 1966.

1218)   Kessel, N. , McCulloch, J. W. , and Simpson, Esme.
        "Psychiatric service in a centre for the treatment of
        poisoning, " British Medical Journal, 2:985-988, 1963.

1219)   Kikel, H. D.   "A group member's suicide--treating
        collective trauma, " International Journal of Group
        Psychotherapy, 23:42-53, Jan. 1973.

1220)   Kiev, A.   "New directions for suicide prevention

centers," American Journal of Psychiatry, 127:87-88, 1970.

1221) Kim, Zoung Soul. "A Rorschach study on attempted suicides," Theses of Catholic Medical College (Seoul, Korea), 9:71-75, 1965.

1222) Kim, Zoung Soul and Kim, Chong-Eun. "A follow-up study on attempted suicides," Theses of Catholic Medical College (Seoul, Korea), 9:63-69, 1965.

1223) King, J. W. "Depression and suicide in children and adolescents," GP 36:95-104, 1969.

1224) King, M. "Evaluation and treatment of suicide-prone youth," Mental Hygiene, 55:344-50, July 1971.

1225) Kirtley, Donald D. and Sacks, Joseph M. "Reactions of a psychotherapy group to ambiguous circumstances surroundings the death of a group member," Journal of Consulting & Clinical Psychology, 33(2):195-199, 1969.

1226) Kirven, L. E., Jr. "A study of suicides in a State Mental Hospital System," Virginia Medical Monthly, 93:350-354, 1966.

1227) Klintworth, G. K. "Suicide and suicide attempts," South African Medical Journal, 34:358-364, 1960.

1228) Klugman, David J. "The behavioral scientist in the Medical Examiner-Coroner's office," Bulletin of Suicidology, No. 6:45-49, 1970.

1229) Klugman, David J., Litman, Robert E., and Wold, Carl I. "Suicide: answering the cry for help," Social Work, 10(4):43-50, 1965.

1230) Knight, G. "Stereotactic surgery for the relief of suicidal and severe depression and intractable psychoneurosis," Postgraduate Medical Journal, 45:1-13, 1969.

1231) Kockelmans, Joseph J. "On suicide: reflections upon Camus' view of the problem," Psychoanalytic Review, 54(3):31-48, 1967.

1232) Kohn, P. "Investigations of a rising suicide rate,"
       British Journal of Social Psychiatry, 3(3):137-143, 1969.

1233) Kolegar, Ferdinand. "T. G. Masaryk's contribution to
       sociology," Journal of the History of the Behavioral
       Sciences, 3(1):27-37, 1967.

1234) Koller, K. M. and Castanos, J. N. "Attempted sui-
       cide and alcoholism," Medical Journal of Australia,
       2(19):835-837, 1968.

1235) Koller, K. M. and Castanos, J. N. "The influence
       of childhood parental deprivation in attempted suicide,"
       Medical Journal of Australia, 1(10):396-399, 1968.

1236) Koller, K. M. and Castanos, J. N. "Parental de-
       privation and attempted suicide in prison populations,"
       Medical Journal of Australia, 1(17):858-861, Apr. 1969.

1237) Kostrubala, Thaddeus and McInerney, Marcia. "Suicide
       in Chicago: a preliminary statistical and attitudinal
       survey," Social Psychiatry, 1(3):121-123, 1966.

1238) Kranitz, Lionel, Abrahams, Joel, Spiegel, Don, and
       Keith-Speigel, Patricia. "Religious beliefs of suicidal
       patients," Psychological Reports, 22(3, Pt. 1):936,
       1968.

1239) Krassner, M. B. "The suicidal patient in general
       practice," Chicago Medical School Quarterly, 21(4):
       173-189, 1961.

1240) Kraus, J. "Use of Bayes's theorem in clinical deci-
       sion. Suicidal risk, differential diagnosis, response
       to treatment," British Journal of Psychiatry, 120:561-
       7, May 1972.

1241) Kraus, R. F. "Emergency evaluation of suicide
       attempters," Pennsylvania Medicine, 75:60-2, Apr.
       1972.

1242) Krauss, Herbert H. "Social development and suicide,"
       Journal of Cross-Cultural Psychology, 1(2):159-167,
       1970.

1243) Krauss, Herbert H. and Krauss, Beatrice J. "Cross-
       cultural study of the thwarting-disorientation theory of

suicide, " Journal of Abnormal Psychology, 73(4):353-357, 1968.

1244) Krauss, Herbert H. and Tesser, Abraham. "Social contexts of suicide, " Journal of Abnormal Psychology, 78(2):222-228, Oct. 1971.

1245) Kreeger, I. S. "Initial assessment of suicidal risk, " Proceedings of the Royal Society of Medicine, 59:92-96, 1966.

1246) Kreitman, N. "Attempted suicide as language, " British Journal of Psychiatry, 117:476, 1970. [Correspondence]

1247) Kreitman, N., Philip, A. E., Greer, S., and Bagley, C. R. "Parasuicide, " British Journal of Psychiatry, 115:746-747, 1969. [Correspondence]

1248) Kreitman, Norman, Smith, Peter, and Tan, Eng-Seong. "Attempted suicide as language: an empirical study, " British Journal of Psychiatry, 116(534):465-473, May 1970.

1249) Kreitman, N., Smith, P., and Tan, E. S. "Attempted suicide in social networks, " British Journal of Preventive and Social Medicine, 23:116-123, 1969.

1250) Krieger, George. "Biochemical predictors of suicide, " Diseases of the Nervous System, 31(7):478-482, July 1970.

1251) Krieger, George. "Psychological autopsies of hospital suicides, " Hospital & Community Psychiatry, 19(7): 218-220, 1968.

1252) Krieger, George. "Suicides, drugs, and the open hospital, " Hospital & Community Psychiatry, 17(7): 196-199, 1966.

1253) Kubie, Lawrence S. "Multiple determinants of suicidal efforts, " Journal of Nervous and Mental Disease, 138(1):3-8, 1964.

1254) Kubli, R. "Health aspects of safety, " Journal of Occupational Medicine, 9:163-9, Apr. 1967.

1255)   Kumler, Fern R.   "Communication between suicide
        attemptors and significant others: an exploratory
        study, "   Nursing Research,   13(3):268-270,   1964.

1256)   Kunasaka, Y.   "Case study with particular attention
        to the 'here-and-now', "   Journal of Existentialism,   6:
        147-160,   1965-1966.

1257)   Lalli, M. and Turner, S. H.   "Suicide and homicide:
        a comparative analysis by race and occupation levels,"
        Journal of Criminal Law,   Criminology and Police Sci-
        ence,   59(2):191-200,   1968.

1258)   Lamb, Charles W.   "Telephone therapy: some common
        errors and fallacies, "   Voices: The Art & Science of
        Psychotherapy,   5(4):42-46,   1969-1970.

1259)   Lampe, J. M.   "Suicide in children and adolescents,"
        Journal of School Health,   34(8):390-391,   1964.

1260)   La Polla, A. and Nash, L. R.   "Two suicide attempts
        with chlorpromazine, "   American Journal of Psychiatry,
        121:920-2,   March   1965.

1261)   Last, P. M.   "Attempted suicide, "   Medical Journal
        of Australia,   1:708-710,   1967.

1262)   Lawler, R. H. , Narielny, W. , and Wright, Nancy A.
        "Suicidal attempts in children, "   Canadian Medical
        Association Journal,   89:751-754,   1963.

1263)   Layton, McCurdy R. , Blanton, E. B. , and Christo-
        pher, Caston J.   "Suicide in South Carolina, 1955 to
        1966, "   Journal of the South Carolina Medical Associ-
        ation,   65(3):76-80,   1969.

1264)   Leese, Stephanie M.   "Suicide behavior in twenty ado-
        lescents, "   British Journal of Psychiatry,   115(521):
        479-480,   1969.

1265)   Lehmann, H. E. and Ban, T. A.   "The nature and
        frequency of the suicide syndrome,   twenty years ago
        and today,   in the English-speaking community of
        Quebec, "   Laval Médical,   38:93-95,   1967.

1266)   Leonard, C. V.   "Bender-gestalt as an indicator of
        suicidal potential, "   Psychological Reports,   32:665-6,
        Apr. 1973.

1267) Leonard, C. V. and Flinn, D. E. "Suicidal ideation and behavior in youthful nonpsychiatric populations, " Journal of Consult. Clin. Psychology, 38:366-71, June 1972.

1268) LeShan, Lawrence. "Cancer mortality rate: some statistical evidence of the effect of psychological factors, " Archives of General Psychiatry, 6(5):333-335, 1962.

1269) Leslie, M. D. "Nursing care of the suicidal patient," Canadian Nurse, 62:39-41, 1966.

1270) Lesse, S. "Apparent remissions in depressed suicidal patients, " Journal of Nervous and Mental Disease, 144(4):291-296, 1967.

1271) Lesse, S. "Combined drug and psychotherapy of severely depressed ambulatory patients, " Canadian Psychiatric Association Journal, II (Supplement):123-130, 1966.

1272) Lesse, S. "Management of apparent remissions in suicidal patients, " Current Psychiatric Therapy, 7:73-6, 1967.

1273) Lesse, Stanley. "The psychotherapist and apparent remissions in depressed suicidal patients, " American Journal of Psychotherapy, 19(3):436-44, 1965.

1274) Lesse, Stephanie M. "Suicide behaviour in twenty adolescents, " British Journal of Psychiatry, 115(521):479-480, 1969. [Abstract]

1275) Lester, David. "Anomie and the suicidal individual, " Psychological Reports, 26(2):532, 1970.

1276) Lester, David. "Adolescent suicide and pre-marital sexual behavior, " Journal of Social Psychology, 82(1): 131-132, Oct. 1970.

1277) Lester, David. "The antisuicide pill, " Journal of the American Medical Association, 208:1908, 1969.

1278) Lester, David. "Attempted suicide and body image, " Journal of Psychology, 66(2):287-290, 1967.

1279)   Lester, David.   "Attempted suicide as a hostile act, "
        Journal of Psychology, 68(2):243-248, 1968.

1280)   Lester, David.   "Attempts to predict suicidal risk
        using psychological tests, " Psychological Bulletin,
        74(1):1-17, 1970.

1281)   Lester, David.   "Attitudes toward death and suicide in
        a nondisturbed population, " Psychological Reports, 29
        (2):386, Oct. 1971.

1282)   Lester, David.   "Attitudes toward death held by staff
        of a suicide prevention center, " Psychological Re-
        ports, 28:650, Apr. 1971.

1283)   Lester, David.   "Bibliography on suicide: 1968, "
        Crisis Intervention, 2(2):55-60, 1970.

1284)   Lester, David.   "Bibliography on suicide: 1969, "
        Crisis Intervention, 2(4):101-105, 1970.

1285)   Lester, David.   "Bibliography on suicide: 1970, "
        Crisis Intervention, 3(2):45-52, 1971.

1286)   Lester, David.   "Choice of method for suicide and
        personality: a study of suicide notes, " Omega, 2:76-
        80, 1971.

1287)   Lester, David.   "Cognitive complexity of the suicidal
        individual, " Psychological Reports, 28(1):158, Feb.
        1971.

1288)   Lester, David.   "Completed suicide and females in
        the labor force, " Psychological Reports, 32:730, June
        1973.

1289)   Lester, David.   "Completed suicide and latitude, "
        Psychological Reports, 27(3):818, 1970.

1290)   Lester, David.   "Completed suicide and longitude, "
        Psychological Reports, 28(2):662, Apr. 1971.

1291)   Lester, David.   "Ellen West's suicide as a case of
        psychic homicide, " Psychoanalytic Review, 58(2):251-
        263, Summer 1971.

1292)   Lester, David.   "The evaluation of suicide prevention centers, " International Behavioral Scientist, 3:40-47, 1971.

1293) Lester, David. "Factors affecting choice of method of suicide, " Journal of Clinical Psychology, 26(4): 437, Oct. 1970.

1294) Lester, David. "Fear of death of suicidal persons, " Psychological Reports, 20(3, Pt. 2):1077-1078, 1967.

1295) Lester, David. "Fetal suicide, " Journal of the American Medical Association, 209:1367, 1969.

1296) Lester, David. "Geographical location of callers to a suicide prevention center: note on the evaluation of suicide prevention programs, " Psychological Reports, 28(2):421-422, Apr. 1971.

1297) Lester, David. "Henry and Short on suicide: a critique, " Journal of Psychology, 70(2):179-186, 1968.

1298) Lester, David. "How common is suicidal behavior?", Crisis Intervention, 2(2, Suppl):48-50, 1970.

1299) Lester, David. "Hysteria and suicide, " Journal of the American Medical Association, 224:902, May 7, 1973.

1300) Lester, David. "The incidence of suicide and fear of the dead in non-literate societies, " Journal of Cross-Cultural Psychology, 2(2):207-208, June 1971.

1301) Lester, David. "Migration and suicide, " Medical Journal of Australia, 1:941-2, Apr. 29, 1972.

1302) Lester, David. "MMPI scores of old and young completed suicides, " Psychological Reports, 28(1):146, Feb. 1971.

1303) Lester, David. "The myth of suicide prevention, " Compr. Psychiatry, 13:555-60, Nov.-Dec. 1972.

1304) Lester, David. "Need for affiliation in suicide notes," Perceptual & Motor Skills, 33(2):550, Oct. 1971.

1305) Lester, David. "Niagara Falls suicides, " Journal of the American Medical Association, 215:797-8, Feb. 1, 1971.

1306) Lester, David. "Note on the inheritance of suicide, "
Psychological Reports, 22(1):320, 1968.

1307) Lester, David. "The obscene caller, " Crisis Intervention, 2(4):92-96, 1970.

1308) Lester, David. "The patient nobody wants, " Crisis
Intervention, 2(4):85-86, 1970.

1309) Lester, David. "Personality correlates associated
with choice of method of committing suicide, " Personality, 1(3):261-264, 1970.

1310) Lester, David. "Psychology and death, " Continuum,
5(3):550-559, 1967.

1311) Lester, David. "Punishment experiences and suicidal
preoccupation, " Journal of Genetic Psychology, 113(1):
89-94, 1968.

1312) Lester, David. "Recruitment of a counselor, " Crisis
Intervention, 2(2 Suppl.):34-37, 1970.

1313) Lester, David. "Relation between attempted suicide
and completed suicide, " Psychological Reports, 27(3):
719-722, 1970.

1314) Lester, David. "Relationship of mental disorder to
suicidal behavior: review of recent issues, " New York
State Journal of Medicine, 71(12):1503-1505, June 1971.

1315) Lester, David. "Resentment and dependency in the
suicidal individual, " Journal of General Psychology,
81(1):137-145, 1969.

1316) Lester, David. "Residential segregation and completed
suicide, " Crisis Intervention, 3(1):7-9, 1971.

1317) Lester, David. "Seasonal variation in suicidal deaths,"
British Journal of Psychiatry, 118(597):627-628, June
1971.

1318) Lester, David. "Sibling position and suicidal behavior, " Journal of Individual Psychology, 22(2):204-207,
1966.

1319) Lester, David. "Social disorganization and completed

suicide, " Social Psychiatry, 5(3):175-176, July 1970.

1320) Lester, David. "Status integration and suicide, " Psychological Reports, 26(2):492, 1970.

1321) Lester, David. "Steps toward the evaluation of a suicide prevention center. I, " Crisis Intervention, 2 (2 Suppl.):42-45, 1970.

1322) Lester, David. "Steps toward the evaluation of a suicide prevention center. II, " Crisis Intervention, 2 (1, Suppl.):12-18, 1970.

1323) Lester, David. "Steps toward the evaluation of a suicide prevention center. III, " Crisis Intervention, 2 (1, Suppl.):19-21, 1970.

1324) Lester, David. "Steps toward the evaluation of suicide prevention centers. IV, " Crisis Intervention, 2 (4, Suppl.):20-22, 1970.

1325) Lester, David (ed.) "Suicidal behavior: a summary of research findings, " Crisis Intervention, 2 (3 Suppl.): 219, 1970.

1326) Lester, David. "Suicidal behavior after restoration of sight, " Journal of the American Medical Association, 214:916, 1970.

1327) Lester, David. "Suicidal behavior and external constraints, " Psychological Reports, 27(3):777-778, 1970.

1328) Lester, David. "Suicidal behavior in men and women," Mental Hygiene, 53:340-345, 1969.

1329) Lester, David. "Suicidal behavior, sex, and mental disorder, " Psychological Reports, 27(1):61-62, Aug. 1970.

1330) Lester, David. "Suicide, " Journal of the Medical Society of New Jersey, 64:665-7, Aug. 1972.

1331) Lester, David. "Suicide after restoration of sight. II, " Journal of the American Medical Association, 219(6):757, Feb. 1972.

1332) Lester, David. "Suicide: aggression or hostility?",

Crisis Intervention, 3(1):10-14, 1971.

1333) Lester, David. "Suicide and homicide: bias in the examination of the relationship between suicide and homicide rates," Social Psychiatry, 6(2):80-82, May 1971.

1334) Lester, David. "Suicide and homicide in open and closed societies," Psychological Reports, 29(2):430, Oct. 1971.

1335) Lester, David. "Suicide and homicide rates and the society's need for affiliation," Journal of Cross-Cultural Psychology, 2(4):405-406, Dec. 1971.

1336) Lester, David. "Suicide and mutilation behaviors in non-literate societies," Psychological Reports, 28(3): 801-802, June 1971.

1337) Lester, David. "Suicide and sibling position," Journal of Individual Psychology, 26:203-4, Nov. 1970.

1338) Lester, David. "Suicide and unemployment. A reexamination," Archives of Environmental Health (Chicago), 20:277-8, Feb. 1970.

1339) Lester, David. "Suicide as a positive act," Psychology, 6(3):43-48, 1969.

1340) Lester, David. "Suicide as an aggressive act," Journal of Psychology, 66(1):47-50, 1967.

1341) Lester, David. "Suicide as an aggressive act. A replication with a control for neuroticism," Journal of General Psychology, 79(1):83-86, 1968.

1342) Lester, David. "The suicide prevention contribution to mental health," Psychological Reports, 28(3):903-905, June 1971.

1343) Lester, David. "Suicide rate," British Medical Journal, 4:612, Dec. 9, 1972.

1344) Lester, David. "A telephone service for the elderly," Crisis Intervention, 2(4):86-87, 1970.

1345) Lester, David. "Temporal perspective and completed

suicide," Perception and Motor Skills, 36:760, June 1973.

1346) Lester, David and Alexander, M. "Suicide and dangerous sports--parachuting," Journal of the American Medical Association, 215:485, Jan. 18, 1971.

1347) Lester, David and Brockopp, Gene W. "Chronic callers to a suicide prevention center," Community Mental Health Journal, 6(3):246-250, June 1970.

1348) Lester, David, Brockopp, Gene W., and Priebe, Kitty. "Association between a full moon and completed suicide," Psychological Reports, 25(2):598, 1969.

1349) Lester, David and Perdue, W. C. "Suicide, homicide, and color-shading response on the Rorschach," Perception and Motor Skills, 35:562, Oct. 1972.

1350) Lester, David, Reeve, Calvin, I., and Priebe, Kitty. "Completed suicide and month of birth," Psychological Reports, 27(1):210, 1970.

1351) Lester, David and Williams, Tim. "The volunteer in suicide prevention," Crisis Intervention, 3(4):87-91, 1971.

1352) Lester, David and Wright, T. "Suicide and overcontrol," Psychological Reports, 32:1278, June 1973.

1353) Levenson, Marvin and Neuringer, Charles. "Intropunitiveness in suicidal adolescents," Journal of Projective Techniques & Personality Assessment, 34(5): 409-411, Oct. 1970.

1354) Levenson, M. and Neuringer, Charles. "Phenomenal environmental oppressiveness in suicidal adolescents," Journal of Genetic Psychology, 120:253-6, June 1972.

1355) Levenson, Marvin and Neuringer, Charles. "Problem-solving behavior in suicidal adolescents," Journal of Consulting and Clinical Psychology, 37(3):433-436, Dec. 1971.

1356) Levi, L. David, Fales, Catherine H., Stein, Marvin, and Sharp, Vernon H. "Separation and attempted suicide," Archives of General Psychiatry, 15(2):158-164, 1966.

1357)   Levin, Edmund C.   "Epidemiology of suicide, "   New
Physician, 11:108-110.

1358)   Leviton, D.   "A course on death education and suicide
prevention--implications for health education, " Journal
of American College Health Association, 19:217-20,
Apr. 1971.

1359)   Leviton, D.   "The need for education on death and
suicide, "   Journal of School Health, 39:270-274, 1969.

1360)   Levy, J.   "Navajo suicide, "   Human Organization, 24:
308-318, 1965.

1361)   Lewin, J. F. , Norris, R. S. and Hughes, J. T.
"Three cases of maldison (malathion) poisoning, "
Forensic Science, 2:101-5, Feb. 1973.

1362)   Lewis, D. J.   "Depression.   3. Suicide, "   Applied
Therapeutics, 9:990-993, 1967.

1363)   Lewis, J. M.   "The family doctor and the suicidal
crisis, "   Texas Medicine, 64:52-56, 1968.

1364)   Lewis, W. S. , Lee, A. B. , Jr. , and Grantham, S. A.
" 'Jumpers syndrome. ' The trauma of high free fall as
seen at Harlem Hospital, "   Journal of Trauma, 5:812-
818, 1965.

1365)   Li, F. P.   "Suicide among chemists, "   Archives of
Environmental Health, 19:518-520, 1969.

1366)   Light, D. W. J.   "Psychiatry and suicide--the management of a mistake, "   American Journal of Sociology,
77:821-38, Mar. 1972.

1367)   Linehan, Marsha M.   "Toward a theory of sex differences in suicidal behavior, "   Crisis Intervention,
3(4):93-101, 1971.

1368)   Link, Ruth.   "Suicide: the deadly game, "   Sweden
Now, 3(12)/4(1):40-46, 1969-1970.

1369)   Litman, Robert E.   "Acutely suicidal patients, management in general medical practice, "   California Medicine, 104:168-74, March 1966.

1370) Litman, Robert E.   "Emergency response to potential suicide," Journal of the Michigan State Medical Society, 62:68-72, 1963.

1371) Litman, Robert E.   "Immobilization response to suicidal behavior," Archives of General Psychiatry, 11 (3):282-285, 1964.

1372) Litman, R. E.   "The prevention of suicide," Current Psychiatric Therapies, 6:268-276, 1966.

1373) Litman, Robert E.   "Psychiatric hospitals and suicide prevention centers," Comprehensive Psychiatry, 6(2): 119-127, 1965.

1374) Litman, R. E.   "Presuicidal states in adolescents," American Journal of Orthopsychiatry, 39:315-316, 1969.

1375) Litman, Robert E.   "Psychological-psychiatric aspects in certifying modes of death," Journal of Forensic Sciences, 13:46-54, 1968.

1376) Litman, Robert E.   "Sigmund Freud on suicide," Bulletin of Suicidology, July 1968, pp. 11-23.

1377) Litman, R. E.   "Sigmund Freud on suicide," Psychoanalytic Forum, 2:206-221, 1966.

1378) Litman, Robert E.   "Suicide Prevention Center patients: A follow-up study," Bulletin of Suicidology, No. 6:12-17, Spring 1970.

1379) Litman, Robert E.   "When patients commit suicide," American Journal of Psychotherapy, 19(4):570-576, 1965.

1380) Litman, Robert E., Curphey, T., Shneidman, E. S., Farberow, N. L., and Tabachnick, N.   "Investigation of equivocal suicides," Journal of the American Medical Association, 184:924-929, 1963.

1381) Litman, Robert E. and Farberow, Norman L.   "The hospital's obligation toward suicide-prone patients," Hospitals, 40:64-68 passim, 1966.

1382) Litman, R. E. and Farberow, N. L.   "Suicide prevention in hospitals," Zeitschrift für Präventivmedizin, 10:488-498, 1965.

1383)   Litman, R. E., Farberow, N. L., Shneidman, E. S.,
        Heilig, S. M., and Kramer, J. A. "Suicide-prevention
        telephone service," Journal of the American Medical
        Association, 192:21-5, Apr. 5, 1965.

1384)   Litman, R. E., Shneidman, E. S., and Farberow,
        N. L. "A Los Angeles suicide prevention center,"
        American Journal of Psychiatry, 117:1084-1087, 1961.

1385)   Litman, R. E., Shneidman, E. S., and Farberow,
        N. L. "A suicide prevention center," Current Psy-
        chiatric Therapies, 1:8-16, 1961.

1386)   Litman, Robert E. and Swearingen, C. "Bondage and
        suicide," Archives of General Psychiatry, " 27:80-5,
        July 1972.

1387)   Litman, Robert E. and Tabachnick, Norman. "Fatal
        one-car accidents," Psychoanalytic Quarterly, 36(2)
        248-259, 1967.

1388)   Littunen, Yrjo and Gaier, Eugene L. "Social control
        and social integration," International Journal of Social
        Psychiatry 9(3):165-173, 1963.

1389)   Long, R. H. "Barbiturates, automatism and suicide,"
        Postgraduate Medicine, 28:A-56, 1960.

1390)   Lordi, Wm. "Suicide in children and adolescents,"
        Virginia Medical Monthly, 98:209-13, Apr. 1971.

1391)   "The Los Angeles Suicide Prevention Center," Nurs-
        ing Outlook, 13(11):61, 1965.

1392)   Lourie, R. S. "Clinical studies of attempted suicide
        in childhood," Clinical Proceedings of Children's Hos-
        pital of the District of Columbia, 22:163-173, 1966.

1393)   Lourie, R. S. "Suicide and attempted suicide in
        children and adolescents," Texas Medicine, 63:58-63,
        1967.

1394)   Lucero, Joseph R., Brantner, John P., Brown, Byron
        W., and Olson, Gordon W. "Weather, crime and
        mental illness," Journal of the Minnesota Academy of
        Science, 32(3):223-226, 1965.

1395)   Luke, J. L.   "Asphyxial deaths by hanging in New
        York City, 1964-1965, " Journal of Forensic Sciences,
        12:359-369, 1967.

1396)   Lukianowicz, N.   "Attempted suicide in children, "
        Acta Psychiatrica Scandinavica, 44:415-435, 1968.

1397)   Lukianowicz, N.   "Suicidal behavior--an attempt to
        modify the environment, " British Journal of Psychi-
        atry, 121:387-90, Oct. 1972.

1398)   Lurie, L.   "The hospital's responsibility for the care
        of the suicidal patient, " Medico-Legal Bulletin, 180:
        1-5, 1968.

1399)   Lyman, J. L.   "Student suicide at Oxford University,"
        Student Medicine, 10(2):218-234, 1961.

1400)   Lynn, R. A.   "National rates of economic growth,
        anxiety and suicide, " Nature (London), 222:494, 1969.

1401)   Lyster, W. R.   "Seasonal variations in suicide rates,"
        Lancet, 1:725, Mar. 31, 1973.

1402)   McCandless, Frederick D.   "Suicide and the com-
        munication of rage: a cross-cultural case study, "
        American Journal of Psychiatry, 125(2):197-205, 1968.

1403)   McCarthy, P. D. and Walsh, D.   "Suicide in Dublin,"
        British Medical Journal, 1(5500):1393-1396, 1966.

1404)   McCartney, J. L.   "Suicide as a complication to group
        psychotherapy, " Military Medicine, 126:895-898, 1961.

1405)   McClean, L. J.   "The rescue system, " Perspectives
        in Psychiatric Care, 10:173-7, 1972.

1406)   McClure, James N. , Reich, Theodore, and Wetzel,
        Richard D.   "Premenstrual symptoms as an indicator
        of bipolar affective disorder, " British Journal of Psy-
        chiatry, 119(552):527-528, Nov. 1971.

1407)   McConaghy, N. , Linnane, J. , and Buckle, R. C.
        "Parental deprivation and attempted suicide, " Medical
        Journal of Australia, 1:886-892, 1966.

1408)   McConnell, Theodore.   "Suicide ethics in cross-disci-

plinary perspectives, " Journal of Religion and Health,
7(1):7-25, 1968.

1409)   McCulloch, J. W. and Philip, Alistair E.   "Social
factors associated with attempted suicide: a review
of the literature, " British Journal of Psychiatric Social Work, 9(1):30-36, 1967.

1410)   McCulloch, J. W. and Philip, Alistair E.   "The social
prognosis of persons who attempt suicide, " Social Psychiatry, 5(3):177-182, July 1970.   (15 ref.)

1411)   McCulloch, J. W. and Philip, Alistair E.   "Social
variables in attempted suicide, " Acta Psychiatrica
Scandinavica, 43(3):341-346, 1967.

1412)   McCulloch, J. W. , Philip, A. E. , and Carstairs,
G. M.   "The ecology of suicidal behavior, " British
Journal of Psychiatry, 113(496):313-319, 1967.

1413)   McDonald, James K.   "An unusual attempt at suicide,"
American Journal of Psychiatry, 118(8):746, 1962.

1414)   MacDonald, John M.   "Homicidal threats, " American
Journal of Psychiatry, 124(4):475-482, 1967.

1415)   MacDonald, John M.   "Suicide and homicide by automobile, " American Journal of Psychiatry, 121(4):366-
370, 1964.

1416)   McDowall, Arthur W. , Brooke, Eileen M. , Freeman-
Browne, Dorothy L. , and Robin, Ashley A.   "Subse-
quent suicide in depressed in-patients, " British
Journal of Psychiatry, 114(511):749-754, 1968.

1417)   MacFee, M.   "The attitude of the hospital staff to the
patient, " Nursing Times, 61:1083-4 contd. , Aug. 6,
1965.

1418)   McGee, Richard K.   "Community mental health concepts as demonstrated by suicide prevention programs
in Florida, " Community Mental Health Journal, 4(2):
144-152, 1968.

1419)   McGee, Richard K.   "Report of a regional workshop, "
Bulletin of Suicidology, Dec. 1967, pp. 43-45.

1420) McGee, R. K. "The suicide prevention center as a model for community mental health programs," Community Mental Health Journal, 1(2):162-170, 1965.

1421) McGee, Richard K. "Suicide prevention programs and mental health associations," Mental Hygiene, 55(1): 60-67, Jan. 1971.

1422) McGee, Richard K. and McGee, Jean P. "Profile of a pioneer: Louis I. Dublin, Ph.D. (1882-1969)," Bulletin of Suicidology, No. 7: 5-8, 1970.

1423) McGuire, F. L. "Suicidal impulses in the operation of motor vehicles," Journal of the Mississippi Medical Association, 2:331-334, 1961.

1424) McGuire, June. "A cry for help: suicide and accident proneness," Journal of Psychiatric Nursing, 2(5):500-508, 1964.

1425) McIntire, Matilda S. and Angle, C. R. "Is the poisoning accidental," Clinical Pediatrics (Philadelphia), 10: 414-7, July 1971.

1426) McIntire, Matilda S. and Angle, C. R. "'Suicide' as seen in poison control centers," Pediatrics, 48:914-22, Dec. 1971.

1427) McIntire, Matilda S. and Angle, C. R. "The taxonomy of suicide as seen in poison control centers," Pediatric Clinics of North America, 17:697-706, 1970.

1428) McKerracher, D. W., Loughnane, T., and Watson, R. A. "Self-mutilation in female psychopaths," British Journal of Psychiatry, 114(512):829-832, 1968.

1429) McLean, F. A. "An inquest quashed," Lancet, 2:146, 1970.

1430) McLean, L. J. "Action and reaction in suicidal crisis," Nursing Forum, 8:28-41, 1969.

1431) Macmahon, B., Johnson, S., and Pugh, T. F. "Relation of suicide rates to social conditions," Public Health Reports, 78:285-293, 1963.

1432) Macmahon, B. and Pugh, T. F. "Suicide in the

widowed, " American Journal of Epidemiology, 81:23-31, Jan. 1965.

1433) McNeal, Benjamin F. and Johnston, Roy. "Problems in assessing suicide potential among psychiatric patients, " Psychiatric Quarterly, 40(4):729-736, 1966.

1434) McPartland, T. S. and Hornstra, R. K. "The depressive datum, " Comprehensive Psychiatry, 5(4):253-261, 1964.

1435) Maddison, David and Mackey, Kenneth H. "Suicide: the clinical problem, " British Journal of Psychiatry, 112(488):693-703, 1966.

1436) Maddocks, P. D. "A five-year follow-up of untreated psychopaths, " British Journal of Psychiatry, 116(534):511-515, May 1970.

1437) Maire, Frederick W. "Van Gogh's suicide, " Journal of the American Medical Association, 217(7):938-939, Aug. 1971.

1438) Maller, Octav. "Suicide and migration, " Israel Annals of Psychiatry & Related Disciplines, 4(1):67-77, 1966.

1439) Malleson, Nicolas. "Acute adverse reactions to LSD in clinical and experimental use in the United Kingdom, " British Journal of Psychiatry, 118(543):229-230, Feb. 1971.

1440) Malmquist, C. P. "Suicide and related clinical problems, " Minnesota Medicine, 52:1597-1602, 1969.

1441) "Management of attempted suicide, " British Medical Journal, 5261:1202-1203, 1961.

1442) Mancuso, T. F. and Locke, B. Z. "Carbon disulphide as a cause of suicide. Epidemiological study of viscose rayon workers, " Journal of Occupational Medicine, 14:595-606, Aug. 1972.

1443) Mandell, Arnold J. and Mandell, Mary P. "Suicide and the menstrual cycle, " Journal of the American Medical Association, 200(9):792-793, 1967.

1444) Mann, J. "EEG changes and psychiatric findings in
       suicidal carbon-monoxide poisoning," Diseases of the
       Nervous System, 26:508-11, Aug. 1965.

1445) Maretzki, Thomas W. "Suicide in Okinawa: prelimi-
       nary explorations," International Journal of Social
       Psychiatry, 11(4):256-263, 1965.

1446) Margolin, N. L. and Teicher, J. D. "Thirteen ado-
       lescent male suicide attempts. Dynamic considera-
       tions," Journal of the American Academy of Child
       Psychiatry, 7:296-315, 1968.

1447) Margolis, P. M. "M.D. suicides. Why?" Michigan
       Medicine, 67:589, 1968.

1448) Margolis, Philip M. "Suicide," University of Michi-
       gan Medical Center Journal, 35(1):10-12, 1969.

1449) Margolis, Philip M., Meyer, George G., and Louw,
       Jan C. "Suicidal precautions," Archives of General
       Psychiatry, 13:224-231, 1965.

1450) Margoshes, A., Litt, S., and Green, R. "Scandina-
       vian suicide in America," Mental Hygiene, 51(4):524-
       526, 1967.

1451) Maris, Ronald. "Age, sex, marital status and the
       suicide rate," Yale Scientific, 42(4):6 passim, 1968.

1452) Maris, Ronald W. "Deviance as therapy: the paradox
       of the self-destructive female," Journal of Health &
       Social Behavior, 12(2):113-124, June 1971.

1453) Maris, Ronald W. "The sociology of suicide preven-
       tion: policy implications of differences between suicidal
       patients and completed suicides," Social Problems,
       17(1):132-149, 1969.

1454) Maris, Ronald W. "Suicide. The nondiminishing
       rate," Minnesota Medicine, 51:723-726, 1968.

1455) Maris, Ronald W. "Suicide, status and mobility in
       Chicago," Social Forces, 46(2):246-256, 1967.

1456) Marjot, D. H. "Aggressive psychopathy. A clinical
       description of sixteen psychopathic females in a Special

Hospital, " Journal of the Royal Naval Medical Service, 52:71-77, 1966.

1457) Martin, M. J. "Suicide: a continuing problem, " Journal of the Iowa Medical Society, 55:533-536, 1965.

1458) Martin, Nancy. "New light on how you can save a colleague's life, " Medical Economics, November 23, 1970, pp. 177-195.

1459) Massey, J. T. "Suicide in the United States, " Vital Health Statistics, 20:1-34, 1967.

1460) "Maternal deaths involving suicide. By the OSMA Committee on Maternal Health, with comment of consulting psychiatrist, " Ohio Medical Journal, 62:1294-5, Dec. 1966.

1461) Matthew, H. "Acute poisoning, " Scottish Medical Journal, 11:1-6, 1966.

1462) Matthew, H. "Self-poisoning, " Scottish Medical Journal, 16:362-3, Aug. 1971.

1463) Matthew, H. and Lawson, A. A. H. "Acute barbiturate poisoning--a review of two years' experience, " Quarterly Journal of Medicine, 35:539-552, 1966.

1464) Matthews, P. C. "Epidemic self-injury in an adolescent unit, " International Journal of Social Psychiatry, 14(2):125-133, 1968.

1465) Mattson, Ake, Seese, Lynne R., and Hawkins, James W. "Suicidal behavior as a child psychiatric emergency: clinical characteristics and follow-up results," Archives of General Psychiatry, 20(1):100-109, 1969.

1466) Maultsby, M. C., Jr. "A behavioral approach to irrational anxiety and insomnia, " (Decreasing prescription suicides), Journal of American Medical Women's Association, 27:416-9, Aug. 1972.

1467) Maxmen, J. S. and Lucker, G. T. "No exit--the persistently suicidal patient, " Comparative Psychiatry, 14:71-9, Jan.-Feb. 1973.

1468) Maycock, E. "Depression, despair and suicide, "

(London) Times Educational Supplement, February 11, 1966, No. 2647, p. 407.

1469) Mayer, D. Y. "A psychotherapeutic approach to the suicidal patient," British Journal of Psychiatry, 119: 629-33, Dec. 1971.

1470) Mayfield, D. G. and Montgomery, P. "Alcoholism, alcohol intoxication and suicide attempts," Archives of General Psychiatry, 27:349-53, Sept. 1972.

1471) Mazrin, Ali. "Sacred suicide," Atlas, March 1966, pp. 164-169.

1472) "Medical contributions to suicide," British Medical Journal, 3(5671):610, Sept. 1969.

1473) Medlicott, R. W. and Medlicott, P. A. W. "Suicide in and after discharge from a private psychiatric hospital over a period of eighty-six years," Australian and New Zealand Journal of Psychiatry, 3(3):137-144, 1969.

1474) Meerloo, J. A. M. "The diencephalization of the reactive depression. [The suicidal implications of euphemist names.]," American Journal of Psychiatry, 121(4):376-377, 1964.

1475) Melges, Frederick T. and Bowlby, John. "Types of hopelessness in psychopathological process," Archives of General Psychiatry, 20:690-699, 1969.

1476) Melges, Frederick T. and Weisz, Alfred E. "The personal future and suicidal ideation," Journal of Nervous & Mental Disease, 153(4):244-250, Oct. 1971.

1477) Mendlewicz, J. and Wilmotte, J. "Suicide by physicians," American Journal of Psychiatry, 128:364-5, Sept. 1971.

1478) Menon, I. S. "A review of 216 cases of attempted suicide in a British hospital," Journal of the Indian Medical Association, 47:22-26, 1966.

1479) "Mental disturbance in doctors," British Medical Journal, 4(5681):448, Nov. 1969.

1480)   Merskey, H.   "Attempted suicide, "   British Journal
        of Psychiatry,   115:1227,   1969.

1481)   Messer, M. H.   "Suicide prevention--Adlerian con-
        tribution, "   Journal of Individual Psychology,   29:54-71,
        May 1973.

1482)   Michaux, Mary H., Suziedelis, Antanas, Garmize,
        Karen, and Rossi, J. Antoinette.   "Depression factors
        in depressed and in heterogeneous in-patient samples,"
        Journal of Neurology, Neurosurgery & Psychiatry, 32
        (6):609-613, 1969.

1483)   Middleton, G. D., Ashby, D. W., and Clark, F. "An
        analysis of attempted suicide in an urban industrial
        district, "   Practitioner,   187:776-782, 1961.

1484)   Mikawa, J. K.   "An alternative to current analyses
        of suicidal behavior, "   Psychological Reports,   32:323-
        30, Feb. 1973.

1485)   Miley, J. D. and Michelin, M.   "Structural change
        and the Durkheimian legacy--a macrosocial analysis
        of suicide rates, "   American Journal of Sociology,   78:
        657-73, Nov. 1972.

1486)   Miller, Dorothy H.   "Suicidal careers: case analysis
        of suicide mental patients, "   Social Work,   15(1):27-36,
        Jan. 1970.

1487)   Miller, Dorothy H. and Godman, Daniel.   "Predicting
        post-release risk among hospitalized suicide attempt-
        ers, "   Omega,   1(1):71-84,   1970.

1488)   Miller, E. R. and Shaskan, D. A.   "A note on the
        group management of a disgruntled suicidal patient, "
        International Journal of Group Psychotherapy,   13:216-
        218, 1963.

1489)   Miller, H.   "Depression, "   British Medical Journal,
        1:257-62, Feb. 4, 1967.

1490)   Miller, S. I. and Schoenfeld, L. S.   "Suicide attempt
        patterns among the Navajo Indians, "   International
        Journal of Social Psychiatry,   17:189-93, Summer 1971.

1491)   Milner, G.   "The absconder, " Comprehensive Psychiatry,

7(3):147-151, 1966.

1492) Minkoff, K., Bergman, E., Beck, A. T. and Beck, R.
       "Hopelessness, depression and attempted suicide, "
       American Journal of Psychiatry, 130:455-9, Apr. 1973.

1493) Mintz, Ronald S.   "Basic considerations in the psycho-
       therapy of the depressed suicidal patient, " American
       Journal of Psychotherapy, 25(1):56-73, Jan. 1971.

1494) Mintz, R. S.   "Depression and suicide, " International
       Psychiatry Clinics, 3:183-195, 1966.

1495) Mintz, Ronald S.   "Prevalence of persons in the city
       of Los Angeles who have attempted suicide: a pilot
       study, " Bulletin of Suicidology, No. 7:9-16, Fall 1970.

1496) Mintz, Ronald S.   "Psychotherapy of the suicidal
       patient, " American Journal of Psychotherapy, 15:38-
       67, 1961.

1497) Mintz, Ronald S.   "Some practical procedures in the
       management of suicidal persons, " American Journal
       of Orthopsychiatry, 36:896-903, 1966.

1498) Miskimins, R. W. and Wilson, Lowell T.   "Revised
       Suicide Potential Scale, " Journal of Consulting &
       Clinical Psychology, 33:258, 1969.

1499) "Misuse of valuable therapeutic agents--barbituates,
       tranquilizers and amphetamines, " Bulletin of the New
       York Academy of Medicine, 40:972-9, Dec. 1964.

1500) Mitchell, A. R.   "Suicidal reaction in the service en-
       vironment, " Journal of the Royal Army Medical Corps,
       109:215-219, 1963.

1501) Modan, B., Nissenkorn, I., and Lewkowski, S. R.
       "Comparative epidemiologic aspects of suicide and
       attempted suicide in Israel, " American Journal of
       Epidemiology, 91:393-399, 1970.

1502) Modan, B., Nissenkorn, I., and Lewkowski, S. R.
       "Suicide in a heterogeneous society, " British Journal
       of Psychiatry, 116(530):65-68, 1970.

1503) Modlin, Herbert C.   "Cues and clues to suicide, "

Menninger Perspective, 2(2):2-5, Feb. 1971.

1504)   Montgomery, Frederick A. and Stephens, Michael.
        "Suicide gestures at Fort Leonard Wood: a follow-up
        study, " Military Medicine, 137(2):59-60, Feb. 1972.

1505)   Morphew, J. A.   "Religion and attempted suicide, "
        International Journal of Social Psychiatry, 14(3):188-
        192, 1968.

1506)   Morris, J. , Selkin, J. , and Yost, J.   "Home treat-
        ment program by an indigenous professional, the visit-
        ing nurse, with a group of adolescents who have
        attempted suicide, " American   Journal of Orthopsy-
        chiatry, 40:340-341, 1970.

1507)   Morrison, Gilbert C. and Collier, Jenny G.   "Family
        treatment approaches to suicidal children and adoles-
        cents, " Journal of the American Academy of Child
        Psychiatry, 8(1):140-153, 1969.

1508)   Morrison, Gilbert C. and Smith, Wiley R. , Jr.
        "Emergencies in child psychiatry: a definition and
        comparison of two groups, " American Journal of
        Orthopsychiatry, 37(2):412-413, 1967.

1509)   Moss, Leonard M.   "Psychotherapy of suicidal pa-
        tient," New York State Journal of Medicine, 66(23):
        3020-3023, 1966.

1510)   Motto, Jerome A.   "Development of standards for
        suicide prevention centers, " Bulletin of Suicidology,
        Mar. 1969, pp. 33-37.

1511)   Motto, Jerome A.   "Newspaper influence on suicide: a
        controlled study, " Archives of General Psychiatry, 23
        (2):143-148, Aug. 1970.

1512)   Motto, Jerome A.   "Responsibilities in suicide pre-
        vention, " California's Health, 29(1):6-7, 17, July,
        1971.

1513)   Motto, Jerome A.   "Suicide and suggestibility: the
        role of the press, " American Journal of Psychiatry,
        124(2):252-256, 1967.

1514)   Motto, Jerome A.   "Suicide attempts: a longitudinal

view, " Archives of General Psychiatry, 13(6):516-
520, 1965.

1515) Motto, Jerome A. "Toward suicide prevention in
       medical practice, " Journal of the American Medical
       Association, 210(7):1229-1232, 1969.

1516) Munck, O. and Quaade, F. "Suicide attempted with
       insulin, " Danish Medical Bulletin, 10(4):139-141, 1963.

1517) Munson, B. E. "Relationship between economic activ-
       ity and critical community dimensions, " American
       Journal of Economics & Sociology, 27:225-237, 1968.

1518) Murphy, G. E. "Clinical identification of suicidal
       risk, " Archives of General Psychiatry, 27:356-9,
       Sept. 1972.

1519) Murphy, G. E. "Recognition of suicidal risk: the
       physician's responsibility, " Southern Medical Journal,
       62:723-728, 1969.

1520) Murphy, G. E. "Suicide and the right to die, "
       American Journal of Psychiatry, 130:472-3, Apr. 1973.

1521) Murphy, G. E. and Robins, E. "Social factors in
       suicide, " Journal of the American Medical Associa-
       tion, 199(5):303-308, 1967.

1522) Murphy, George E., Wetzel, Richard D., Swallow,
       Carolyn S., and McClure, James N., Jr. "Who calls
       the suicide prevention center: a study of 55 persons
       calling on their own behalf, " American Journal of
       Psychiatry, 126(3):314-324, 1969.

1523) Murray, Neville and Murray, Betty. "Recognition and
       management of group self-destruction in psychodrama,"
       Group Psychotherapy, 15(3):200-202, 1962.

1524) Murrell, Stanley A. "Community involvement in mental
       health programs: the Wyandotte County Mental Health
       and Guidance Center, " Community Mental Health
       Journal, 5(1):82-87, 1969.

1525) Murthy, Vinoda N. "Attempted suicide and goal set-
       ting behavior, " Transactions of All-India Institute of
       Mental Health, 6:69-78, 1966.

1526) Murthy, Vinoda N.   "Personality and the nature of
       suicidal attempts, "   British Journal of Psychiatry, 115
       (524):791-795, 1969.

1527) Mutty, Lawrence B.   "Aspects of psychiatry in a Viet-
       namese General Hospital.   Suicide in Vietnam, "
       Journal of the American Medical Association, 206(5):
       1152-1153, 1968.

1528) "Mythology of suicide, "   British Medical Journal,
       1(5699):770, Mar. 1970.

1529) Naftulin, D. H.   "The potentially suicidal patient, "
       California Medicine, 111:169-176, 1969.

1530) Nahum, L. H.   "The somatic mask of depression, "
       Conn. Med. , 30:608 passim, Sept. 1966.

1531) Nashold, R. D.   "Attempted suicide by chemical
       agents, "   Wisconsin Medical Journal, 64:327-328, 1965.

1532) Nathan, P. , Smith, S. , and Rossi, A. M.   "Experi-
       mental analysis of a brief psychotherapeutic relation-
       ship, "   American Journal of Orthopsychiatry, 38:482-
       492, 1968.

1533) Nawas, M. Mike and Worth, James W.   "Suicidal con-
       figurations in the Bender-Gestalt, "   Journal of Pro-
       jective Techniques & Personality Assessment, 32(4):
       392-394, 1968.

1534) Neiberg, Norman A.   "Murder and suicide, "   Archives
       of Criminal Psychodynamics, 4:253-268, 1961.

1535) Neiswander, A. C.   "Suicide--to be or not to be, "
       Journal of the American Institute of Homeopathy, 58:
       42-5, Jan. -Feb. 1965.

1536) Nelson, B.   "Suicide prevention: NIHM wants more
       attention for 'taboo' subject, "   Science, 161:766-767,
       1968.

1537) Nelson, Scott H. and Grunebaum, Henry.   "A follow-
       up study of wrist-slashers, "   American Journal of
       Psychiatry, 127(10):1345-1349, Apr. 1971.

1538) Nelson, Zane P. and Smith, Wilford E.   "The law en-

forcement profession: an incident of high suicide, "
Omega, 1(4):293-299, 1970.

1539) Neumann, M. "Suicide proneness: research based on
a study of 38 patients who committed suicide, " Israel
Annals of Psychiatry & Related Disciplines, 9(1):39-
51, Apr. 1971.

1540) Neuringer, Charles. "Changes in attitudes towards
life and death during recovery from a serious suicide
attempt, " Omega, 1(4):301-309, 1970.

1541) Neuringer, Charles. "The cognitive organization of
meaning in suicidal individuals, " Journal of General
Psychology, 76(1):91-100, 1967.

1542) Neuringer, Charles. "Dichotomous evaluations in suicidal individuals, " Journal of Consulting Psychology,
25(5):445-449, 1961.

1543) Neuringer, Charles. "Divergencies between attitudes
towards life and death among suicidal, psychosomatic,
and normal hospitalized patients, " Journal of Consulting & Clinical Psychology, 32(1):59-63, 1968.

1544) Neuringer, Charles and Kolstoe, Ralph H. "Suicide
research and non-rejection of the null hypothesis, "
Perceptual and Motor Skills, 22(1):115-118, 1966.

1545) Neuringer, Charles. "Methodological problems in suicide research, " Journal of Consulting Psychology, 26
(3):273-278, 1962.

1546) Neuringer, Charles. "The problem of suicide, "
Journal of Existential Psychiatry, 2(9):69-74, 1962.

1547) Neuringer, Charles. "Reactions to interpersonal
crises in suicidal individuals, " Journal of General
Psychology, 71(1):47-55, 1964.

1548) Neuringer, Charles. "Rigid thinking in suicidal individuals, " Journal of Consulting Psychology, 28(1):54-
58, 1964. (27 ref.)

1549) Neuringer, Charles. "The Rorschach test as a research device for the identification, prediction and understanding of suicidal ideation and behavior, " Journal

of Projective Techniques and Personality Assessment,
29(1):71-82, 1965.

1550) Neuringer, Charles, McEvoy, Theodore L., and
Schlesinger, Richard J. "The identification of suicidal
behavior in females by the use of the Rorschach,"
Journal of General Psychology, 72(1):127-133, 1965.

1551) Newby, John H., Jr. and Van Der Heide, C. J. "A
review of 139 suicidal gestures: discussion of some
psychological implications and treatment techniques,"
Military Medicine, 133(8):629-637, 1968.

1552) Niccolini, R. "Reading the signals for suicide risk,"
Geriatrics, 28:71-2, May 1973.

1553) Nicholson, W. A. "Self-inflicted and accidental poisoning in adults admitted to a general hospital," Practitioner, 190:230, 1963.

1554) Nomura, Akichika. "Treatment of depression in relation to suicidal attempt," Diseases of the Nervous
System, 21(12):701-703, 1960.

1555) Northcutt, T. "Answering cries for help," Journal
of the Florida Medical Association, 51:301-302, 1964.

1556) Noyes, Russell, Jr. "Shall we prevent suicide?", Comprehensive Psychiatry, 11(4):361-370, July 1970.

1557) Noyes, Russell, Jr. "Suicide: motivation and prevention," Postgraduate Medicine, 47:182-187, 1970.

1558) Noyes, Russell, Jr. "The taboo of suicide," Psychiatry, 31(2):173-183, 1968.

1559) Noyes, R., Jr. "Toward understanding suicide,"
Journal of the Iowa Medical Society, 58:1147-1152, 1968.

1560) Offenkrantz, W. "Depression and suicide in general
medical practice," American Practitioner, 13:427-
430, 1962.

1561) Offer, D. and Barglow, P. "Adolescent and young
adult self-mutilation incidents in a general psychiatric
hospital," Archives of General Psychiatry, 3(2):194-
204, 1960.

1562) Ogden, M., Spector, M. I., and Hill, C. A., Jr. "Suicides and homicides among Indians," Public Health Reports, 85:75-80, 1970.

1563) Ogilvie, Daniel M., Stone, Philip J., and Shneidman, Edwin S. "Some characteristics of genuine versus simulated suicide notes," Bulletin of Suicidology, March 1969, pp. 27-32.

1564) Ohara, K. "Characteristics of suicides in Japan, especially of parent-child double suicide," American Journal of Psychiatry, 120(4):382-385, 1963.

1565) Ohara, K. "A study on the factors contributing to suicide from the standpoint of psychiatry," American Journal of Psychiatry, 120:798-799, 1964.

1566) Ohara, Kenshiro and Reynolds, David K. "Love-pact suicide," Anthropology UCLA, 2:49-53, 1969.

1567) Ohara, K. and Reynolds, D. "Love-pact suicide," Omega, 1(3):159-166, 1970.

1568) Ohara, K., Shimizu, M., and Aizawa, S. "A follow-up survey of unsuccessful love-pact suicides," Psychiatria et Neurologia Japonica, 64(12):1216-1224, 1962.

1569) Ohara, K., Shimizu, M., and Kojima, H. "Suicide in children," Psychiatria et Neurologia Japonica, 65:468, 1963.

1570) Ohio State Medical Association Committee on Maternal Health. "Maternal deaths involving suicide," Ohio State Medical Journal, 62(1):1294-1295, 1966.

1571) Oki, T., Sakai, T., Otsuka, F., Kizu, M., Higashi, H., Asano, N., and Asano, N. "The psychological investigation of child suicide," Bulletin of the Osaka Medical School, 6(2):86-90, 1960.

1572) Oltman, J. E. and Friedman, S. "Study of suicidal attempts in patients admitted to a state psychiatric hospital," Diseases of the Nervous System, 23:433-439, 1962.

1573) Oltman, J. E. and Friedman, S. "Life cycles in patients with manic-depressive psychosis," American

Journal of Psychiatry, 119(2):174-176, 1962.

1574) Opler, M. K. "International and cultural conflicts
       affecting mental health.   Violence, suicide and with-
       drawal, " American Journal of Psychotherapy, 23:608-
       620, 1969.

1575) Opler, M. K. and Small, S. M. "Cultural variables
       affecting somatic complaints and depressions, " Psy-
       chosomatics, 9:261-266, 1968.

1576) Osmond, Humphry and Hoffer, Abram. "Schizophrenia
       and suicide, " Journal of Schizophrenia, 1(1):54-64,
       1967.

1577) Ostow, Mortimer. "Suicide and social responsibility,"
       Israel Annals of Psychiatry & Related Disciplines, 7
       (2):138-144, Nov. 1969.

1578) Oswald, I. and Rosen, D. H. "Suicide attempts--
       validation of the data, " American Journal of Psychi-
       atry, 128:900-1, Jan. 1972.

1579) Otto, Ulf. "Changes in the behavior of children and
       adolescents preceding suicidal attempts, " Acta Psy-
       chiatrica Scandinavica, 40(4):386-400, 1964.

1580) Otto, Ulf. "Suicidal acts by children and adolescents.
       A follow-up study, " Acta Psychiatrica Scandinavica
       Suppl. , 233:7-123, 1972.

1581) Otto, U. "Suicidal attempts in adolescence and child-
       hood.   States of mental illness and personality vari-
       ables, " Acta Paedopsychiatrica, 31(12):397-411, 1964.

1582) Otto, Ulf. "Suicidal attempts made by children and
       adolescents because of school problems, " Acta Paedi-
       atrica Scandinavica, 54(4):348-356.

1583) Otto, Ulf. "Suicidal attempts made by children, "
       Acta Paediatrica Scandinavica, 55(1):64-72, 1966.

1584) Otto, Ulf. "Suicidal attempts made by psychotic
       children and adolescents, " Acta Paediatrica Scandi-
       navica, 56(40):349-356, 1967.

1585) Otto, Ulf. "Suicidal attempts made during compulsory

military service, " Acta Psychiatrica Scandinavica,
39(2):298-308, 1963.

1586) Paerregard, G. "Is attempted suicide more common
in Denmark than elsewhere?", Danish Medical Bulletin, 10:136-138, 1963.

1587) Paerregaard, G. "Suicide in a 'Welfare State, '" International Anesthesiology Clinics, 4:373-377, 1966.

1588) Paffenbarger, R. S., Jr. and Asnes, D. P. "Chronic
disease in former college students. 3. Precursors of
suicide in early and middle life, " American Journal
of Public Health, 56:1026-1036, 1966.

1589) Paffenbarger, R. S., Jr., King, S. H. and Wing, A.
L. "Chronic disease in former college students. IX.
Characteristics in youth that predispose to suicide and
accidental death in later life, " American Journal of
Public Health, 59(6):900-908, 1969.

1590) Pai, D. N. "Epidemiology of suicide, homicide and
accidents, " Indian Journal of Medical Sciences, 21:
117-122, 1967.

1591) Palola, E. G., Jackson, J. K., and Kelleher, D.
"Defensiveness in alcoholics: measures based on the
Minnesota Multiphasic Personality Inventory," Journal
of Health and Human Behavior, 2:185-189, 1961.

1592) Pandey, R. E. "The suicide problem in India, " International Journal of Social Psychiatry, 14(3):193-200,
1968.

1593) Pao, Ping-Nie. "The syndrome of delicate self-cut-
ting, " British Journal of Medical Psychology, 42:195-
206, 1969.

1594) Parker, Seymour. "Eskimo psychopathology in the
context of Eskimo personality and culture, " American
Anthropologist, 64:76-96, 1962.

1595) Parkin, D. and Stengel, E. "Incidence of suicide
attempts in an urban community, " British Medical
Journal, 2:133-138, 1965.

1596) Parks, F. M. and Wolf, D. "A suicide prevention

center in Chicago, " Illinois Medical Journal, 133:306-310 passim, 1968.

1597) Parr, H. "Suicide by poisoning. 5. Nursing in the general ward for the first 24 hours, " Nursing Times, 61:1112-3 contd. , Aug. 13, 1965.

1598) Patrick, Jerry H. and Overall, John E. "Multivariate analysis of clinical rating profiles of suicidal psychiatric inpatients, " Journal of Projective Techniques & Personality Assessment, 33(2):138-145, 1969.

1599) Pauker, J. D. "Base rates in the prediction of suicide: a note on Appelbaum's and Holzman's 'the color-shading response and suicide, ' " Journal of Projective Techniques, 26:429-430, 1962.

1600) Paul, Louis. "The suicidal self, " Psychotherapy: Theory, Research, and Practice, 7(3):177-180, Fall 1970.

1601) Paykel, Eugene S. and Dienelt, Marcia N. "Suicide attempts following acute depression, " Journal of Nervous and Mental Disease, 153(4):234-243, Oct. 1971.

1602) Paykel, Eugene S. , Klerman, Gerald L. , and Prusoff, Brigitte A. "Treatment setting and clinical depression, " Archives of General Psychiatry, 22(1):11-21, 1970.

1603) Peck, M. L. and Schrut, A. "Suicidal behavior among college students, " HSMHA Health Reports, 86:149-56, Feb. 1971.

1604) Peck, Michael L. "Research and training in prevention of suicide in adolescents and youths, " Bulletin of Suicidology, No. 6:35-40, Spring 1970.

1605) Peck, Michael L. "Suicide motivations in adolescents, " Adolescence, 3(9):109-118, 1968.

1606) Peck, Michael. "The Suicide Prevention Center, " School Health Review, September 1970.

1607) Perlin, Seymour and Schmidt, Chester W. "Fellowship program in suicidology: a first report, " Bulletin of Suicidology, pp. 38-42, Mar. 1969.

1608) Perlstein, A. P. "Suicide in adolescence," New York State Journal of Medicine, 66(23):3017-3020, 1966.

1609) Perr, H. M. "Suicide and the doctor-patient relationship," American Journal of Psychoanalysis, 28(2):177-188, 1968.

1610) Perr, Irwin N. "Liability of hospital and psychiatrist in suicide," American Journal of Psychiatry, 122:631-638, 1965.

1611) Peterson, Robert F. and Peterson, Linda R. "The use of positive reinforcement in the control of self-destructive behavior in a retarded boy," Journal of Experimental Child Psychology, 6(3):351-360, 1968.

1612) Petrovsky, C. C. "Suicide in a general hospital. Launceston General Hospital," Medical Journal of Australia, 2:669-672, 1967.

1613) Philip, Alistair E. "Personality and attempted suicide: traits related to having a prior history of suicidal attempts," Applied Social Studies, 2:35-39, 1970.

1614) Philip, Alistair E. "Traits, attitudes and symptoms in a group of attempted suicides," British Journal of Psychiatry, 116:475-482, 1970.

1615) Philip, Alistair E. and McCulloch, J. W. "Ecological correlates of attempted suicide," Bulletin of the British Psychological Society, 20:23A-24A, 1967.

1616) Philip, Alistair E. and McCulloch, J. W. "Social pathology and personality in attempted suicide," British Journal of Psychiatry, 113(505):1405-1406, 1967. [Abstract]

1617) Philip, Alistair E. and McCulloch, J. W. "Some psychological features of persons who have attempted suicide," British Journal of Psychiatry, 114(515):1299-1300, 1968.

1618) Philip, Alistair E. and McCulloch, J. W. "Test-retest characteristics of a group of attempted suicide patients," Journal of Consulting and Clinical Psychology, 34(2):144-147, 1970.

1619) Phillips, R. H. and Alkan, M.   "Recurrent self-muti-
       lation, " Psychiatric Quarterly, 35:424-431, 1961.

1620) Phillips, R. H. and Muzaffer, A.   "Some aspects of
       self-mutilation in the general population of a large
       psychiatric hospital, " Psychiatric Quarterly, 35:421-
       423, 1961.

1621) Phillipson, B. R.   "Alcoholism, " Royal Society Health
       Journal, 84:267-71, Sept. -Oct. 1964.

1622) "Physician's responsibility for suicide prevention, "
       Journal of the Medical Society of New Jersey, 64:101-
       102, 1967.

1623) Pierce, Albert.   "The economic cycle and the social
       suicide rate, " American Sociological Review, 32(3):
       457-462, 1967.

1624) Pierce, James I.   "Suicide and mortality amongst
       heroin addicts in Britain, " British Journal of Addic-
       tion, 62:391-8, Dec. 1967.

1625) Pitts, Ferris N. and Winokur, George.   "Affective
       disorder: III. Diagnostic correlates and incidence of
       suicide, " Journal of Nervous and Mental Disease,
       137(2):176-181, 1964.

1626) Planansky, K. and Johnston, K.   "The occurrence and
       characteristics of suicidal preoccupation and acts in
       schizophrenia, " Acta Psychiatrica Scandinavica, 47:
       473-83, 1971.

1627) Pokorny, Alex D.   "Characteristics of forty-four
       patients who subsequently committed suicide, " AMA
       Archives of General Psychiatry, 2:314-323, 1960.

1628) Pokorny, Alex D.   "A follow-up study of 618 suicidal
       patients, " American Journal of Psychiatry, 122(10):
       1109-1116, 1966.

1629) Pokorny, Alex D.   "Human violence: a comparison of
       homicide, aggravated assault, suicide, and attempted
       suicide, " Journal of Criminal Law, Criminology, and
       Police Science, 56(4):488-497, 1965.

1630) Pokorny, Alex D.   "Moonphase, suicide and homicide,"

American Journal of Psychiatry, 121:66-67, 1964.

1631) Pokorny, Alex D. "Moon phases and mental hospital admissions, " Journal of Psychiatric Nursing & Mental Health Services, 6(6):325-327, 1968.

1632) Pokorny, Alex D. "Suicide and weather, " Archives of Environmental Health, 13:255-256, 1966.

1633) Pokorny, Alex D. "Suicide in war veterans: rates and methods, " Journal of Nervous and Mental Disease, 144(3):224-229, 1967.

1634) Pokorny, Alex D. "Suicide rates in various psychiatric disorders, " Journal of Nervous and Mental Disease, 139(6):499-506, 1964.

1635) Pokorny, Alex D. "Sunspots, suicide and homicide," Diseases of the Nervous System, 27:347-348, 1966.

1636) Pokorny, Alex D. , Davis, Fred, and Harberson, Wayne. "Suicide, suicide attempts and weather, " American Journal of Psychiatry, 120(4):377-381, 1963.

1637) Pokorny, Alex D. and Mefferd, R. B. "Geomagnetic fluctuations and disturbed behavior, " Journal of Nervous and Mental Disease, 143(2):140-151, 1966.

1638) Pollack, S. "Problems of suicide in medical practice," California Medicine, 89:343, 1958.

1639) Porterfield, Austin L. and Gibbs, Jack P. "Occupational prestige and social mobility of suicides in New Zealand, " American Journal of Sociology, 66:147-152, 1960.

1640) Porterfield, Austin L. "Traffic fatalities, suicide and homicide, " American Sociological Review, 25:897-901, 1960.

1641) "Prediction and prevention of suicide, " Canadian Medical Association Journal, 100:867-868, 1969.

1642) Prendergast, F. G. "Poisonings and prescribing habits, " Medical Journal of Australia, 1:614-5, Mar. 13, 1971.

1643)   Preston, Caroline E.   "Accident-proneness in at-
        tempted suicide and in automobile accident victims, "
        Journal of Consulting Psychology, 28(1):79-82, 1964.

1644)   Pretzel, Paul W.   "Philosophical and ethical consid-
        erations of suicide prevention, " Bulletin of Suicidol-
        ogy, July 1968, pp. 30-38.

1645)   Pretzel, Paul W., et al.   "Psychological autopsy: 1.
        From the files of the Los Angeles Suicide Prevention
        Center, " Bulletin of Suicidology, No. 7:27-35, Fall
        1970.

1646)   Pretzel, Paul W.   "The volunteer clinical worker at
        the Suicide Prevention Center, " Bulletin of Suicid-
        ology, No. 6:29-34, Spring 1970.

1647)   "Preventing suicides, " Medical Officer, 107:320, 1962.

1648)   Primost, N.   "Definition of suicide, " Lancet, 1:326,
        1967.

1649)   Proctor, R. C.   "Psychotheological treatise on death,"
        North Carolina Medical Journal, 28:467-468, 1967.

1650)   Proudfoot, A. T. and Wright, N.   "The physical con-
        sequences of self-poisoning by the elderly, " Geron-
        tological Clin. (Basel), 14:25-31, 1972.

1651)   "Psychological autopsy, No. 1: From the files of the
        Los Angeles Suicide Prevention Center, " Bulletin of
        Suicidology, No. 7:27-33, 1970.

1652)   "Psychotherapy and the danger of suicide, " American
        Journal of Psychotherapy, 15(2):181-183, 1961. [Edi-
        torial]

1653)   Quinney, Richard.   "Suicide, homicide, and economic
        development, " Social Forces, 43(3):401-406, 1965.

1654)   Rabinowitz, S.   "Developmental problems in Catholic
        seminarians, " Psychiatry, 32:107-117, 1969.

1655)   Rachlis, David.   "Suicide and loss adjustment in the
        aging, " Bulletin of Suicidology, No. 7:23-26, Fall
        1970.

1656) Raft, D., Newman, M. and Spencer, R. "Suicide on L-Dopa," Southern Medical Journal, 65:312 passim, March 1972.

1657) Ralph, D. M. "Attempted suicide," Nursing Times, 63:688-690, 1967.

1658) Randall, K. J. "An unusual suicide in a thirteen-year-old boy," Medicine, Science and the Law, 6:45-46, 1966.

1659) Randell, John H. "A nightwatch program in a Suicide Prevention Center," Bulletin of Suicidology, No. 6: 50-55, Spring 1970.

1660) Raphling, David L. "Dreams and suicide attempts," Journal of Nervous & Mental Disease, 151(6):404-410, Dec. 1970.

1661) Rascovsky, A. and Rascovsky, M. "On the genesis of acting out and psychopathic behaviour in Sophocles' Oedipus. Notes on filicide," International Journal of Psycho-Analysis, 49:390-394, 1968.

1662) Ravensborg, M., Hon, R., and Foss, Adeline. "Suicide and natural death in a state hospital population: a comparison of admission complaints, MMPI profiles, and social competence factors," Journal of Consulting & Clinical Psychology, 33(4):466-471, 1969.

1663) Rawlings, J., Jr. "Seattle coroner documents three suicides," Traffic Digest and Review, 12(2):5-6, 1964.

1664) Reay, Donald T. and Hazelwood, Robert R. "Death in military police custody and confinement," Military Medicine, 135(9):765-771, 1970.

1665) "Recent trends in suicide," Statistical Bulletin of the Metropolitan Life Insurance Company, 51:10-11, 1970.

1666) Reeve, A. M. "Death by their own hands--a statistical study of suicides in Nebraska during 1968," Nebraska State Medical Journal, 55:680-683, 1970.

1667) Reich, G. A. and Welke, J. O. "Death due to a pesticide," New England Journal of Medicine, 274: 1432, 1966.

1668) Reich, T. , Clayton, P. J. , and Winokur, G. "Family
       history studies: V. The genetics of mania," American
       Journal of Psychiatry, 125:1358-1369, 1969.

1669) Reiheld, Robert E. "A physician looks at suicide,"
       Ohio's Health, 17(2):30-36, 1965.

1670) Reiss, David. "The suicide six: observations on sui-
       cidal behavior and group function," International
       Journal of Social Psychiatry, 14(3):201-212, 1968.

1671) Resnik, H. L. P. "A community anti-suicidal organi-
       zation," Current Psychiatric Therapy, 4:253-9, 1964.

1672) Resnik, H. L. P. "Psychological resynthesis: a
       clinical approach to the survivors of a death by sui-
       cide," International Psychiatry Clinics, 6:213-224,
       1969.

1673) Resnik, H. L. P. "Suicide attempt by a 10-year-old
       after quadruple amputations," Journal of the American
       Medical Association, 212:1211-1212, 1970.

1674) Resnik, H. L. P. "Suicide prevention and niacin,"
       Journal of the American Medical Association, 208:2164,
       1969.

1675) Resnik, H. L. P. "Urban problems and suicide pre-
       vention," American Journal of Psychiatry, 125(12):
       1723-1724, 1969.

1676) Resnik, H. L. P. and Cantor, J. M. "Suicide and
       aging," Journal of the American Geriatric Society,
       18:152-158, 1970.

1677) Resnik, H. L. P. , Davison, W. T. , Schuyler, D. , and
       Christopher, P. "Videotape confrontation after at-
       tempted suicide," American Journal of Psychiatry,
       130:460-3, Apr. 1973.

1678) Resnik, H. L. P. and Dizmang, Larry H. "Observa-
       tions on suicidal behavior among American Indians,"
       American Journal of Psychiatry, 127(7):882-887, Jan.
       1971.

1679) Resnik, H. L. P. and Dizmang, Larry H. "Suicidal
       behavior among American Indians," Sandoz Psychiatric

Spectator, 6(9):7, 1970. [Abstract]

1680) Resnik, H. L. P., Sullivan, F. J., and Wilkie, C. H.
"Insurability and suicidal behaviors--issues for the
seventies," Trans. Assoc. Life Ins. Med. Dir. Am.,
55:132-48, 1972.

1681) Resnik, H. L. P. and Wittlin, Byron J. "Abortion and
suicidal behaviors: observations on the concept of 'en-
dangering the mental health of the mother,'" Mental
Hygiene, 55(1):10-20, Jan. 1971.

1682) Resnick, J. H. and Kendra, J. M. "Predictive value
of the 'scale for assessing suicide risk' (SASR) with
hospitalized psychiatric patients," Journal of Clinical
Psychology, 29:187-90, Apr. 1973.

1683) Reynolds, David K. and Ohara, Kenshiro. "Morita
therapy and attempted suicide," Anthropology UCLA,
2:45-48, 1969.

1684) Richman, A. and Orlan, R. "Barbiturate mortality as
an index of barbiturate use, Canada, 1950-1963,"
Canadian Medical Association Journal, 93:1336-9, Dec.
25, 1965.

1685) Richman, Joseph and Rosenbaum, Milton. "A clinical
study of the role of hostility and death wishes by the
family and society in suicidal attempts," Israel Annals of Psychiatry & Related Disciplines, 8(3):213-231,
Dec. 1970.

1686) Richman, Joseph and Rosenbaum, Milton. "The family
doctor and the suicidal family," Psychiatry in Medicine, 1(1):27-35, 1970.

1687) Ridout, A. B. "Suicide as a factor in public health,"
Journal of the Royal Institute of Public Health and
Hygiene, 25:115-128, 1962.

1688) Riegel, Klaus F., Riegel, Ruth M., and Meyer, Gün-
ther. "A study of the dropout rates in longitudinal
research on aging and the prediction of death," Journal
of Personality and Social Psychology, 5(3):342-348,1967.

1689) Rieger, W. "Suicide attempts in a federal prison,"
Archives of General Psychiatry, 24:532-5, June 1971.

1690) Rinzler, C. and Shapiro, D. A.   "Wrist-cutting and
       suicide, " Journal of the Mt. Sinai Hospital (New
       York), 35(5):485-488, 1968.

1691) "Rise in frequency of suicide, " Statistical Bulletin,
       Metropolitan Life Insurance Co., 45:8-10, 1964.

1692) Ritson, E. B.   "Suicide amongst alcoholics, " British
       Journal of Medical Psychology, 41(3):235-242, 1968.

1693) Ritz, E., Andrassy, K., Ziegler, M., and Krempien,
       B.   "Suicide by eating bananas, " German Medical
       Monthly, 14:529-530, 1969.

1694) Roberts, Albert R.   "An organizational study of suicide
       prevention agencies in the United States, " Police, 14:
       64-72, May-June 1970.

1695) Roberts, Albert R. and Grau, Joseph J.   "Procedures
       used in crisis intervention by suicide prevention agen-
       cies, " Public Health Reports, 85(8):691-697, 1970.

1696) Roberts, John and Hooper, Douglas.   "The natural his-
       tory of attempted suicide in Bristol, " British Journal
       of Medical Psychology, 42(4):303-312, 1969.

1697) Robin, A. A., Brooke, Eileen M., and Freeman-
       Browne, Dorothy L.   "Some aspects of suicide in psy-
       chiatric patients in Southend, " British Journal of Psy-
       chiatry, 114(511):739-747, 1968.

1698) Robin, A. A. and Freeman-Browne, D. L.   "Drugs
       left at home by psychiatric inpatients, " British Med-
       ical Journal, 3(5615):424-425, 1968.

1699) Robins, Eli.   "Recognition and management of the
       seriously suicidal patient, " Medical Science, 42:78-
       94, 1960.

1700) Robinson, P. I.   "Suicide: causes and prevention,
       statistics and public health significance, " Postgrad-
       uate Medicine, 32:154-159, 1962.

1701) Roche, D. A.   "Suicide and euthanasia, " British
       Medical Journal, 3:50, July 3, 1971.

1702) Roche, L., et al.   "Considerations on the suicidal

behavior of 239 minors admitted to the Poisons Department during a 24-month period, " Lyon Medical,
214:35-37, 1965.

1703) Rogow, Arnold A.   "Private illness and public policy:
the case of James Forrestal and John Winant, "
American Journal of Psychiatry, 125(8):1093-1098, 1969.

1704) Roisum, B. H.   "The family physician and the problem of suicide, " General Practitioner, 33:87-93, 1966.

1705) Ropschitz, D. H.   "Dealing with attempted suicide, "
British Medical Journal, 2:117-118, 1968.

1706) Ropschitz, D. H. and Ovenstone, Irene M.   "A two
years' survey on self-aggressive acts, suicides and
suicidal threats in the Halifax district between 1962
and 1964; Part I: Self-aggressive acts in the Halifax
area, " International Journal of Social Psychiatry, 14
(3):165-177, 1968.

1707) Ropschitz, D. H. and Ovenstone, Irene M.   "A two
years' survey on self-aggressive acts, suicides and
suicidal threats in the Halifax district between 1962
and 1964; Part II: Suicides in the Halifax area 1962-
1964, " International Journal of Social Psychiatry, 14
(3):177-187, 1968.

1708) Rosen, David H.   "The serious suicide attempt: epidemiological and follow-up study of 886 patients, "
American Journal of Psychiatry, 127(6):764-770, Dec.
1970.

1709) Rosen, D. H.   "Suicide rates among psychiatrists, "
Journal of the American Medical Association,   224:
246-7, Apr. 9, 1973.

1710) Rosen, G.   "History in the study of suicide, " Psychol.
Med., 1:267-85, Aug. 1971.

1711) Rosenbaum, Milton and Richman, Joseph.   "Suicide
prevention in the military, " Military Medicine, 135
(6):500-501, 1970.   [Editorial]

1712) Rosenbaum, Milton and Richman, Joseph.   "Suicide:
the role of hostility and death wishes from the family:
a preliminary report, " Proceedings of the 77th An-

nual Convention of the American Psychological Association, 4(Pt. 2):551-552, 1969.

1713) Rosenbaum, Milton and Richman, Joseph. "Suicide:
the role of hostility and death wishes from the family
and significant others," American Journal of Psychiatry, 126(11):1652-1655, May, 1970.

1714) Rosenberg, A. J. and Silver, E. "Suicide, psychiatrists and therapeutic abortion," California Medicine,
102(6):407-411, 1965.

1715) Rosenberg, Mervin. "On accidents and incidents: a
study of self-destruction," Comprehensive Psychiatry,
8(12):108-118, 1967.

1716) Rosenberg, P. H. and Latimer, Ruth. "Suicide attempts by children," Mental Hygiene, 50(3):354-359,
1966.

1717) Rosenthal, Saul H. and Gudeman, Jon E. "The en-
dogenous depressive pattern: an empirical investigation," Archives of General Psychiatry, 16(2):241-249,
1967.

1718) Rosenthal, Saul H. and Reiss, D. "Suicide and uri-
nary tract infections," American Journal of Psychiatry,
122:574-576, 1965.

1719) Ross, M. "The practical recognition of depressive
and suicidal states," Annals of Internal Medicine, 64
(5):1079-1086, 1966.

1720) Ross, M. "The presuicidal patient: recognition and
management," Southern Medical Journal, 60:1094-
1098, 1967.

1721) Ross, Mathew. "Death at an early age," Canada's
Mental Health, 18(6):7-10, 1970.

1722) Ross, Mathew. "Suicide among college students,"
American Journal of Psychiatry, 126(2):220-225, 1969.

1723) Ross, Mathew. "Suicide among physicians," Psychiatry in Medicine, 2(3):189-198, July, 1971.

1724) Roth, M. "Cerebral disease and mental disorders of

old age as causes of antisocial behaviour, " International Psychiatry Clinics, 5:35-58, 1968.

1725) Roth, M.   "Suicide and the aged, " Canada's Mental
Health, 2, 1963.

1726) Rotov, Michail.   "Death by suicide in the hospital: an
analysis of 20 therapeutic failures, " American Journal
of Psychotherapy, 25(2):216-227, 1970.

1727) Rubinstein, D.   "Critical incidents in the context of
family therapy.   Critical incident no. 5, " International
Psychiatry Clinics, 7:309-326, 1970.

1728) Rudestan, K. E.   "Stockholm and Los Angeles--a
cross-cultural study of the communication of suicidal
intent, " Journal of Consult. Clin. Psychology, 36:82-
90, Feb. 1971.

1729) Rudin, S. A.   "National motives predict psychogenic
death rates 25 years later, " Science, 160(3830):901-
903, 1968.

1730) Rupp, J. C.   "Suicidal garrotting and manual self-
strangulation, " Journal of Forensic Sciences, 15:71-
77, 1970.

1731) Rushing, William A.   "Alcoholism and suicide rates
by status set and occupation, " Quarterly Journal of
Studies on Alcohol, 29(2):399-412, 1968.

1732) Rushing, William A.   "Deviance, interpersonal relations and suicide, " Human Relations, 22(1):61-76,
1969.

1733) Rushing, William A.   "Income, unemployment and
suicide: an occupational study, " Sociological Quarterly,
9(4):493-503, 1968.

1734) Rushing, William A.   "Suicide and the interaction of
alcoholism (liver cirrhosis) with the social situation,"
Quarterly Journal of Studies on Alcohol, 30(1-A):93-
103, 1969.

1735) Russell, Harold E. , Conroy, Robert W. , and Werner,
John J.   "A study of suicidal behavior in the military
setting, " Military Medicine, 136(6):549-552, June 1971.

1736) Ryan, Hewitt F., et al. "Increase in suicidal thoughts
       and tendencies: association with diazepam therapy,"
       Journal of the American Medical Association, 203(13):
       1137-1139, 1968.

1737) Ryle, Anthony. "A repertory grid study of the mean-
       ing and consequences of a suicidal act," British
       Journal of Psychiatry, 113(505):1393-1403, 1967.

1738) Sabbath, Joseph C. "Parental collusion in adolescent
       suicidal behavior," Sandoz Psychiatric Spectator, 5(9):
       17-18, 1969. [Abstract]

1739) Sabbath, Joseph C. "The role of the parents in ado-
       lescent suicidal behavior," Acta Paedopsychiatrica,
       38(7-8):211-220, July 1971.

1740) Sabbath, Joseph C. "The suicidal adolescent: the ex-
       pendable child," Journal of the American Academy of
       Child Psychiatry, 8(2):272-285, 1969.

1741) Saghir, Marcel T., Robins, Eli, Walbran, Bonnie, and
       Gentry, Kathye A. "Homosexuality: IV. Psychiatric
       disorders and disability in the female homosexual,"
       American Journal of Psychiatry, 127(2):147-154, 1970.

1742) Sainsbury, P. "The social relations of suicide. The
       value of a combined epidemiological and case study
       approach," Social Science Medicine, 6:189-98, Apr.
       1972.

1743) Sainsbury, P. "Suicide and depression," British
       Journal of Psychiatry, Spec. pub. No. 2, 1968, pp. 1-
       13.

1744) Sainsbury, P. "Suicide in later life," Gerontologia
       Clinica (Basel), 4(3):161-170, 1962.

1745) Sainsbury, P. "Suicide in old age," Proceedings of
       the Royal Society of Medicine, 54(4):266-268, 1961.

1746) Sainsbury, P. and Barraclough, B. "Differences be-
       tween suicide rates," Nature (London), 220:1252, 1968.

1747) Saint, E. G. "Suicide in Australia," Medical Journal
       of Australia, 52(1):911-920, 1965.

1748) Salako, L. A. "Self-poisoning by drugs. A survey of admissions in Nigeria," Tropical and Geographical Medicine, 22:397-402, 1970.

1749) Salmon, J. H. "Hanging in childhood," Journal of the American Medical Association, 201:204-205, 1967.

1750) Sanborn, Donald E., Casey, Thomas, M., and Niswander, G. D. "Drug abusers, suicide attempters, and the MMPI," Diseases of the Nervous System, 32: 183-7, Mar. 1971.

1751) Sanborn, Donald E., Casey, Thomas M., and Niswander, G. D. "Monthly patterns of suicide and mental illness," Diseases of the Nervous System, 36 (8):551-552, 1969.

1752) Sanborn, Donald E., Casey, Thomas M., and Niswander, G. D. "Suicide: seasonal patterns and related variables," Diseases of the Nervous System, 31(10):702-704, Oct. 1970.

1753) Sanborn, Donald E., Niswander, G. Donald, and Casey, Thomas M. "The family physician and suicide prevention," American Family Physician/GP, 1(3):75-78, 1970.

1754) Sanborn, Donald E., Sanborn, Charlotte J., and Niswander, G. D. "Role of education in reporting attempted suicide," Diseases of the Nervous System, 32(7):467-471, July 1971.

1755) Sapolsky, A. "An indicator of suicidal ideation on the Rorschach test," Journal of Projective Techniques & Personality Assessment, 27(3):332-335, 1963.

1756) Sarwer-Foner, G. J. "Depression and suicide. On some particularly high risk suicidal patients," Diseases of the Nervous System, 30 (Suppl.):104-110, 1969.

1757) Sathyavathi, K. "Male and female suicides in Bangalore: a longitudinal study over a ten-year period," Transactions of All-India Institute of Mental Health, No. 10:105-108, Dec. 1970.

1758) Sathyavathi, K. "A study of attempted suicides in general population of Bangalore through police records,"

Transactions of All-India Institute of Mental Health,
No. 10:99-103, Dec. 1970.

1759) Satterfield, J.   "Successful suicide in a patient with a
       conversion reaction, " American Journal of Psychiatry,
       118:1047, 1962.

1760) Sawyer, John B.   "An incidence study of military per-
       sonnel engaging in suicidal behavior, " Military Medi-
       cine, 134(12):1440-1444, 1969.

1761) Sawyer, John B.   "The suicidal patient in the general
       ward, " Nursing Times, 58:1587-1589, 1962.

1762) Saylor, L. F.   "Suicide prevention--the physician's
       role, " California Medicine, 112:102-103, 1970.

1763) Schechter, M. D. and Sternlof, R. E.   "Suicide in
       adolescents, " Postgraduate Medicine, 47:220-223, 1970.

1764) Schneer, H. I., Kay, P., and Brozousky, M.   "Events
       and conscious ideation leading to suicidal behavior in
       adolescence, " Psychiatric Quarterly, 35:507-15, 1961.

1765) Schneer, H. I.   "Phase developmental approach to sui-
       cidal behavior, " American Journal of Orthopsychiatry,
       39:317-318, 1969.

1766) Schonfeld, William A.   "Socioeconomic affluence as a
       factor, " New York State Journal of Medicine, 67(14):
       1981-1990, 1967.

1767) Schroeder, O. C., Jr.   "Suicide--a dilemma for medi-
       cine, law and society, " Postgraduate Medicine, 53:
       55-7, Jan. 1973.

1768) Schrut, Albert.   "Some typical patterns in the behavior
       and background of adolescent girls who attempt sui-
       cide, " American Journal of Psychiatry, 125:69-74,
       July 1968.

1769) Schrut, Albert.   "Suicidal adolescents and children, "
       Journal of the American Medical Association, 188(13):
       1103-1107, 1964.

1770) Schrut, Albert and Michels, Toni.   "Adolescent girls
       who attempt suicide: comments on treatment, " Ameri-

can Journal of Psychotherapy, 23(2):243-251, 1969.

1771) Schuckit, Marc. "The alcoholic woman: a literature review, " Psychiatry in Medicine, 3(1):37-43, Jan. 1972.

1772) Schulman, Robert. "Suicide prevention and the volunteer, " Menninger Perspective, 3(3):15-18, Apr. 1972.

1773) Schwab, J. J., Bialow, M. R., and Holzer, C. E. "A comparison of two rating scales for depression, " Journal of Clinical Psychology, 23(1):94-96, 1967.

1774) Schwab, J. J., Warheit, G. J., and Holzer, C. E. 3rd. "Suicidal ideation and behavior in a general population, " Diseases of the Nervous System, 33:745-8, Nov. 1972.

1775) Seagull, Arthur A. "Two cases illustrating different approaches to the treatment of a suicide threat, " Psychotherapy: Theory, Research and Practice, 4(1): 41-43, 1967.

1776) Seale, A. L. and McNichol, R. W. "Treatment of the suicidal patient: community psychiatry approach, " Southern Medical Journal, 58(9):1159-1162, 1965.

1777) Segal, Bernard E. "Comment on Jack Gibb's 'Marital status and suicide, ' " American Journal of Sociology, 75:405-411, 1969.

1778) Segal, Bernard E. "Suicide and middle age, " Sociological Symposium, No. 3:131-140, Fall, 1969.

1779) Segal, Bernard E. and Humphrey, John. "A comparison of suicide victims and suicide attempters in New Hampshire, " Diseases of the Nervous System, 31(12): 830-838, Dec. 1970.

1780) Seiden, Richard H. "The Bridge and its suicides, " California's Health, 27(7):1-2 passim, 1970.

1781) Seiden, Richard H. "Campus tragedy: a study of student suicide, " Journal of Abnormal Psychology, 71(6):389-399, 1966.

1782) Seiden, Richard H. "The problem of suicide on col-

lege campuses, " Journal of School Health, 41:243-8,
May 1971.

1783) Seiden, Richard H. "Suicide capital? A study of the
San Francisco suicide rate, " Bulletin of Suicidology,
pp. 1-10, Dec. 1967.

1784) Seiden, Richard H. "We're driving young blacks to
suicide, " Psychology Today, 4(3):24-28, Aug. 1970.

1785) Seiden, Richard H. "Why are suicides of young blacks
increasing?" HSMHA Health Reports, 87:3-8, Jan.
1972.

1786) Seitz, Frank C. "A behavior modification approach to
depression: a case study, " Psychology, 8(1):58-63,
Feb. 1971.

1787) "Self-poisoning, " British Medical Journal, 5474:1323-
1324, 1965.

1788) Selzer, M. L., Payne, C. E., Westervelt, F. H.,
and Quinn, J. "Automobile accidents as an expression
of psychopathology in an alcoholic population, " Quarterly Journal of Studies on Alcohol, 38:505-516, 1967.

1789) Selzer, Melvin L. and Payne, Charles E. "Automobile accidents, suicide and unconscious motivation, "
American Journal of Psychiatry, 119(3):237-240, 1962.

1790) Senay, Edward C. "Therapeutic abortion: clinical
aspects, " Archives of General Psychiatry, 23(5):408-
415, 1970.

1791) Sendbuehler, J. M. "Attempted suicide--a description
of the pre and post suicidal states, " Canadian Psychiatric Association Journal, 18:113-6, April 1973.

1792) Sendbuehler, J. M. "Attempted suicide: facts and
theories, " Diseases of the Nervous System, 30
(Suppl.):111-114, 1969.

1793) Sendbuehler, J. M., Bernstein, J., and Nemeth, G.
"Attempted suicide and social class. I, " Canadian
Psychiatric Association Journal, Suppl. 2-SS185, 1972.

1794) Sendbuehler, J. M., Bland, B. A., and Nemeth, G.

"Attempted suicide: I. Some statistical and psychiatric parameters, " Diseases of the Nervous System, 31 (11, Suppl.):59-68, Nov. 1970.

1795) Sen Gupta, B. K. "Studies on 101 cases of death due to hanging, " Journal of the Indian Medical Association, 45:135-140, 1965.

1796) Senseman, L. A. "Attempted suicide in adolescents. Suicide prevention center in Rhode Island is an urgent need, " Rhode Island Medical Journal, 52(8):449-451, 1969.

1797) Shah, J. H. "Causes and prevention of suicides, " Indian Journal of Social Work, 21(2):167-176, 1960.

1798) Shanholtz, M. I. "Suicide in Virginia and the nation," Virginia Medical Monthly, 95(9):583-584, 1968.

1799) Shaw, Charles R. and Schelkun, Ruth F. "Suicidal behavior in children, " Psychiatry, 28(2):157-169, 1965.

1800) Shaw, David M. , Frizel, Doris, Camps, Francis E. , and White, Stuart. "Brain electrolytes in depressive and alcoholic suicides, " British Journal of Psychiatry, 115(518):69-79, 1969.

1801) Shein, Harvey M. and Stone, Alan A. "Monitoring and treatment of suicidal potential within the context of psychotherapy, " Comprehensive Psychiatry, 10(1):59-70, 1969.

1802) Shein, Harvey M. and Stone, Alan A. "Psychotherapy designed to detect and treat suicidal potential, " American Journal of Psychiatry, 125(9):1247-1251, 1969.

1803) Shevrin, Howard, Voth, Harold, and Gardner, Riley W. "Research perspectives on treatment and diagnosis, " Bulletin of the Menninger Clinic, 35(6):461-478, Nov. 1971.

1804) Shibata, Joseph I. "Limits of application of autogenic training to schizophrenia and selection of the patients," American Journal of Clinical Hypnosis, 11(2):99-100, 1968.

1805) Shneidman, Edwin S. "Classifications of suicidal

phenomena, " Bulletin of Suicidology, July 1968, pp. 1-9.

1806) Shneidman, Edwin S. "Orientations toward death: a vital aspect of the study of lives, " International Journal of Psychiatry, 2(2):167-190, 1966.

1807) Shneidman, Edwin S. "Orientation toward cessation, " Journal of Forensic Sciences, 13:33-45, 1968.

1808) Shneidman, Edwin S. "Precursors of suicide, " Medical Insight, Nov. 1969, pp. 41-47.

1809) Shneidman, Edwin S. "Preventing suicide, " American Journal of Nursing, 65(5):111-116, 1965.

1810) Shneidman, Edwin S. "Preventing suicide, " Bulletin of Suicidology, pp. 19-25, Dec. 1968.

1811) Shneidman, Edwin S. "The role of psychotherapy in the treatment of suicidal persons. On the deromanticization of death, " American Journal of Psychotherapy, 25:4-17, Jan. 1971.

1812) Shneidman, Edwin S. "Some current developments in suicide prevention, " Bulletin of Suicidology, Dec. 1967, pp. 31-34.

1813) Shneidman, Edwin S. "Some logical psychological and ecological environments of suicide, " California's Health, 17:193-196, 1960.

1814) Shneidman, Edwin S. "Some reflections on death and suicide, " Folia Psychiatrica et Neurological Japonica, 19:317-325, 1965.

1815) Shneidman, Edwin S. (ed.). "Special issue commemorating the tenth anniversary of the Los Angeles Suicide Prevention Center, " Bulletin of Suicidology, Spring 1970, pp. 1-65.

1816) Shneidman, Edwin S. "Suicide among adolescents, " California School Health, 2(3):1-4, 1966a.

1817) Shneidman, Edwin S. "Suicide, lethality, and the psychological autopsy, " International Psychiatry Clinics, 6(2):225-280, 1969.

1818)   Shneidman, Edwin S.   "Suicide, sleep and death: some
        possible interrelations among cessation, interruption,
        and continuous phenomena, " Journal of Consulting
        Psychology, 28(2):95-106, 1964.

1819)   Shneidman, Edwin S. and Farberow, N. L.   "The Los
        Angeles Suicide Prevention Center: a demonstration of
        public health feasibilities, " American Journal of Pub-
        lic Health, 55(1):21-26, 1965.

1820)   Shneidman, Edwin S. , Farberow, Norman L. , and
        Litman, Robert E.   "Comprehensive suicide prevention
        program, " California Mental Health Research Digest,
        3(1):37, 1965.

1821)   Shocket, B. R.   "Attempted suicide: experience in a
        general hospital emergency service, " Maryland State
        Medical Journal, 13(3):107-112, 1964.

1822)   Shocket, B. R.   "Recognizing the suicidal patient, "
        Maryland State Medical Journal, 18(9):65-67, 1969.

1823)   Shore, James H.   "Suicide and suicide attempts among
        Indians of the Pacific Northwest, " International Journal
        of Social Psychiatry, 18:91-6, Summer 1972.

1824)   Shore, James H. , Bopp, John F. , Dawes, James W. ,
        and Waller, Thelma R.   "A suicidal prevention center
        on an Indian reservation, " American Journal of Psy-
        chiatry, 128(9):1088-1091, Mar. 1972.

1825)   Short, C. A.   "Attempted suicide, " Nursing Times,
        66:1067-1068, 1970.

1826)   Shubin, Herbert and Weil, Max H.   "The mechanism
        of shock following suicidal doses of barbiturates, nar-
        cotics and tranquilizer drugs, with observations on the
        effects of treatment, " American Journal of Medicine,
        38:853-863, 1965.

1827)   Siddiqui, J. Y. , Fitz, A. E. , Lawton, R. L. , and
        Kirkendall, W. M.   "Causes of death in patients re-
        ceiving long-term hemodialysis, " Journal of the
        American Medical Association, 212:1350-1354, 1970.

1828)   Sifneos, Peter E.   "The doctor/patient relationship in
        manipulative suicide: a common psychosomatic dis-

ease, " Psychotherapist & Psychosomatics, 18(1-6):
40-46, 1970.

1829)   Sifneos, Peter E.   "Manipulative suicide, " Psychiatric
        Quarterly, 40(3):525-537, 1966.

1830)   Sifneos, Peter E.   "Wishes for life and death in some
        patients who attempted suicide, " Mental Hygiene, 46
        (4):543-552, 1962.

1831)   Silver, M. A. , Bohnert, M. , Beck, A. T. , and
        Marcus, D.   "Relation of depression of attempted sui-
        cide and seriousness of intent, " Archives of General
        Psychiatry, 25:573-6, Dec. 1971.

1832)   Simon, Julian.   "The effect of income on the suicide
        rate: a paradox resolved, " American Journal of So-
        ciology, 74(3):302-303, 1968.

1833)   Simon, Werner and Lumry, Gayle K.   "Alcoholism and
        drug addiction among physicians--chronic self-destruc-
        tion?", Bulletin of Suicidology, July 1969, pp. 11-14.

1834)   Simon, Werner.   "The suicidal physician, " Minnesota
        Medicine, 55:729-32, Aug. 1972.

1835)   Simon, Werner and Lumry, Gayle K.   "Suicide among
        physician-patients, " Journal of Nervous and Mental
        Disease, 147(2):105-112, 1968.

1836)   Simon, Werner and Lumry, Gayle K.   "Suicide of the
        spouse as a divorce substitute, " Diseases of the
        Nervous System, 31(9):608-612, Sept. 1970.

1837)   Simms, L. and Ball, M. J.   "Suicide among univer-
        sity students, " Journal of the American College Health
        Associations, 21:336-8, Apr. 1973.

1838)   Singer, Richard G. and Blumenthal, Irving J.   "Suicide
        clues in psychotic patients, " Mental Hygiene, 53(3):
        346-350, 1969.

1839)   Singh, A. N. and Brown, J. H.   "Suicide prevention.
        Review and evaluation, " Canadian Psychiatric Asso-
        ciation Journal, 18:117-21, Apr. 1973.

1840)   Slaikeu, K. , Lester, D. , and Tulkin, S. R.   "Show

versus no show--a comparison of referral calls to a
suicide prevention and crisis service, " Journal of
Consulting Clinical Psychology, 40:481-6, June 1973.

1841) Sletten, I. W. and Evenson, R. C. "The suicidal
patient, " Missouri Medicine, 69:864-7, Nov. 1972.

1842) Slorach, J. "Suicide as catharsis, " Lancet, 2:971,
Nov. 4, 1972.

1843) Small, I. F. and DeArmond, M. M. "The clinical
assessment and management of the potential suicide, "
Journal of the Indiana Medical Association, 59(11):1301-
1306, 1966.

1844) Small, Joyce G. "The six per second spike and wave:
a psychiatric population study, " Electroencephalography
& Clinical Neurophysiology, 24(6):561-568, 1968.

1845) Smith, A. J. "Self-poisoning with drugs--a worsening
situation, " British Medical Journal, 4:157-9, Oct. 21,
1972.

1846) Sokolow, Lloyd, et al. "The effect of distribution of
information about crisis intervention services on num-
ber of calls to a suicide prevention center, " Crisis
Intervention, 3(4):91-92, 1971.

1847) Solomon, P. "The burden of responsibility in suicide
and homicide, " Journal of the American Medical Association, 199:321-324, 1967.

1848) Soreff, S. "The suicidal patient. Some considerations
in evaluation and management, " Journal of Maine
Medical Association, 63:225-6, Oct. 1972.

1849) Sorrel, W. E. "Violence toward self. A study in
suicide, " Diseases of the Nervous System, 33:501-8,
Aug. 1972.

1850) Spalt, Lee and Weisbuch, Jonathan B. "Suicide: an
epidemiologic study, " Diseases of the Nervous System,
33(1):23-29, Jan. 1972.

1851) Spark, Derek and Papp, Peggy. "Critical incidents in
the context of family therapy. Critical incident no. 6,"
International Psychiatry Clinics, 7(4):327-334, 1970.

1852)   Spiegel, Donald. "Autonomic reactivity in relation to
        the affective meaning of suicide, " Journal of Clinical
        Psychology, 24(4):359-362, 1969.

1853)   Spiegel, Donald, Keith-Spiegel, Patricia, Abrahams,
        Joel, and Kranitz, Lionel. "Humor and suicide: fa-
        vorite jokes of suicidal patients, " Journal of Consult-
        ing and Clinical Psychiatry, 33(4):504-505, 1969.

1854)   Spiegel, Donald E. and Neuringer, Charles. "Role of
        dread in suicidal behavior, " Journal of Abnormal So-
        cial Psychology, 66(5):507-511, 1963.

1855)   Spiers, P. S. "Seasonal variation in suicide rates, "
        Lancet, 2:428-9, Aug. 26, 1972.

1856)   Stajduhar-Carlc, Z. "Acute phenol poisoning. Singu-
        lar findings in a lethal case, " Journal of Forensic
        Medicine, 15:41-42, 1968.

1857)   Stanley, E. James and Barter, James T. "Adolescent
        suicidal behavior, " American Journal of Orthopsy-
        chiatry, 40(1):87-96, Jan. 1970.

1858)   Stanley, W. J. "Attempted suicide and suicidal ges-
        tures, " British Journal of Preventive and Social Med-
        icine, 23(3):190-195, 1969.

1859)   Starer, E. "The effects of two simultaneous cognitive
        and affective stimuli on a group of chronic schizo-
        phrenic patients with suicidal ideation, " Journal of
        Clinical Psychology, 16(3):341-343, 1960.

1860)   Stein, Marvin, Glasberg, H. Mark, and Levy, Michael.
        "Childhood separation experiences and suicide attempts,"
        Sandoz Psychiatric Spectator, 5(9):5, 7, 1969.
        [Abstract]

1861)   Steinberg, H. R., Green, R., and Durell, J. "De-
        pression occurring during the course of recovery from
        schizophrenic symptoms, " American Journal of Psy-
        chiatry, 124(5):699-702, 1967.

1862)   Steinhilber, R. M. "Suicide, " Minnesota Medicine,
        51:1205, 1968.

1863)   Stenback, Asser and Blumenthal, M. "Relationship of alcoholism, hypochondria and attempted suicide, " Acta Psychiatrica Scandinavica, 40(2):133-140, 1964.

1864) Stenback, Asser, Achté, K. A., and Rimón, R. H. "Physical disease, hypochondria, and alcohol addiction in suicides committed by mental hospital patients, " British Journal of Psychiatry, 111(479):933-937, 1965.

1865) Stengel, Erwin. "Attempted suicide, " British Journal of Psychiatry, 116:237-238, 1970.

1866) Stengel, Erwin. "Attempted suicide: its management in the general hospital, " Lancet, Feb. 2, 1963, pp. 233-235.

1867) Stengel, Erwin. "The complexity of motivations to suicidal attempts, " Journal of Mental Science, 106 (445):1388-1393, 1960.

1868) Stengel, Erwin. "Old and new trends in suicide research, " British Journal of Medical Psychology, 33: 283-286, 1960.

1869) Stengel, Erwin. "Recent progress in suicide research and prevention, " Israel Annals of Psychiatry & Related Disciplines, 7(2):127-137, 1969.

1870) Stengel, E. "Recent research into suicide and attempted suicide, " American Journal of Psychiatry, 118:725-727, 1962.

1871) Stengel, Erwin. "Self-destructiveness and self-preservation, " Bulletin of the Menninger Clinic, 26(1):7-17, 1962.

1872) Stengel, Erwin. "Some unexplored aspects of suicide and attempted suicide, " Comprehensive Psychiatry, 1(2):71-79, 1960.

1873) Stengel, Erwin. "The suicidal patient in the general hospital, " Nursing Times, 59(35):1083-1084, 1963.

1874) Stengel, Erwin. "Suicide and attempted suicide, " New Society, 2(45):7-9, 1963.

1875) Stengel, E. "Suicide and social isolation, " Twentieth Century, 173:24-36, 1964.

1876) Stengel, Erwin. "Suicide by poisoning. 6. Some con-
       troversial aspects of attempted suicide," Nursing
       Times, 61:1143-4, Aug. 20, 1965.

1877) Stengel, Erwin. "The suicide problem in general
       practice," Medical World, 99(1):21-24, 1963.

1878) Stengel, Erwin. "The suicide problem up to date,"
       Current Medicine and Drugs, 6:3-17, 1966.

1879) Stengel, Erwin and Cook, Nancy G. "Contrasting sui-
       cide rates in industrial communities," Journal of
       Mental Science, 107:1011-1019, 1961.

1880) Stern, Roy. "Standard operating procedures and insti-
       tutionalization on the psychiatric unit," American
       Journal of Orthopsychiatry, 40(5):744-750, 1970.

1881) Sternlicht, Manny, Pustel, Gabriel, and Deutsch,
       Martin R. "Suicidal tendencies among institutionalized
       retardates," Journal of Mental Subnormality, 16(31,
       Pt. 2):93-102, Dec. 1970.

1882) Stevens, Barbara J. "A phenomenological approach to
       understanding suicidal behavior," Journal of Psychi-
       atric Nursing & Mental Health Services, 9(5):33-35,
       Sept. 1971.

1883) Stevenson, E. K., Hudgens, R. W., Held, C. P.,
       Meredith, C. H., Hendrix, M. E., and Carr, D. L.
       "Suicidal communication by adolescents. Study of two
       matched groups of 60 teenagers," Diseases of the
       Nervous System, 33:112-22, Feb. 1972.

1884) Stewart, I. "Suicide. The influence of organic dis-
       ease," Lancet, 2:919, 1960.

1885) Stoller, Robert J. and Estes, Floyd M. "Suicides in
       medical and surgical wards of general hospitals,"
       Journal of Chronic Diseases, 12:592-599, 1960.

1886) Stone, Alan A. "Suicide precipitated by psychotherapy:
       a clinical contribution," American Journal of Psycho-
       therapy, 25(1):18-26, Jan. 1971.

1887) Stone, Alan A. "A syndrome of serious suicidal in-
       tent," Archives of General Psychiatry, 3:331-3, 1960.

1888) Stone, Alan A. "Treatment of the hospitalized suicidal patient," Current Psychiatric Therapies, 9:209-217, 1969.

1889) Stone, Alan A. and Shein, H. M. "Psychotherapy of the hospitalized suicidal patient," American Journal of Psychotherapy, 22:15-25, 1968.

1890) Strahm, W. J. "Clues to suicide," Journal of the Kansas Medical Society, 64:6-8, 1963.

1891) Strange, Robert E. and Brown, Dudley E. "Home from the war: a study of psychiatric problems in Viet Nam returnees," American Journal of Psychiatry, 127 (4):488-492, 1970.

1892) Stross, Lawrence. "Impulse-defense implications in a case of amnesia," International Journal of Clinical and Experimental Hypnosis, 14(2):89-103, 1966.

1893) Sudak, Howard S., Hall, S. Richard, and Sawyer, John B. "The suicide prevention center as a coordinating facility," Bulletin of Suicidology, No. 7:17-22, 1970.

1894) Sudnow, David. "Dead on arrival," New Society, 11 (280):187-189, 1968.

1895) "Suicidal attempts and poisonings involving infants," New York State Journal of Medicine, 60:2145-2149, 1960.

1896) "Suicidal psychiatrists," Medical Journal of Australia, 2(19):858, 1968.

1897) "Suicide," Lancet, 1:508, 1969.

1898) "Suicide [1951-1959]," Epidemiological and Vital Statistics Report, 14:144-73, Nov. 1961.

1899) "Suicide: a neglected problem," WHO Chronicle, 14: 196-198, 1960.

1900) "Suicide among the Blackfeet Indians," Bulletin of Suicidology, No. 7:42-43, Fall 1970.

1901) "Suicide among doctors," British Medical Journal, 1:789-790, 1964.

1902) "Suicide and its prevention," WHO Chronicle, 22:489-491, 1968.

1903) "Suicide and social decline," British Medical Journal, 5286:1194-1195, 1962.

1904) "Suicide and student stress," Moderator, 5(4):8-15, 1966.

1905) "Suicide and suicidal attempts in children and adolescents," Lancet, 7364:847-849, 1964.

1906) "Suicide and the Fatal Accidents Act," British Medical Journal, 5198:610, 1960.

1907) "Suicide and the press," Lancet, 2:731-2, Oct. 4, 1969.

1908) "Suicide for surcease," Journal of the Medical Association of Alabama, 34:177-9, Dec. 1964.

1909) "Suicide patterns in the elderly," Geriatrics, 22:68, 1967.

1910) "Suicide prevention," British Medical Journal, 4 (5682):513-514, Nov. 1969.

1911) "Suicide statistics," Medico-Legal Journal, 37:49-50, 1969.

1912) "Suicide: the patient's viewpoint," Nursing Times, 61:1700, 1965.

1913) "Suicides and the weather," Journal of the American Medical Association, 195:955, 1966. [Editorial]

1914) "Suicides in Italy and abroad: trend over the past ten years," Italian Affairs, 11:3845-8, Mar./Apr. 1962.

1915) Swanson, D. W. "Suicide in identical twins," American Journal of Psychiatry, 116(1):934-935, 1960.

1916) Swanson, W. C. "Anti-suicide service in New Orleans," Journal of Louisiana State Medical Society, 123:83-90, March 1971.

1917) Swartzburg, M., Schwartz, A. H., Lieb, J., and Slaky, A. E. "Dual suicide in homosexuals," Journal

of Nervous and Mental Disorders, 155:125-30, Aug.
1972.

1918) Swenson, David D. "First Annual Conference on Suicidology, " Bulletin of Suicidology, Dec.1968, pp. 46-48.

1919) Swenson, David D. "Western regional seminar on suicide prevention, " Bulletin of Suicidology, Dec. 1967,
pp. 41-42.

1920) "Symposium on impulsive self-mutilation: discussion, "
British Journal of Medical Psychology, 42:223-229, 1969.

1921) Szabo, D. "Sociological aspects of suicide, " Canadian
Nurse, 62:33-38, 1966.

1922) Tabachnick, Norman, et al. "Comparative psychiatric
study of accidental and suicidal death, " Archives of
General Psychiatry, 41(1):60-68, 1966.

1923) Tabachnick, Norman. "Countertransference crisis in
suicidal attempts, " Archives of General Psychiatry,
4:572-578, 1961.

1924) Tabachnick, Norman. "The crisis treatment of suicide, " California Medicine, 112:1-8, 1970.

1925) Tabachnick, Norman. "The crisis treatment of suicide, " Northwest Medicine, 69:1-8, 1970.

1926) Tabachnick, Norman. "Interpersonal relations in suicidal attempts: some psychodynamic considerations and
implications for treatment, " Archives of General Psychiatry, 4:16-21, 1961.

1927) Tabachnick, Norman. "The psychoanalyst as accident
investigator, " Behavioral Research in Highway Safety,
1(1):18-25, 1970.

1928) Tabachnick, Norman. "Sex and suicide, " Medical Aspects of Human Sexuality, 4(5):6p., 1970.

1929) Tabachnick, Norman. "A theoretical approach to
'accident' research, " Bulletin of Suicidology, No. 6:
18-23, 1970.

1930) Tabachnick, Norman and Klugman, David. "Anonymous

suicidal telephone calls: a research critique, " Psychiatry, Washington, D. C., 33(4):526-532, Nov. 1970.

1931) Tabachnick, Norman and Klugman, David J. "No
       name: a study of anonymous suicidal telephone calls, "
       Psychiatry, 28(1):79-87, 1965.

1932) Tabachnick, N. D. and Klugman, D. J. "Suicide re-
       search and the death instinct, " Yale Scientific Maga-
       zine, 6:12-15, 1967.

1933) Tabachnick, Norman. "Theories of self-destruction, "
       American Journal of Psychoanalysis, 32:53-61, 1972.

1934) Tallent, N., Kennedy, G. F., and Hurley, W. T. "A
       program for suicidal patients, " American Journal of
       Nursing, 66(9):2014-2016, 1966.

1935) Tarbox, R. "A note on M. D. Faber's essay, 'Suicide
       and the "Ajax" of Sophocles, '" Psychoanalytic Review,
       56:453-460, 1969.

1936) Tarrant, B. "Report on the crisis intervention and
       suicide prevention centre for Greater Vancouver, "
       Canadian Journal of Public Health, 61:66-67, 1970.

1937) Tarrant, B. "A suicide prevention center in Van-
       couver, " Canada's Mental Health, 18:3-4, 11-14, 1970.

1938) Tate, B. G. and Baroff, G. S. "Aversive control of
       self-injurious behavior in a psychotic boy, " Behaviour
       Research and Therapy, 4(4):281-287, 1966.

1939) Tausk, V. and Kanzer, M. "Victor Tausk, the cre-
       ativity and suicide of a psychoanalyst, " Psychoanal.
       Quarterly, 41:556-84, 1972.

1940) Tayal, S. S. "The communication of suicidal ideation
       in art therapy, " Psychiatry & Art, 2:205-209, 1969.

1941) Taylor, D. J. E., Hart, F. D., and Burley, D. "Sui-
       cide in South London. An analysis of the admissions
       for attempted suicide in one medical unit of a general
       hospital, " Practitioner, 192:251-256, 1964.

1942) Taylor, Dale. "Expressive emphasis in the treatment
       of intropunitive behavior, " Journal of Music Therapy,

6(2):41-43, 1969.

1943) Taylor, Graham C. "Self-destruction and self-crea-
       tion: multiple commitments to the irrelevant, " Hu-
       manitas, 6(1):69-79, 1970.

1944) Teele, James E. "Suicidal behavior, assaultiveness,
       and socialization principles, " Social Forces, 43(4):
       510-518, 1965.

1945) Teicher, Joseph D. "Children and adolescents who
       attempt suicide, " Pediatric Clinics of North America,
       17:687-696, 1970.

1946) Teicher, Joseph D. and Jacobs, Jerry. "Adolescents
       who attempt suicide: preliminary findings, " American
       Journal of Psychiatry, 122(11):1248-1257, 1966.

1947) Teicher, Joseph D. and Jacobs, Jerry. "The physician
       and the adolescent suicide attempter, " Journal of
       School Health, 36(9):406-415, November 1966.

1948) Teicher, Joseph D. , Jacobs, Jerry, Margolin, N.
       Leonel, Walker, Marilee, and Katz, Donna. "Factors
       in adolescent suicide attempts, " California Mental
       Health Research Digest, 3(1):38, 1965.

1949) Temoche, Abelardo, Pugh, Thomas F. , and MacMahon,
       Brian. "Suicide rates among current and former men-
       tal institution patients, " Journal of Nervous and Men-
       tal Disease, 138(2):124-130, 1964.

1950) Templeton, B. "Suicide by anaphyloxis attempted with
       penicillin, " Journal of the American Medical Associa-
       tion, 192:264, Apr. 19, 1965.

1951) Tenenbaum, Samuel. "The threat of suicide in psy-
       chotherapy, " Psychotherapy: Theory, Research and
       Practice, 1(3):124-128, 1964.

1952) Thomas, C. B. "Suicide among us: can we learn to
       prevent it?", Johns Hopkins Medical Journal, 125:276-
       285, 1969.

1953) Thomas, C. B. and Greenstreet, R. L. "Psychobi-
       ological characteristics in youth as predictors of five
       disease states--suicide, mental illness, hypertension,

coronary heart disease and tumor, " Johns Hopkins
Medical Journal, 132:16-43, Jan. 1973.

1954)   Thomas, Captane P.   "Suicide prevention in a rural
        area, " Bulletin of Suicidology, July 1968, pp. 49-52.

1955)   Thomson, W. A.   "Therapeutic poisoning, " Medicine,
        Science and the Law, 5:210-215, 1965.

1956)   Tonks, C. M. , Rack, P. H. , and Rose, M. J.   "At-
        tempted suicide and the menstrual cycle, " Journal of
        Psychosomatic Research, 11(4):319-323, 1968.

1957)   Toolan, James M.   "Suicide and suicidal attempts in
        children and adolescents, " American Journal of Psy-
        chiatry, 118:719-724, 1962.

1958)   Toole, J. F.   "Danger ahead: problems in defining
        life and death, " North Carolina Medical Journal, 28:
        464-466, 1967.

1959)   Trautman, Edgar C.   "Drug abuse and suicide attempt
        of an adolescent girl: a social and psychiatric evalua-
        tion, " Adolescence, 1(4):381-392, 1966.

1960)   Trautman, Edgar C.   "Suicide attempts of Puerto
        Rican immigrants, " Psychiatric Quarterly, 35:544-
        554, 1961.

1961)   Trautman, Edgar C.   "The suicidal fit: a psychobi-
        ologic study on Puerto Rican immigrants, " Archives
        of General Psychiatry, 5:76-83, 1961.

1962)   Trautman, Edgar C.   "Suicide as a psychodramatic
        act, " Group Psychotherapy, 15(2):159-161, 1962.

1963)   "Treatment and prevention of poisoning, " British
        Medical Journal, 4:787-788, 1968.

1964)   Trowell, H.   "Suicide and euthanasia, " British Medical
        Journal, 2:275, May 1, 1971.

1965)   Tsoi, Wing Foo.   "Attempted suicides, " Singapore
        Medical Journal, 11:258-263, 1970.

1966)   Tsutsumi, S. , Tsujino, S. , Tsude, K. , Nagao, S. ,
        and Imamichi, H.   "A study on suicides in families of

psychotics, " Bulletin of the Osaka Medical School, 12(Suppl.):399+, 1967.

1967) Tucker, B. J. , Megenity, D. , and Vigil, L.   "Anatomy of a campus crisis center, " Personnel Guidance Journal, 48:343-348, 1970.

1968) Tucker, Gary J. and Gorman, E. R.   "The significance of the suicide gesture in the military, " American Journal of Psychiatry, 123(7):854-861, 1967.

1969) Tuckman, Jacob.   "Emergency rescue services, " Bulletin of Suicidology, No. 7:36-37, 1970.

1970) Tuckman, Jacob.   "Philadelphia Suicide Prevention Center, " Crisis Intervention, 2(4):88-92, 1970.

1971) Tuckman, Jacob and Connor, Helen E.   "Attempted suicide in adolescents, " American Journal of Psychiatry, 119(3):228-232, 1962.

1972) Tuckman, Jacob, Kleiner, Robert J. , and Lavell, Martha.   "Credibility of suicide notes, " American Journal of Psychiatry, 116:1104-1106, 1960.

1973) Tuckman, Jacob and Youngman, William F.   "Attempted suicide and family disorganization, " Journal of Genetic Psychology, 105(2):187-193, 1964.

1974) Tuckman, J. and Youngman, W. F.   "Identifying suicide risk groups among attempted suicides, " Public Health Reports, 78(9):763-766, 1963.

1975) Tuckman, J. , Youngman, W. F. , and Bleiberg, Beulah M.   "Attempted suicide by adults, " Public Health Reports, 77:605-614, 1962.

1976) Tuckman, Jacob and Youngman, William F.   "A scale for assessing suicide risk of attempted suicides, " Journal of Clinical Psychology, 24(1):17-19, 1968.

1977) Tuckman, J. and Youngman, W. F.   "Suicide and criminality, " Journal of Forensic Science, 10:104-7, Jan. 1965.

1978) Tuckman, J. and Youngman, W. F.   "Suicide risk among persons attempting suicide, " Public Health Reports, 78:585-587, 1963.

1979) Tuckman, Jacob, Youngman, William F., and Kreizman, Garry. "Multiple suicide attempts," Community Mental Health Journal, 4(2):164-170, 1968.

1980) Tuckman, J., Youngman, W. F., and Kreizman, G.
"Occupation and suicide," Indus. Med. Surg., 33:818-
20, Nov. 1964.

1981) Tuckman, Jacob, Youngman, William F., and Kreizman, Garry. "Suicide and physical illness," Journal
of General Psychology," 75(2):291-295, 1966.

1982) Tuckman, Jacob, Youngman, W. F., and Leifer, Betty.
"Suicide and family disorganization," International
Journal of Social Psychiatry, 12(3):187-191, 1966.

1983) Tuckman, Jacob and Ziegler, Ralph. "A comparison
of single and multiple note writers among suicides,"
Journal of Clinical Psychology, 24(2):179-80, 1968.

1984) Tuckman, Jacob and Ziegler, Ralph. "Language usage
and social maturity as related to suicide notes,"
Journal of Social Psychology, 68(1):139-142, 1966.

1985) Turner, D. A. "Survival or suicide," American Sociologist, 5(1):43, 1970.

1986) Tuteur, Werner and Glotzer, Jacob. "Further observations on murdering mothers," Journal of Forensic
Sciences, 11(3):373-383, 1966.

1987) Udsen, P. "Prognosis and follow-up of attempted suicide," International Anesthesiology Clinics, 4:379-388,
1966.

1988) Uematsu, M. "A statistic approach to the host factor
of suicide in adolescence," Acta Medica et Biologica
(Niigata), 8(4):279-286, 1961.

1989) Umscheid, T. "With suicidal patients; caring for is
caring about," American Journal of Nursing, 67:1230-
1232, 1967.

1990) "Unemployment and suicide," British Medical Journal,
2:965, 1966.

1991) Urban, William H. "Suicide: a cultural and semantic view, " Mental Hygiene, 46(3):377-381, 1962.

1992) Usher, A. "The case of the disembowelled doll--a multiple murder, " Medicine, Science and the Law, 7(4):211-212, 1967.

1993) Van Dellen, T. R. "Suicide among physicians, " Illinois Medical Journal, 133:622, 1968.

1994) "Vanderbilt University Hospital--dual personality, " Journal of the Tennessee Medical Association, 56:443-9, Nov. 1963.

1995) Varah, Chad. "How 'The Samaritans' combat suicide," Mental Health, 21:132-4, Oct. 1962.

1996) Varah, Chad. "Sexual and religious conflicts in suicidal young people, " Zeitschrift für Präventivmedizin, 10:487, 1965.

1997) Varma, P. "Accidental deaths and suicides in India, " Social Welfare, 16:16-17, 1970.

1998) Veevers, J. E. "Parenthood and suicide--an examination of a neglected variable, " Social Science Medicine, 7:135-44, Feb. 1973.

1999) Victor, Leonard B. , Gordon, Elmer L. , and Greendyke, Robert M. "Therapeutic implications of autopsy findings in acute barbiturate intoxication, " New York State Journal of Medicine, 68(15):2090-2092, 1968.

2000) Vincent, M. O. "Doctor and Mrs. : their mental health, " Canadian Psychiatric Association Journal, 14(5):509-515, 1969.

2001) Vincent, M. O. "The doctor's life and practice, " NS Medical Bulletin, 50:139-42, Dec. 1971.

2002) Vincent, M. O. , Robinson, E. A. , and Latt, L. "Physicians and patients: private psychiatric hospital experience, " Canadian Medical Association Journal, 100(9):403-412, 1969.

2003) Vinoda, K. S. "A comparative study of the personality characteristics of attempted suicides, psychiatric pa-

tients and normals," Transactions of All-India Institute
of Mental Health, 5:67-74, 1965.

2004) Vinoda, K. S. "Personality characteristics of attempted
suicides, " British Journal of Psychiatry, 112(492):
1143-1150, 1966.

2005) Virkkunen, M. "Suicides among alcoholics on social
welfare rolls, " Acta Sociomed. Scandinavica, 3:51-8,
1971.

2006) Virkkunen, M. "On suicides committed by disability
pensioners, " Acta Sociomed. Scandinavica, 4:1-8, 1972.

2007) Virkkunen, M. and Alha, A. "On suicides committed
under the influence of alcohol in Finland in 1967, "
British Journal of Addiction, 63:317-323, 1970.

2008) Voth, Harold M., Voth, Albert C., and Cancro, Robert.
"Suicidal solution as a function of ego-closeness--ego-
distance, " Archives of General Psychiatry, 21(5):536-
545, 1969.

2009) Wagner, F. F. "Suicide notes, " Danish Medical Bulletin, 7:62-64, 1960.

2010) Wagner, F. F. "Suicide prevention and social clubs,"
International Journal of Social Psychiatry, 11:116-7,
Spring 1965.

2011) Walk, David. "Suicide and community care, " British
Journal of Psychiatry, 113(505):1381-1391, 1967.

2012) Wallace, M. A. "The nurse in suicide prevention, "
Nursing Outlook, 14:55-57, 1967.

2013) Wallace, Mary A. and Morley, Wilbur E. "Teaching
crisis intervention, " American Journal of Nursing,
70(7):1484-1487, 1970.

2014) Wallis, G. G. "Attempted suicide, " Journal of the
Royal Naval Medical Service, 50:155-158, 1964.

2015) Walsh, D., and McCarthy, P. D. "Suicide in Dublin's
elderly, " Acta Psychiatrica Scandinavica, 41(2):227-
235, 1965.

2016) Waltzer, H. "Depersonalization and self-destruction,"
       American Journal of Psychiatry, 125(3):399-401, 1968.

2017) Waltzer, Herbert and Hankoff, Leon D. "One year's
       experience with a suicide prevention telephone service,"
       Community Mental Health Journal, 1(4):309-315, 1965.

2018) "Wanting to die," Nursing Times, 62:1253-1258, 1966.

2019) Warnes, H. "Suicide in schizophrenics," Diseases
       of the Nervous System, 29(5, Suppl.):35-40, 1968.

2020) Watanake, T., Kobayashi, Y., and Hata, S. "Hara-
       kiri and suicide by sharp instruments in Japan,"
       Forensic Sciences, 2:191-9, May 1973.

2021) Watkins, Charles, Gilbert, J. E., and Bass, William.
       "The persistent suicidal patient," American Journal
       of Psychiatry, 125(11):1590-1593, 1969.

2022) Watson, Robert L., Jennette, Arthur H., and Hansen,
       Herman R. "Adult drug intoxications and treatment in
       an Army Hospital," Military Medicine, 133(10):793-
       798, 1968.

2023) Watts, C. A. H. "The problem of suicide in general
       practice," Proceedings of the Royal Society of Medi-
       cine, 54(4):264-266, 1961.

2024) "Ways to prevent suicide," Nature (London), 220:417-
       418, 1968.

2025) Wechsler, H. "Community growth, depressive dis-
       orders, and suicide," American Journal of Sociology,
       67:9-17, 1961.

2026) Weddige, R. L. and Stenhilker, R. M. "Attempted
       suicide by drug overdose," Postgraduate Medicine,
       49:184-6, May 1971.

2027) Weikel, Charles P. "The life you can save," Har-
       vest Years, Jan. 1970, pp. 7-11.

2028) Weill, J. "Child suicide," Semaine des Hôpitaux de
       Paris, 40(54):2950-2955, 1964.

2029) Weinberg, S. "Suicidal intent in adolescence: a hypo-

thesis about the role of physical illness, " Journal of
Pediatrics, 77:579-586, 1970.

2030)   Weiner, Irving B.   "Cross-validation of a Rorschach
check list associated with suicidal tendencies, " Journal
of Consulting Psychology, 25(4):312-315, 1961.

2031)   Weiner, I. W.   "The effectiveness of a suicide prevention program, " Mental Hygiene, 53:357-363, 1969.

2032)   Weisfogel, Jerry.   "A psychodynamic study of an
attempted suicide, " Psychiatric Quarterly, 43(2):257-
284, 1969.

2033)   Weisman, Avery.   "Discussion of suicide and appropri-
ate death, " International Journal of Psychiatry, 2:190-
193, 1966.

2034)   Weisman, Avery D.   "Importance of following the hospitalized suicidal patient, " Sandoz Panorama, 8(2):24-
28, 1970.

2035)   Weisman, Avery D.   "The psychological autopsy and
the potential suicide, " Bulletin of Suicidology, Dec.
1967, pp. 15-24.

2036)   Weisman, Avery D. and Worden, J. W.   "Risk-rescue
rating in suicide assessment, " Archives of General
Psychiatry, 26:533-60, June 1972.

2037)   Weiss, Hilda.   "Durkheim, Denmark, and suicide. A
sociological interpretation of statistical data, " Acta
Sociologica, 7(4):264-278, 1964.

2038)   Weiss, James M. A.   "Suicide and common sense, "
Journal of Operational Psychiatry, 1(2):50-51, 1970.

2039)   Weiss, Samuel A.   "Therapeutic strategy to obviate
suicide, " Psychotherapy: Theory, Research and Practice, 6(1):39-42, 1969.

2040)   Weiss, S. W.   "Cry wolf: a case study of suicide and
homicide, " Delaware Medical Journal, 35:293-297,
1963.

2041)   Weissman, M., Fox, K., and Klerman, G. L.   "Hostility and depression associated with suicide attempts, "

American Journal of Psychiatry, 130:450-5, Apr. 1973.

2042) Welu, T. C. "Broadening the focus of suicide prevention activities utilizing the public health model, "
American Journal of Public Health, 62:1625-8, Dec.
1972.

2043) West, D. J. "Murder, then suicide," New Society,
6(167):7-9, 1965.

2044) Westermeyer, J. "Disorganization--its role in Indian
suicide rates," American Journal of Psychiatry, 128:
123-4, July 1971.

2045) Wetzel, R. D. and McClure, J. N., Jr. "Suicide and
the menstrual cycle--a review," Comparative Psychiatry, 13:369-74, July-Aug. 1972.

2046) Wetzel, Richard D., McClure, James N., and Reich,
Theodore. "Premenstrual symptoms in self-referrals
to a suicide prevention service," British Journal of
Psychiatry, 119(552):525-526, Nov. 1971.

2047) Wetzel, Richard D., Reich, Theodore, and McClure,
James N. "Phase of the menstrual cycle and self-
referrals to a suicide prevention service," British
Journal of Psychiatry, 119(552):523-524, Nov. 1971.

2048) Wexler, Murray and Adler, Leta M. "When the patient has attempted suicide," Hospital Physician, June
1970, pp. 62-67.

2049) Whalley, Elsa A. "Self-destructive and self-creative
philosophies of life," Humanitas, 6(1):95-115, 1970.

2050) Wharton, C. F. P. "Attempted suicide by digoxin
self-administration and its management," Guy's Hospital Reports, 119(3):242-251, 1970.

2051) Wheat, W. D. "Motivational aspects of suicide in
patients during and after psychiatric treatment,"
Southern Medical Journal, 53(3):273-278, 1960.

2052) Whitehead, P. C. "Notes on the association between
alcoholism and suicide," International Journal of Addiction, 7:525-32, 1972.

2053) Whitehead, P. C., Johnson, F. G., and Terrence, K. "Measuring the incidence of self-injury--some methodological and design considerations," American Journal of Orthopsychiatry, 43:142-8, Jan. 1973.

2054) Whitely, J. M. "Student stress, suicide and the role of the university," Journal of the National Association of Women Deans and Counselors, 30(3):120-124, 1967.

2055) Whitis, P. R. "The legacy of a child's suicide," Family Process, 7(2):159-169, 1968.

2056) Whitlock, F. A. "The epidemiology of drug overdosage," Medical Journal of Australia, 1:1195-1199, 1970.

2057) Whitlock, F. A. "Migration and suicide," Medical Journal of Australia, 2:840-8, Oct. 23, 1971.

2058) Whitlock, F. A. "Suicide in today's society," Medical Journal of Australia, 1:361-362, 1969.

2059) Whitlock, F. A. and Broadhurst, A. D. "Attempted suicide and the experience of violence," Journal of Biosocial Science, 1(4):353-368, Oct. 1969.

2060) Whitlock, F. A. and Edwards, J. E. "Pregnancy and attempted suicide," Comprehensive Psychiatry, 9(1): 1-12, 1968.

2061) Whitlock, F. A. and Fama, P. G. "Hyoscine poisoning in psychiatric practice," Medical Journal of Australia, 2(16):763-764, 1966.

2062) Whittemore, K. R., Nugent, J., and Boom, P. "Suicide and the physician--experience and attitudes in the community," Journal of the Medical Association of Georgia, 61:307-11, Sept. 1972.

2063) "Who commits suicide?" Postgraduate Medicine, 43 (6):198, 1968.

2064) Wilkins, James. "A follow-up study of those who called a suicide prevention center," American Journal of Psychiatry, 127(2):155-161, 1970.

2065) Wilkins, James. "Suicidal behavior," American Sociological Review, 32(2):286-298, 1967.

2066) Wilkins, James. "Suicide and anonymity," Psychiatry, 32(3):303-312, 1969.

2067) Wilkins, James. "Suicide calls and identification of suicide callers," Medical Journal of Australia, 2:923-9, Oct. 21, 1972.

2068) Wilkins, James. "Suicide prevention centers: comparison of clients in several cities," Comprehensive Psychiatry, 10(6):443-451, 1969.

2069) Wilkins, J. L. "Experience in suicide prevention. 'Calls for help in Chicago,'" Illinois Medical Journal, 137:257-260 passim, 1970.

2070) Wilkins, J. L. "Producing suicides," American Behavioral Scientist, 14(2):185, 1970.

2071) Williams, Christene B. and Nickels, James B. "Internal-external control dimension as related to accident and suicide proneness," Journal of Consulting and Clinical Psychology, 33(4):485-494, 1969.

2072) Williams, L. N. "Responsibility for the depressive," Lancet, 1:1441, 1964.

2073) Williams, Mary. "Changing attitudes to death: a survey of contribution in 'Psychological Abstracts' over a thirty-year period," Human Relations, 19(4):405-423, 1966.

2074) Williams, R. H. "Our role in the generation, modification, and termination of life," Transactions of the Association of American Physicians, 82:1-22, 1969.

2075) Wilson, George C., Jr. "Suicide in psychiatric patients who have received hospital treatment," American Journal of Psychiatry, 125(6):752-757, 1968.

2076) Wilson, Lowell T., Braucht, G. Nicholas, Miskimins, R. W., and Berry, K. L. "The severe suicide attempter and self-concept," Journal of Clinical Psychology, 27(3):307-309, July 1971.

2077) Winek, C. L., Collom, W. D., and Wecht, C. H. "Suicide with plastic bag and ethyl ether," Lancet, 1(7642):365, 1970.

2078)   Winn, Don and Halla, Rode.   "Observations of children
        who threaten to kill themselves, " Canadian Psychiatric
        Association Journal, 11(Suppl.):283-294, 1966.

2079)   Winn, J. A.   "Psychiatrists who kill themselves, "
        American Journal of Psychiatry, 124:1270, 1968.

2080)   Wold, Carl I.   "Characteristics of 26, 000 Suicide Pre-
        vention Center patients, " Bulletin of Suicidology, No.
        6:24-28, Spring 1970.

2081)   Wold, Carl I.   "Social and medical responsibility in
        suicide prevention, " Wisconsin Medical Journal, 66:
        535-539, 1967.

2082)   Wold, Carl I. and Litman, R. E.   "Suicide after con-
        tact with a suicide prevention center, " Archives of
        General Psychiatry, 28:735-9, May 1973.

2083)   Wolff, K.   "Depression and suicide in the geriatric
        patient, " Journal of the American Geriatric Society,
        17(7):668-672, 1969.

2084)   Wolff, K.   "The treatment of the depressed and sui-
        cidal geriatric patient, " Geriatrics, 26:65-9, July 1971.

2085)   Wolfgang, M. E.   "Who kills whom?", Psychology
        Today, 3(5):54-56, 72-75, 1969.

2086)   Wolford, Helen G.   "A psychiatric nurse in a suicide
        outreach program, " Psychiatric Quarterly Supple-
        ment, 39:88-94, 1965.

2087)   Woodruff, R. A. , Jr. , Clayton, P. J. , and Guze,
        S. B.   "Suicide attempts and psychiatric diagnosis, "
        Diseases of the Nervous System, 33:617-21, Sept. 1972.

2088)   Woods, L. W.   "Disaster during psychiatric treatment.
        An intrapsychic problem for the physician, " Canadian
        Psychiatric Association Journal, 18:67-70, Feb. 1973.

2089)   Yacoubian, J. H. and Lourie, R. S.   "Suicide and
        attempted suicide in children and adolescents, " Clin-
        ical Proceedings of the Children's Hospital (Washing-
        ton, D. C.), 25:325-344, 1969.

2090)   Yamada, H.   "Pre-suicidal mental states estimated

from the records kept at police stations (Japanese), "
Journal of the Yonago Medical Association, 13(3):209-
215, 1962.

2091) Yessler, Paul G. , Gibbs, James J. , and Becker,
Herman. "On the communication of suicidal ideas:
I. Some sociological and behavioral considerations, "
Archives of General Psychiatry, 3:612-631, 1960.

2092) Yessler, Paul G. , Gibbs, James J. , and Becker,
Herman. "On the communication of suicidal ideas:
II. Some medical considerations, " Archives of Gen-
eral Psychiatry, 5:12-29, 1961.

2093) Yufit, Robert I. , Benzies, Bonnie, Fonte, Mary E. ,
and Fawcett, Jan. A. "Suicide potential and time
perspective, " Archives of General Psychiatry, 23(2):
158-163, Aug. 1970.

2094) Zamcheck, N. and Geisler, M. A. "Homicides and
suicides of World War II, " Journal of Forensic Science, 5:84-101, 1960.

2095) Zee, H. J. "Blindspots in recognizing serious suicidal
intentions, " Bulletin of the Menninger Clinic, 36:551-
5, Sept. 1972.

2096) Zmuc, M. "Alcohol and suicide, " Alcoholism, 4:38-
44, 1968.

IX. LITERARY WORKS

CRITICISM

2097) Camus, A. The Myth of Sisyphus and Other Essays.
New York: Vintage, 1955. (Originally pub. 1942.)

2098) Dettmering, Peter. "The theme of suicide in the work
of Thomas Mann, " Humanitas, 6(1):23-44, 1970.

2099) Faber, M. D. "Some remarks on the suicide of King
Lear's eldest daughter, " University Review, 33(4):
313-317, 1967.

2100) Faber, M. D. Suicide and Greek Tragedy. New
York: Sphinx Press, 1970.

2101) Glicksberg, C. I. "To be or not to be; the literature
of suicide, " Queen's Quarterly, 67:384-95, Autumn
1960.

2102) Jones, C. "Suicide--a disease that can be treated, "
Maclean's Magazine, 74:21, 38-9, Apr. 8, 1961.

2103) Kornbluth, Alice Fox. A Suicidal Ending in Virginia
Woolf. Kentucky Microcards, Series A, Modern
Languages Series No. 48. South Atlantic Modern
Language Association, Knoxville, 1957.

2104) Rankin, H. D. "Socrates' approach to Thanatos, "
American Imago, 21(3-4):111-128, 1964.

2105) Sprott, Samuel Ernest. The English Debate on Suicide: from Donne to Hume. La Salle, Ill. : Open
Court, 1961. 168pp.

NOVELS

2106) Aldington, Richard. Death of a Hero. New York: Covici, 1929.

2107) Barjola y Nessi, P. The Tree of Knowledge. New York: Knopf, 1928. (Trans. from Spanish.)

2108) Barth, John. The Floating Opera. New York: Doubleday, 1967.

2109) Bates, Herbert Ernest. The Sleepless Moon. Boston: Little, Brown, 1956.

2110) Bates, Sylvia Chatfeld. Floor of Heaven. New York: Harcourt, Brace, 1941.

2111) Borden, M. The Hungry Leopard. London: Longmans, 1956.

2112) Brown, J. D. Kings Go Forth. New York: Morrow, 1956.

2113) Butler, William. The House at Akiya. New York: Scribner, 1969.

2114) Colette. The Last of Chère. New York: Farrar, Straus, 1953. In: Colette, 7 by Colette, v2, pp. 157-296.

2115) Deeping, Warwick. Doomsday. New York: Knopf, 1927.

2116) Derleth, August William. Restless is the River. New York: Scribner, 1939.

       Faulkner, The Sound & the Fury
2117) Field, Herman. Angry Harvest. New York: Crowell, 1958.

2118) Flaubert, Gustave. Madame Bovary. New York: Random House, 1957.

2119) Gide, Andre. The Counterfeiters. New York: Modern Library, 1951. (Originally pub. 1926.)

2120) Goethe, Johann Wolfgang von. The Sorrows of Young Werter, ed. by Frank G. Ryder. Chapel Hill: Univ. of North Carolina Press, 1952.

2121) Greenaway, Emily. Sweepstakes. New York: Houghton, 1941.

2122) Hardy, Thomas. Jude the Obscure. New York: Modern Library, 1923.

2123) Harrison, William. In a Wild Sanctuary. New York: Morrow, 1969.

2124) Hurst, Fannie. Five and Ten. New York: Harper, 1929.

2125) Lenn, James W. Winds Over the Campus. New York: Bobbs, 1936.

2126) Locke, Wm. J. Stella Maris. New York: Grosset, 1915.

2127) Lofts, Nora. White Hell of Pity. New York: Knopf, 1937.

2128) McFee, William. Harbourmaster. New York: Doubleday, 1931.

2129) Martinez, Zoviriá Gustavo A. Peach Blossom. London: Longmans, 1929. (Trans. from Spanish.)

2130) Maugham, William S. Moon and Sixpence. New York: Modern Library, 1919.

2131) Maugham, William S. Narrow Corner. Garden City, N.Y.: Doubleday, 1932.

2132) Maugham, William S. Up at the Villa. London: W. Heinemann, 1941.

2133) Mora, Ferenc. Song of the Wheatfields. New York: Brewer, 1930. (Trans. from Hungarian.)

2134) Murphy, Dennis. The Sergeant. New York: Viking, 1958.

2135) Murray, David Leslie. Regency: A Quadruple Portrait. New York: Knopf, 1936.

2136) O'Brien, Kate. The Anteroom. New York: Doubleday, 1934.

2137) O'Faolain, Sean. Bird Alone. New York: Viking, 1936.

2138) Ostenso, Martha. Young May Moon. New York: Dodd, 1941.

2139) Parrish, Arne. Perennial Bachelor. New York: Harper, 1925.

2140) Pavese, C. "Among women only." In: Pavese, C., The Selected Works of Cesare Pavese. New York: Farrar, Straus, 1968, pp. 175-275. (Trans. from Italian.)

2141) Pérochon, Ernest. Nêve. New York: Doran, 1922. (Trans. from French.)

2142) Rinehart, Mary Roberts. This Strange Adventure. New York: Doubleday, 1929.

2143) Ross, Ishbel. Promenade Deck. New York: Harper, 1932.

2144) Sandy, Isabell. Andorra. New York: Houghton, 1924. (Trans. from French.)

2145) Sarton, May. Faithful are the Wounds. New York: Holt, Rinehart, 1955.

2146) Sheed, Wilfrid. "Pennsylvania Gothic." In: Sheed, W., The Blacking Factory and Pennsylvania Gothic. New York: Farrar, Straus, 1968, pp. 3-63.

2147) Shute, Nevil. The Breaking Wave. New York: Morrow, 1955.

2148) Smith, Bradford. To the Mountain. New York: Bobbs, 1936.

2149) Sprigge, Elizabeth. Raven's Wing. New York: Macmillan, 1940.

2150) Styron, William. Lie Down in Darkness. New York: Bobbs, 1951.

2151) Sudermann, Hermann. The Mad Professor. New York: H. Liveright, 1928.

2152) Swinnerton, Frank A. Two Wives. New York: Doubleday, 1940.

2153) Tolstoi, Leon N. Anna Karenina. New York: The
Modern Library, 1930.

2154) Vane, Sutton. Outward Bound. New York: Liveright,
1924.

2155) Varandyan, Emmanuel P. Well of Ararat, Pt. 3. New
York: Doubleday, 1938.

2156) Walpole, Sir Hugh. Sea Tower, Pt. 2. New York:
Doubleday, 1939.

2157) Walpole, Sir Hugh. Wintersmoon. New York: Doubleday, 1928.

2158) Wassermann, J. Oberlin's Three Stages. New York:
Harcourt, 1926.

2159) Werfel, Franz V. Class Reunion. New York: Viking,
1929.
       Woolf, Virginia. Mrs. Dalloway

2160) Zweig, Stephen. Beware of Pity. New York: Viking,
1939. (Trans. from German.)

SHORT STORIES

2161) Maupassant, Guy de. "Suicides. " In: Complete Novels
and Short Stories, introd. by Edmund Gasse and Arthur
Symons. New York: Bigelow, Brown, 1922.

2162) Merrick, L. "Suicides in the Rue Sombre. " In:
Merrick, L. , Chair on the Boulevard. New York:
Dutton, 1921.

2163) Merrick, Leonard. "Suicides in the Rue Sombre. "
In: Merrick, Leonard, The Man Who Understood
Women. New York: M. Kennedy, 1911.

2164) Roth, Philip. "The conversion of the Jews. " In:
P. Roth, Goodbye, Columbus. New York: Bantam,
1963, pp. 100-114.

2165) Sedgwick, A. D. "The Suicide. " In: The Nest and

Other Stories. New York: Houghton, 1913.

2166) Stevenson, Robert Louis. "The suicide club." In:
Dr. Jekyll and Mr. Hyde and the Suicide Club. New
York: Arco, 1964.

2167) Thackeray, W. M. "A legend of the Rhine." In:
Thackeray, W. M., Burlesques. London: Macmillan,
1903, pp. 3-36.

PLAYS

2168) Baker, Elizabeth. Miss Tassey. London: Sidgwick &
Jackson, Ltd., 1913.

2169) Blake, Elizabeth. Quiet Cries. Washington, D.C.:
National Institute of Mental Health, 1969.

2170) Boyce, Neith. "Winter's Night." In: Shay, F., ed.
Fifty More Contemporary One-Act Plays. New York:
Appleton, 1928.

2171) Chekhov, A. P. Ivanov. In: Plays, tr. from the
Russian. New York: C. Scribner's Sons, 1912.

2172) Colton, A. and Randolph, C. Rain. New York: Liveright, 1936.

2173) Conkle, Ellsworth P. "Things is that-a-way." In:
Crick Bottom Plays, Five Midwestern Sketches. New
York: S. French, 1928.

2174) Crocker, B. "The last straw." In: Lewis, Benjamin
R., ed., Contemporary One-Act Plays. New York:
Scribner, 1922.

2175) Galloway, J. L. "The Dark." In: Fuller, M. H.,
comp. One-Act Plays for the Amateur Theatre. London: Harrap, 1949.

2176) Geiger, M. "One Special for Doc." In: Cook, Luella
B. and others. Adventures in Appreciation. 3rd ed.
New York: Harcourt, 1947.

2177) Gibson, W. W. "The Millrace." In: Within Four
Walls, New York: Macmillan, 1952.

2178) Hackett, W. A. "The Young Man with the Cream
      Tarts. " In: Plays, 8:75-85, April 1949.

2179) Ibsen, Henrik. The Wild Duck. New York: Modern
      Library, 1961, pp. 103-210.

2180) Kent, Mark. "Let's End It All. " In: One Rehearsal
      Variety Programs. Boston: Baker, 1946.

2181) Kramm, J. The Shrike. New York: Random House,
      1952.

2182) Kyd, T. Spanish Tragedy, with additions, 1602. Lon-
      don, printed for the Malone Society by F. Hail, M. A.
      at the Oxford University Press, 1925.

2183) Laurents, A. Bird Cage. New York: Guild Library,
      1950.

2184) Pertwee, M. Night was Our Friend. New York: Guild
      Library, 1950.

2185) Pierce, Carl W. The Suicide Specialist. Boston:
      Baker, 1924.

2186) Rattigan, Terrence M. Deep Blue Sea. New York:
      Random House, 1953.

2187) Wolas, E. "Look Back on Today!" In: One-Act Play
      Magazine, 3:297-314, May-June 1940.

2188) Zacks, R. A. "The Stranger. " In: One-Act Play
      Magazine, 8:416-423, July-Aug. 1940.

POETRY

2189) Berryman, John. Recovery. New York: Farrar,
      Straus & Giroux, 1973.

2190) Berryman, John. 77 Dream Songs. New York: Far-
      rar, Straus, 1964.

2191) Berryman, John. Short Poems. New York: Farrar,
      Straus & Giroux, 1967.

2192) Chatterton, Thomas. "Last Verses. " In: Taylor,

Donald S. , ed. , Complete Works of Thomas Chatterton: A Bicentenary Edition. Oxford: Clarendon Press,
1971.

2193) Chesterton, G. K. "Ballade of Suicide." In: The
Collected Poems of G. K. Chesterton. London: C.
Palmer, 1927.

2194) Flecker, James E. "Felo-de-Se." In: Collected
Poems, ed. with an introd. by Sir J. Squire. London:
Secker, 1935.

2195) Hood, Thomas. "Bridge of Sighs." In: Hood, Thomas,
Poems. London: E. Moxon, 1871.

2196) Hughes, Ted. Crow: From the Life and Songs of the
Crow. New York: Harper & Row, 1971.

2197) Hughes, Ted. The Earth-Owl and Other Moon-People.
London: Faber and Faber, 1963.

2198) Hughes, Ted. The Hawk in the Rain. London: Faber
and Faber, 1968.

2199) Hughes, Ted. Lupercal. New York: Harper, 1960.

2200) Hughes, Ted. Wodwo. New York: Harper and Row,
1967.

2201) Perhoff, Stuart Z. The Suicide Room; Poems.
Karlsruhe: J. Williams, 1956.

2202) Plath, Sylvia. Winter Trees. London: Faber and
Faber, 1971.

X. FILMS, TAPES, RECORDINGS

2203) A case of suicide. British Broadcasting Corp., London. Released in the U. S. by Peter M. Robeck & Co., 1968. (Film)

2204) The cry for help. Louisiana Association for Mental Health in cooperation with U. S. Public Health Service. Made by George C. Stoney. Released by U. S. Public Health Service, 1963. (Film)

2205) The diagnosis and therapy of sedative overdose. Joel B. Mann and CIBA Pharmaceutical Co. Made by Medical Illustration Dept., University of Miami School of Medicine. Released by CIBA Phamaceutical Co., 1970. (Film)

2206) Journey of mind. Steven Radwan and Bernard Baumohl, 1969. (Film)

2207) Last act for an actor. California Medical Association. Made and released by Lawren Productions, 1962. (Film)

2208) A point of return. Oklahoma State Health Dept., 1964. Made by Motion Picture Production, University of Oklahoma. Released by International Film Bureau, 1965. (Film)

2209) Peck, M. L. Rick: An adolescent suicide. Los Angeles: Suicide Prevention Center, 1969. (Film)

2210) Suicide clinic: a cry for help. National Educational Television. Released by Indiana University, Audio-Visual Center, 1971. (Film)

2211) Suicide prevention in hospitals. U. S. Veterans Administration, 1968. Made by George C. Stoney Associates. (Film)

2212) Suicide prevention: the physician's role. Roche Laboratories, 1967. Made by Visual Projects. (Film)

2213) A thousand red flowers. Paulist Productions, 1969. (Film)

2214) Winter Sunday. Alden McLellan, 1969. (Film)

2215) Suicide. Q & Ed Productions. Released by Cathedral Films and Society for Visual Education, 1970. (Filmstrip)

2216) Gentry, Bobbie. "Ode to Billy Joe." Capitol Records, 1967. (Recording)

2217) On Syliva Plath. Actresses Sondra Lovell, Joy Macintosh, Juliana McCarthy, Constance Pfeiffer, Judith Roberts, Joanne Straus, and Sheri Tyler read examples of the work of the brilliant and tortured poet who committed suicide at the age of 30. Actress Dorothy Dells reads the profile of Elizabeth Hardwick from the New York Review of Books which includes an analysis of the prose and poetry of Ms. Plath. Program produced and directed by Constance Pfeiffer. 89 min. (Tape)

2218) Training Record in Suicidology. Phonograph record of 5 conversations; calls to suicide prevention centers. Write to: Center for Studies of Suicide Prevention, National Institute of Mental Health, 5454 Wisconsin Avenue, Chevy Chase, Md. 20015.

XI. INDEX OF AUTHORS

Maugham, Wm. S. 2130,
2131, 2132
Maultsky, M. C. 1466
Maupassant, G. 2161
Maxmen, J. S. 1467
Maycock, E. 1468
Mayer, D. Y. 302, 1469
Mayfield, D. G. 1470
Mazrin, Ali 1471
Meaker, M. J. 76
Medlicott, R. W. 1473
Meerloo, J. A. M. 77,
303, 464, 1474
Melges, F. T. 1475, 1476
Menard, B. S. 304
Mendlewicz, J. 1477
Menon, I. S. 1478
Merrick, L. 2162, 2163
Merskey, H. 1480
Messer, M. H. 1481
Michaux, Mary H. 1482
Middleton, G. D. 1483
Mikawa, J. K. 1484
Miley, J. D. 1485
Miller, Dorothy H. 163,
1486, 1487
Miller, E. R. 1488
Miller, H. 1489
Miller, S. I. 1490
Milner, A. 581
Milner, G. 1491
Minkoff, K. 1492
Mintz, R. S. 79, 305,
1493, 1494, 1495, 1496,
1497
Miskimins, R. W. 1498
Mitchell, A. R. 1500
Mitrovich, P. 582
Modan, B. 1501, 1502
Modlin, Herbert C. 1503
Mona, F. 2133
Monch, M. F. 164
Montgomery, Frederick A.
1504
Moriyama, I. M. 80, 307
Morphew, J. A. 1505
Morris, J. 1506
Morrisson, Gilbert 1507,
1528

Moss, Leonard 1509
Motto, Jerome A. 308, 309,
1510, 1511, 1512, 1513,
1514, 1515
Muhr, E. 583
Munck, O. 1516
Munson, B. E. 1517
Munter, P. K. 310
Murphy, D. 2134
Murphy, G. E. 311, 312,
313, 1518, 1519, 1520,
1521, 1522
Murphy, K. B. 466
Murray, David 2135
Murray, Neville 1523
Murrell, Stanley A. 1524
Murthy, V. 1525, 1526
Mutty, Lawrence B. 1527
Myra, H. 535
Myrdal, G. 467

Naftulin, D. H. 1529
Nahum, L. H. 1530
Nashold, R. D. 1531
Nathan, P. 1532
Nawas, M. 1533
Neilberg, N. 1534
Neiswander, A. C. 1534
Nelson, B. 468, 1536
Nelson, Scott H. 1537
Nelson, Zane P. 1538
Neumann, M. 1539
Neuringer, Charles 165,
314, 1540, 1541, 1542,
1543, 1544, 1545, 1546,
1547, 1548, 1549, 1550
Newby, J. H. 1551
Niccolini, R. 1552
Nicholson, W. A. 1553
Nomura, A. 1554
Northcutt, T. 1555
Nott, K. 471, 536
Noyes, Russell, Jr. 1556,
1557, 1558, 1559

O'Brien, Kate 2136

Sletten, I. W. 1841
Slorach, J. 1842
Small, I. F. 1843
Small, J. C. 1844
Smith, A. J. 1845
Smith, B. 2148
Smith, G. B. 545
Smith, V. E. 495
Snavely, H. R. 178
Sokolow, L. 1846
Solomon, P. 1847
Soreff, S. 1848
Sorrel, W. E. 1849
Soubrier, J. P. 367, 368
Spalt, L. 1850
Spark, Derek 1851
Speck, R. V. 369
Spencer, S. 370
Spiegel, D. 1852, 1853,
  1854
Spiers, P. S. 1855
Sprigge, E. 2149
Sprott, S. 2105
Stajduhar-Carlc Z. 1856
Stalter, D. 546
Stanley, E. J. 1857
Stanley, W. J. 1858
Starer, E. 1859
Stein, E. V. 547, 548
Stein, M. 1860
Steinberg, H. R. 1861
Steiner, N. H. 110
Steinhilber, R. M. 1862
Stenback, A. 1863, 1864
Stengel, E. 111, 371, 372,
  373, 1865, 1866, 1867,
  1868, 1869, 1870, 1871,
  1872, 1873, 1874, 1875,
  1876, 1877, 1878, 1879
Stern, D. 112
Stern, Roy 1880
Sternlicht, M. 1881
Stevens, B. 1882
Stevenson, E. K. 1883
Stevenson, R. L. 2166
Stewart, I. 1884
Stoller, Robert 1885
Stone, A. A. 1886, 1887,

1888, 1889
Strachan, J. 497
Strahm, W. J. 1890
Strange, R. E. 1891
Stross, L. 1892
Strunk, O. 549
Styron, William 2150
Sudak, H. S. 1893
Sudermann, H. 2151
Sudnow, David 1894
Suinn, R. M. 114
Swanson, D. W. 1915
Swanson, W. C. 1916
Swartzburg, M. 1917
Swenson, D. D. 1918, 1919
Swinnerton, F. 2152
Szabo, D. 1921

Tabachnick, N. 375, 376,
  551, 1922, 1923, 1924,
  1925, 1926, 1927, 1928,
  1929, 1930, 1931, 1932,
  1933
Tallent, N. 1934
Tarbox, R. 1935
Tarrant, B. 1936, 1937
Tate, B. G. 1938
Tausk, V. 1939
Tayal, S. S. 1940
Taylor, D. J. E. 1941
Taylor, Dale 1942
Taylor, G. C. 1943
Teele, James E. 1944
Teicher, J. D. 1945, 1946,
  1947, 1948
Temby, W. B. 377
Temoche, A. 179, 1949
Templeton, B. 1950
Tenenbaum, S. 1951
Thackeray, Wm. 2167
Thakur, A. 115
Thielicke, H. 116
Thilges, R. 378
Thomas, C. B. 1952, 1953
Thomas, K. 379
Thomson, C. P. 380, 1954
Thomson, I. G. 381

217

218 Suicide Bibliography

Attempts (cont.)
2014, 2021, 2032, 2048, 2051, 2059, 2087

Attitudes toward 1068, 1281, 1457, 1540, 1558, 1559, 2073

Australia 1747

Austria 335, 336, 418, 951

Behavior 11, 12, 14, 16, 17, 18, 19, 21, 28, 30, 68, 71,
71a, 76, 78, 79, 85, 87, 93, 97, 99, 101, 104, 114,
117, 120, 126, 130, 138, 139, 146, 148, 149, 150, 155,
163, 164, 172, 176, 199, 292, 303, 339, 343, 438, 459,
474, 477, 513, 647, 859, 887, 889, 891, 895, 897, 990,
1061, 1181, 1228, 1287, 1298, 1325, 1326, 1327, 1329,
1371, 1397, 1412, 1466, 1467, 1484, 1533, 1541, 1542,
1546, 1670, 1680, 1697, 1765, 1774, 1854, 1878, 1882,
1897, 1899, 1912, 1944, 2038, 2065, 2091, 2092

Bibliography and review of literature 33, 95, 632, 702, 870,
1283, 1284, 1285

Biochemistry 200, 351, 797, 1250

Bioelectrical potential differences 164

Biography 7, 72, 83a, 91, 110, 643, 1437, 2208

Biological crises 382

Birth date 1350

Blacks 9, 54, 74, 415, 449, 516, 666, 674, 767, 1089,
1784, 1785

Canada 304, 1265

Cases 7, 215, 227, 237, 251, 304, 370, 408, 409, 428,
437, 483, 495, 522, 851, 932, 1141, 1175, 1190, 1256,
1291, 1402, 1486, 1651, 1703, 1892, 1939, 2040, 2204,
2207, 2208, 2210

Cases, legal 619-624

Causes 4, 6, 14, 16, 17, 18, 19, 23, 28, 30, 32, 48, 49,
65, 73, 79, 101, 103, 104, 142, 148, 188, 235, 268,
321, 422, 458, 490, 502, 513, 573, 667, 719, 757, 773,
794, 830, 838, 886, 904, 931, 939, 940, 974, 1030, 1060,